i

The Best of Adair Lara

Adair, Patrick, and Morgan, at Kirkwood, 1994

The Best of Adair Lara

Award Winning Columns
from the
San Francisco Chronicle

Scottwall Associates, Publishers
San Francisco

Scottwall Associates, Publishers
95 Scott Street
San Francisco, CA 94117
Telephone (415) 861-1956
Fax: (415) 626-6844
e-mail: scottwal@hooked.net

Book design: Lawrence R. Peterson
Cover design: Ed Rachles
Editor: James Heig
Printed in U.S.A.

First edition: 5 4 3 2 1

Library of Congress Catalog Card Number: 99 075742
Cataloging in Publication Data:
Lara, Adair: The Best of Adair Lara, newspaper columnist
1. If You Can Read This, You're Too Close
2. When Children Turn Into Cats
3. The Days of My Life
4. The Mating Game
5. A Few Moments of Clear Peace
6. It's All Relative
7. In Search of a Father

ISBN 0-942087-17-8

Introduction

Why not say what happened?
—Robert Lowell

WHEN THE *Chronicle* hired me, I had just one question. "What do you want me to write about?" I had to almost shout it, because the editor was hard of hearing.

"Write about your life," he said. He had been Charles McCabe's editor, and Stanton Delaplane's. He didn't seem sure about what to do with a female columnist, especially one whose work was so personal.

"About my life?" I repeated. I think I had expected to be a foreign correspondent, or at least get to pontificate on the OP-Ed page. I saw myself going to theater openings and penning savagely funny reviews in time for the first edition.

"Sure." He waved vaguely. "Go to the mall."

I was hired. The managing editor, Rosalie Wright, led me down Fifth Street, past the main building, past the M&M restaurant where staffers from both the *Chronicle* and *Examiner* hung out, past the car parking lots, the coffee shop where the bike messengers congregated, to an anonymous-looking building near Folsom Street, where the Chronicle had rented a floor for critics and columnists.

She showed me a cubicle with a window opening onto Clementina alley, with an old folks' home across the way, and explained that it was Jon Carroll's desk but he never came in, so it would be my desk, too. She showed me how to work the huge brown Coyote in-house computer, told me that my deadlines were Tuesday at four for the Thursday column, and Fridays at four for the Tuesday, and then clicked away in her high heels.

I filed — I loved the word "filed" and started using it right away, as it made me feel like a reporter — my first column. It was, no surprise, a personal column, about getting a newspaper job.

The next thousand or so columns were also personal.

Introduction

To some, this seemed like a frivolous use of newspaper space that should be reserved for more important matters. But others disagree. Patricia Hampf has written, "As writers, we sense that in order to live together we must learn to speak of peace, of history, of meaning and values. Instinctively, we go to our private store of images and associations for our authority to speak of these weighty issues."

What I discovered is that when you write from that private store of images and associations, no one can argue with you. When you say how it felt when you had an abortion at seventeen, no one can say, you didn't have the experience you say you had, and that you don't feel about it the way you say you do.

Philip Lopate said, "I want to record how the world comes at me, because I think that's how it comes at everyone."

So I write about my life. I write about operating a tricky clutch, owning a cat, wishing it would rain, passing the kids off as friends when trying to rent an apartment. I wrote about my dad's efforts to find himself, and my suspicion that several other people were looking for him too.

It's been ten years since Rosalie Wright showed me that desk. But I'm still here, still writing about my life. Why? Because people write back. Over the years the column, wonderfully, has taken on the feeling of personal conversation. I've learned to trust the feeling that if I tell the truth about my own experience, it will have meaning for someone else. I broach a subject, such as raising a teenager, and say this is how this was for me, and people write back, to say, "Oh you too?"

Readers tell me about their lives, their fathers, their kids. One reader, Myra Canizares, told me that my columns made her think that ordinary life has a lot of meaning in it. It doesn't get any better than that.

It's been a conversation, but for those who just came in, I should explain that the book is not linear. It's divided thematically.

For new readers, the picture is this: I have two children, Patrick and Morgan, with my ex-husband Jim, who was once also my college English teacher. When we divorced, I dated for several years, then met Bill, my husband, in the elevator at the *Chronicle* (he's the cookbook editor at Chronicle Books).

Bill and I searched for a house together and ended by buying a flat in Jim's four-story San Francisco Victorian house and moving in underneath him. Today we all live here, with Mike, the cat who used to be mine but who promptly moved upstairs to live with Jim when I got a dog. Morgan now lives in Jim's downstairs apartment, one floor below Bill and me.

I have six brothers and sisters (including a twin sister), a crazy old dad who lived in the desert before moving back to Marin County, and a mom who was the Rock of Gibraltar when he deserted us when I was eleven.

Carl Jung once said, "That which is most personal is most common." From conversations with readers over the years, I've come to believe that's true. You will find me in these pages, but with luck, you may also find yourself.

Dedication

For Bill, with love

Contents

Contents

The Mating Game   131

Contents

In Search of a Father 229

If You Can Read This, You're Too Close

The Night School of Hard Knocks

IT WAS THE second day of the fiction class that I had paid $165 for and given up my Thursday nights to take. An upset at work had made me rethink putting all my eggs in one basket, and I had become obsessed with making my fortune by writing a novel. (I know I'm not the first to get this idea. I try not to think about Erma Bombeck, who once said to a man, admiringly, `When did you first get this idea for not writing a book?')

But I had no idea how to do it. A night class, I decided, would be just the ticket, allowing me to share my first secret stumblings with a sympathetic group who would sip machine coffee out of Styrofoam cups while listening appreciatively to one another's efforts.

I would mention the encouragement of this group when the paperback edition of my novel sold to Bantam for a record amount.

The first class went well, and at the end we got our first assignment — to write the plot outline for whatever opus we were working on, and bring it in for class discussion.

All week, I slaved over my outline. I had had the strikingly original idea of making my first novel largely autobiographical. About my childhood, in fact. I deftly interwove all the elements covered in the first class, not forgetting conflict (the day Dad burned down our house for the insurance and found out too late it had lapsed) or foreshadowing (even our dog, George, left us for a family down the street). Then I made 24 copies on pink Xerox paper, one for each student.

The second evening was stormy — we had moved suddenly from summer to winter — and we had dropped to sixteen people. "The real writers, like snails, come out in the rain," the teacher reassured us. She returned the enrollment slips she collected in a burst of administrative fervor the first day. "I'm sorry," she said, "I had a deep need to collect something."

By eight o'clock everybody was half asleep and doodling while the teacher completed a discussion of suspense, to which she had added some of her own by trying to open a can of Diet Coke with her long red fingernails. The struggle lasted for almost two minutes.

Then she asked for volunteers to read their outlines, and I, not having learned very much yet and determined to get the most mileage out of my $165, read mine first. When I finished, there was a stunned silence.

"Can we really be brutally honest?" asked a distinguished looking man in the in the back row (actually, everybody was in the back). He was there, he had said, to collapse five novels into one on the advice of his agent.

"You had one or two interesting characters, but your novel bored me. The last thing I want to be dragged through is that little girl's childhood. It picked up for me in the scene where Casey almost ladles her grandmother's ashes into her coffee."

The scene with the ashes is the second to last. I wadded my coffee cup until it was the size of a quarter, keeping a smile plastered on my face.

"Can't you make the childhood a sort of prologue?" asked a young man in the seat ahead of me. He wasn't even in the class, but had come to tape it for his girlfriend, who was sick.

"I don't understand what it's about," said a blonde woman across the room. She leaned over to make eye contact with me. "What I'm wondering is, what about it is new?"

"You're next," the teacher said to a man sitting at the back. There were lots of hands in the air.

"I can't be next," he said. "My hearing aid has broken and I can't hear a thing, and I'm very frustrated." He got up and left.

I was squirming in my seat. This was the story of my life they were talking about.

"I agree with the first man," said a woman at the back. "I don't want to hear about the childhood. Nothing happens, and the characters aren't very interesting."

That seemed to sum it up for everybody, and we went on. Jose, a medical supply salesman sitting at the back, with a halo of curly black hair, read the outline for his novel next.

It had enough plot for six books. Every few minutes a trainload of people would be herded out and shot, and then another generation would grow up, move to Texas or Los Angeles to start a restaurant, and then some more people would be herded off a train and shot. Or so it seemed.

The class didn't ask Jose a single question, and the teacher said only, "You certainly have a fine sense of drama."

At the end of class, three or four people followed me out to the parking lot to renew the attack on my plot. Several of them were apparently going to lose sleep at the thought that somewhere, someday, that tedious childhood might find its way into print.

The assignment for next week is to revise the outline. I'm going to put some trainloads of hostages in mine — maybe get them at the local night school — and have them all shot by bandits.

My First Shrink

A T 5 P.M. on a Wednesday night in my 37th spring, I find myself barreling through the city in the dusk, heading for my appointment with the shrink. My first ever.

I did some shopping for this guy, asking candidates how threatened they felt about being interviewed for the position as my analyst. One growled, "What's your problem?" What's yours, buddy?

I arrive at the block of California Street where all the shrinks huddle together. I am obviously repressing some parking spaces and denying others, because it takes a while. While I circle, I decide I resent Dr. Bruce Levin for wanting $90 an hour to talk to me when I am prepared to be fascinating.

Also, I wonder if he will appreciate finding out that I am not preshrunk. I come not from the self-indulgent, self-absorbed, shrink-visiting anal-retentive middle classes, but from the people — the oral-explosive, drinking-class Irish. We don't even know shrinks. They live in another neighborhood.

In short, I am offering Levin a wild and untended orchard. Nobody has been here before him, squinting nearsightedly at my psyche, spraying what needs pruning. He can just stroll around and pick up the fallen apples.

I have, on the drive over, tried to rehearse my little speech. What brings me to your office, doctor? "There's this guy — Neil — who doesn't want me to change but wishes I were different . . . "

Great. To get a guy? That's a real grown-up reason to hie me to a shrinkery. Nah.

"I'm trying to write a book about my family . . . " Nope. True, but too detached.

What brings me here? I guess it's time to kick over a few rocks, see what's under there. God, what an awful image. Must remember to tell the shrink.

Here's the door. I'm right on time, 5:50. If you're early, you're anxious; if you're late, you're hostile; if you're on time, you're compulsive. Pick up that apple.

Sounds of snuffling come from a nearby door — someone is getting her $90 worth. Since I have a few minutes to spare, I fill out the medical form.

"When did the illness begin?" it says. That stumps me. I pause, then write down "January 3, 1952" — my birthdate. It occurs to me that this is what the insurance companies would call a pre-existing condition, so I crumple it up and start a whole new form.

Oh here comes Levin, tall, skinny, halo of curly hair, around my age. Oh, great. My type. Let the transference begin.

We pad down a hallway past soothing watercolors and into a spacious office; then we take armchairs on opposite sides of the room. Discomfort rises in my breast. He's too far away, and the fat blue box of kleenex is too near. It's the only thing on my side of the room, like a challenge. Use me. Cry. Be good at this.

I begin my prattling, hear my own voice in my ears, telling him about Neil, about my family, about what has set me, ever so tentatively, on the path to self-exploration.

Levin smiles and speaks with the familiarity of an old friend. This is hopeless. He says nothing, even though I have asked him to flag me — raise his hand or something — when I am being glib or evasive. I need a woman shrink.

After twenty minutes, he digs out his appointment book and I dig out mine and we discuss the time of the next appointment. I wonder why he feels it necessary to do this on my time.

His childhood is beginning to interest me. He says that at this point in their lives, most people are pretty happy with their characters. I might conclude in a few weeks that I'm OK. This worries me.

But I guess you bring a shrink a vague problem, you get a vague solution. Garbage in, garbage out.

By this time, I have got off myself completely and am rattling on about Neil, and the shrink doesn't even notice. So much for raising his hand. . . . Oops, hour's up. At exactly 6:50, my new friend Bruce abruptly loses interest in my monologue, though I think I am having interesting insights into Neil's character.

Leaving, I notice Bruce has two heavy wooden doors, one right after the other. This guy needs a shrink.

"I noticed you have two doors," I say, brightly. "Did I pass the test?"

I picked up on my own need to pass tests — did Bruce? Did he notice my earlier reference to wanting to do well? Is he there? Hello? Do I like have an attitude problem, and if not, where can I find one, cheap, before next Wednesday?

Blonde Dyes By Her Own Hand

I STOPPED darkening my hair this weekend. It was kind of sudden and not altogether successful. OK, it was a disaster. All I had meant to do was frost my hair, which I've been doing since I was a kid. You buy a kit in the drugstore for ten bucks and lighten selected strands for what you hope will be a sun-streaked effect. Salons will tell you home kits don't work, but they do.

Salons also require appointments, and the thing about frosting your hair is that when the impulse hits, you have to do it right that second. One minute I was peacefully reading a book, and the next I wouldn't be happy until I could pass as a stunt double for Marilyn Monroe.

I asked my neighbor Marjanne to help. She runs a leading executive-search company out of her living room, but was more than happy to abandon the phones and fax for a hair-frosting party. This is female bonding at its finest. Men ought to try this — get together, fiddle with one another's hair, gab a little — it'd lower the old blood pressure right away.

Marjanne came over, accepted a glass of my premium house red and recklessly pulled a thick strand of hair out of every hole in my frosting cap while I sat on the floor with my own glass. Then she remembered she had a turkey in the oven and went tripping home while I finished the wine, smeared on the hair goo and went back to my book.

Hours passed. By the time I recalled I had a corrosive solution on my hair and rushed to wash it off, it was too late. When I lowered the towel, there in the mirror was the new me — a daffodil wearing a shocked expression.

I didn't panic. It was possible, I told myself, that being alone was making me overreact. My hair might look just fine to other people.

Ten minutes later I met my nine-year-old son, Patrick, and his friend Edward in the hallway. "Mom?" said Patrick. "What did you do? Can you bleach it back?"

"It looks as if I could walk over and lift that off your head," remarked Edward.

When Jim, my ex-husband saw my new look, I saw on his face a merry expression I haven't seen there for years. "It isn't really so bad," he grinned.

I was glad I put that spot of joy into his day.

I went to bed wanting to kill whoever it was said blondes have more fun. The next morning I woke at six and realized that I could now do anything I liked to my hair because it couldn't possibly get worse. I drove to the 24-hour Safeway, grabbed a box of Medium Ash Blonde off the shelf, brought it home and sloshed it on.

Twenty-five minutes later I looked in my mirror and thought — hey, not bad. I was very, very blonde still, but this at least was a color occasionally found on human beings.

The reaction has been mixed. Patrick still wants it back the way it was. I don't blame him — Mom is supposed to go on looking like Mom. Other opinions I just listen to and nod.

Jim, trying to talk me out of frosting my hair, used to rhapsodize about the terrific copper highlights I had when I stood under the light, and I would think, "Great, I'll just carry a lamp around with me."

My boyfriend said he liked my hair this way, which he'd better. As Shakespeare said, "Love is not love which alters when it alteration finds."

The heck with the natural look. After all, you can't take credit for what you're born with, only for what you do yourself. Where would Marilyn Monroe be if she'd clung to the hair color God gave her? We'd have a movie called "Gentlemen Prefer Mousy Brown Hair."

First Love and the Impossibly Cool Ian

WHEN I WAS in the third grade, I lived in Lagunitas, out in West Marin, and Ian lived in Forest Knolls, about a mile away. It was 1960. Mother sang along to "Steam Heat" on the record player, Eisenhower was president, my older sister had just got a Hula Hoop, and I was in love with Ian Cooper.

On Valentine's Day, I gave Ian a huge red heart to which I had glued about fifty little candy hearts. From across the classroom, I watched him picking off a candy. When he saw me watching, he scowled. He had given me the smallest possible valentine from his cellophane package, one about two inches across.

I didn't care. Ian was the smartest boy in the class, shorter than I was, with light sandy hair and an impossibly cool gaze. Once he had spilled his milk all over the desk and cried, but I chose not to think about that. He was the first boy I ever loved, and I loved him unreservedly. For the first time in my life, I was glad to have been born a girl because it meant I could grow up to marry Ian.

Ian's own feelings were clear enough — he wished I had never been born, never wound up in his third-grade class, and, above all, never found out where he lived.

I went to see him as often as I could. I'd ring the doorbell over and over. "Oh, it's you," he would say, opening the screen door with an air of resignation that meant his mother had told him to let his little friend in.

Luckily for me, Ian had a price. "Can you come to the store with me?" I'd ask. "I have fifty cents."

You could see the struggle on Ian's face. On the one hand, someone might see him in my company. On the other hand, fifty cents could buy a lot of Charleston Chews and Big Hunks.

"Let's see it," he'd say, and I would have to dig in my jeans pocket for the dimes and nickels I'd made picking blackberries from the bushes above the road and selling them door to door.

The time always came, too soon, when Mrs. Cooper wondered aloud whether my mother was missing me. I'd head home, then call Ian up to assure him I'd arrived safely.

When I learned we were moving away, at the end of that year, I ran to the phone to call Ian. "We're moving to Santa Cruz!" I said.

"Good," he said, and hung up the phone.

I called him back. "This is your last chance to be nice to me," I pointed out.

"Good riddance to bad rubbish," he said in his piping voice, and hung up again.

And that was it.

I never saw Ian again, except for an occasional glimpse across the crowded corridors in high school, but I never forgot him.

What I like remembering about Ian is not Ian, who I now realize was probably a somewhat priggish and uninteresting little boy. My memory of him — maybe everybody's memory of first love — is really of myself as I was then, heading down the hilly, candy-wrapper-strewn trail between our houses with my straight brown bangs high and foolish on my forehead, bearing my heart on my none-too-clean sleeve.

Remembering him means remembering an age when the cold nipping my ears was colder than it would ever be again, when the sky was so blue I stared at it endlessly, wondering where all that blue came from. When blackberries mashed in milk tasted so good I had to walk up and down in the yard as I ate them. When I loved unreservedly and asked for nothing back.

Missing the One Who Will Never Be

THAT'S MAKING me nervous," said the trainer from the Norplant company to my doctor, who had never inserted the capsules in anybody's arm before and thought she'd start with me. They were introducing it at Kaiser, and I was getting it for nothing in exchange for letting them practice on me. Norplant is a contraceptive: Five capsules in your arm will release a low-level hormone, keeping babies at bay for five years.

I was pinned to a bed, with the doctors crowded around. The Norplant representative told me she had one child and tried for years desperately to conceive another before giving up. "And I sell Norplant," she said. "Ironic, isn't it?"

As I lay there, surrounded by the other women, watching the capsules go into my arm one by one, I thought about babies.

Sometimes when Bill and I are alone, the kids off with their friends, the thought comes unbidden: What this place needs is a baby standing in his crib, slobbering on the neck of his T-shirt. Bill has no children, but he's curious.

"What do babies do all day?" he asks, watching one fuss on its mother's lap at a party.

The first one goes in. Wait, I want to cry, wait. These capsules could very well take me right up to menopause. This could be it for me.

But the doctor, getting the hang of it now, is putting in another one. These capsules, fanned out in a semi-circle under the skin of my upper arm, mean that if I decide, one night under a tender moon, to say oh-what-the-hell-let's-have-a- baby, I would have to wait for the night to pass, and make an appointment in the cold light of day to have the capsules removed.

The third capsule goes in. I remember what Bill's brother Ray said when he first saw his newborn daughter: "It's the only legitimate way you can fall in love again."

I watch babies at parties, tipping over on the rug, or cruising hell-bent for the hors d'oeuvres table, and catch sight of a mother sitting on the floor in another room, cradling a blanket. I watch, losing my place in the conversation. For a moment all I want in the world is to be off among the coats, tipping a bottle into a baby's mouth. I can so easily imagine being pulled back into that easiness, the weight of a baby's head on my arm, that series of predictable demands and known pleasures.

I felt like such an animal when I was pregnant. I growled at women who came near my mate, I dreamed of puppies. I even tried in my inept way to make pillows, to line the nest. I stored up fat against the coming famine.

"Really piling on the pounds, aren't we?" said the doctor unkindly, and I would skip breakfast and remove my wedding ring for the next weighing, but I didn't really mind. After they were born, I led my ducklings down to the pond, signing them up for kindergarten.

Though I live in a century riddled with angst, I never wondered what any of it meant, what it was all leading to. It was as another woman remarked: Babies turn your world from black and white to Technicolor.

Still, I have firmly decided, have practically for sure made up my mind, not to have more. I don't want to be pregnant again, don't want to drive to the preschool and sort through thirty little jackets. I want to keep my future hours empty, see what else life fills them with. I want to spend the time with the kids I have before they grow up.

I tell myself all this, but still, as the last capsule goes in, I feel a fleeting sadness. An image comes of a dark-haired child, coming in to throw down his books and chatter about what happened at school, the child I have decided not to spend my next twenty years raising.

When Summer Meant Nobody Got Older

WE ARE WELL into summer now, here in the city. Newspapers skid down the sidewalks, Morgan and her friends come down for breakfast wrapped in blankets, the sun shines somewhere north of Mill Valley. An early morning alarm gets Morgan off to summer school, Patrick's in Minnesota helping at his uncle's fishing resort, and Bill and I have to go to our jobs, cram vacation in somewhere, continue our vigorous program of occasional exercise.

Summer wasn't always like this. When I was growing up in Lagunitas, a perfect stillness waited for us Daly kids when we stepped out of school in June.

We had no summer school, no summer camps, no relatives to go visit. The calendar was a blank. Every day the hills of Lagunitas in West Marin pressed in and the light pressed down, and we had absolutely nothing to do.

It was as if the planet itself had come lazily to a stop, so that we could all hear the buzzing of the dragonflies above the creek, and the beating of our own hearts.

I was so bored I once blindfolded myself and went around bumping into my toys, trying to see them with new eyes. I thought about running away just for the excitement of it. Whenever I heard sirens, I hoped they'd get louder. I hoped our house was burning down.

Time hung heavy on our hands in a way it never would again. June was far away, September a distant blur. Without school to tell us who we were, fifth-graders or sixth-graders, good students or goof-offs, we were free just to be ourselves, to moon around the neighborhood with a head full of fantastical schemes, or build forts or briskly staff lemonade stands.

There was time for everything. Minutes were as big as plums, hours the size of watermelons. You could spend a quarter of an hour noticing the dust motes in the shaft of sunlight from the doorway and wondering if anybody else could see them.

I don't miss those long slow days, not really.

What I miss is summer time, that illusion that the sun is standing still and the future is keeping its distance.

Maybe that's why the two most beautiful words in the language are said to be "summer" and "afternoon" — because that's when nobody gets any older. On summer afternoons, kids don't have to worry about becoming adults, and adults don't have to worry about running out of adulthood. You can lie on your back watching clouds scud across the sky, and maybe later walk down to the store for a Popsicle. You can lose your watch and not miss it for two days.

These busy city kids I'm raising don't know what summertime is. They're on city time. "My life is going too fast," Patrick once grumbled on Sunday night as he got into bed. "This whole day went by just like that, and I didn't have enough fun."

He's a city child, a winter child, a child whose fun is packed into the short blurry weekends. Even in summer his hours grow shorter and begin to run together, faster and faster. It won't be long before an hour, once an eternity, is for him, too, a walk to the grocery store, a few paragraphs, three phone calls, half a movie.

Maybe that's why we still need long school vacations — to anchor kids to the earth, keep them from rocketing too fast out of childhood. If they have enough time on their hands, they might be one of the lucky ones who carry their summertime with them into adulthood, like a woman I once knew who wanted to go to medical school, though she was 56.

"My God, when you finish you'll be sixty!" a friend gasped.

"I'll be sixty anyway," she said.

She's on summer time.

Just Scoot A Little Bit Closer

I HAD MY ANNUAL gyn appointment this morning with the affable Dr. Jones at Kaiser. I have, to my horror, become used to this experience. I could read a book during the exam and actually remember what I read.

It wasn't always this way. I remember my first exam, when I was seventeen. I had been staring unseeingly at magazines for some time when a voice said, "The doctor will see you now."

They didn't have to rub it in, I thought.

I was led into a tiny room, handed a piece of tissue paper, told to put it on.

Left alone, I was confused. Did I take everything off the top, too? What if I did and the doctor looked at me as if to say, "Whoa, we got carried away, didn't we?" Did I leave my socks on? And what was I supposed to do with my clothes, just fling them over the chair as if I were getting ready for bed?

A long time had passed since the nurse left. For all I knew, the doctors had got out of their lease and moved away, forgetting the shivering patient in the second room on the left.

I stuck my underwear in the pockets of my jeans, rolled everything else into a ball, and then experimented with various ways of wearing the piece of tissue paper I had been given. Leave it open in front for the breast exam, or open in back, letting him tear open as needed? Were those armholes, or were they to make the breast exam easier? Forced to decide, I sort of stuck it on in front, then hopped up to the table.

The doctor, when he showed up, started chatting with me about everything under the sun, movies he had seen, the weather, everything. As he began the exam, he seemed not to notice what he was doing at all, except he would say very casually, "Just scoot down a bit."

I moved down the table a half inch or so. It was not the direction I wanted to go in.

"Just a bit more." He squinted, looked and gestured again, like a man guiding a truck backing up to the dock. "Whoa, that's good."

"Now try to relax," he said, taking what looked like dental instruments out of, from the feel of them, a nearby refrigerator. "This will pinch a little," he said. I answered, desperately, that I loved "Midnight Cowboy," what did he think of it?

"That's it," the doctor said after a while, smiling. "Nothing to it. See you next year."

Nothing to it. I'd get the results of my Pap smear in the mail.

He left so I could get dressed. They are allowed to see parts of you that you yourself hadn't got around to having a good look at, but it would be a huge breach of ethics, not to mention embarrassing all around, for them to watch you get dressed.

I got my clothes on and walked into the sunlight. I had had my first gyn checkup. I was a woman.

Now, dozens of such appointments and two kids later, my exams are a piece of cake. Dr. Jones, a real chatterbox, said today that he could find nothing wrong with me, then started to talk cheerfully about how many people my age are dropping dead of colon cancer. "But now we have this great test," he added.

I hoped it would be something men had to come in for this time. Tissue-paper gowns and icy instruments in unfamiliar places (while patient and doctor chat determinedly about those Niners) might tell them what we'd been subjected to all our adult lives.

But no. You mail your sample in.

They couldn't do that for Pap smears, I suppose.

Another Way We Fool Ourselves

I WAS OUT with my friend Mary the other night. I'd just been saying, over dinner, how nice it was not to have to worry about every nickel and dime now. It's especially nice after growing up dirt poor, picking blackberries at twenty cents a basket for pocket money and shopping at the Bargain Box. Mary agreed. We split the bill. It was only $12, since we had had only two Thai dishes and two glasses of water.

I had torn a two-for-one coupon to a North Beach comedy club out of the pink section, and we agreed to meet there after she parked her car at her house on Russian Hill, to save money on parking. The coupon I had ripped out said I could get my ticket validated at a nearby garage, so I drove directly there.

I spotted the garage and swung in. While I was parking, it occurred to me that this garage didn't say "Anchorage" on the sign, as it did on the coupon. When I got out to the sidewalk, my suspicions were confirmed: This was the wrong garage.

The heck with it, I thought. How much can it be, ten bucks? Money is a number in a bank account. So the number changes by a fraction. I didn't feel like driving to another garage. Besides, they'd charge me extravagantly for the two minutes I'd been parked. Better stay a couple of hours and get my money's worth.

I felt good as I crossed the street, being so free of petty anxiety about money that I could throw away ten bucks. I had some time to kill, so I went to some shops. Looked at holograms, tried on a sweater, adjusted my lipstick in a window. I tried to put the garage out of my mind, but it stayed there, a small, nagging worry, like an alarm buzzing in a faraway room.

I met Mary, and we each got in for $5 with my coupon. I mentioned to the guy at the counter where I parked, and he said I should really move my car, I'd save $6. While Mary got us a table, I sprinted over and did it, then hurried back. The car left my mind, and into it came the two-drink minimum.

All you have to do to make me lose all interest in drinking is to tell me I have to. I ordered a light beer and Mary got a Calistoga. I nursed my beer throughout the show, shaking my head every time the cocktail waitress looked over. I felt a little guilty: I had used that two-for-one coupon, and the show with Jake Johansen was a steal at $5. In the end we ordered two Calistogas to go, and put them in our purses to take home.

I like to think of myself as good about money, but my preoccupations with the price of things keep surfacing to refute my sunny opinion of myself. Inconsistency is the main theme: When I was married before, I accepted money from my husband but refused a joint checking account on the grounds that would limit my independence.

I've shared the deepest intimacies between men and women but have never shared a bank account with anyone. It's one thing to share your body, your house, your heart; it's another to let them have a gander at your spending habits.

There's inconsistency, too, in the way I rocket between wild extravagance and extreme penury, between $200 leather jackets I don't need and peculiar little economies like making long-distance calls from the office.

I'm not alone in this: A friend blasts the heat in her house night and day, yet washes out plastic sandwich baggies for re-use. Another gives $500 at a time to friends who need it, yet arrives empty-handed at parties.

I don't mind being inconsistent, but I would like to think of myself as good about money. I'm not alone in this, either: Everybody wants to think of himself as good about money, just as we all want to think we have a good sense of humor. Actually, no one is good about money, least of all me.

And least of all you. You were spotted picking up that BART card with 35 cents remaining value.

All the Lists I've Loved Before

AT 32, when my second marriage was coming apart, I made lists of furniture to divide: lamps, couches, bunk beds. Breaking up a marriage was a long ordeal, complicated and emotional, but a list was short and manageable. If I could separate the furniture, I could get through the next step, and the next.

I've been making lists all my life, but the kinds of things I note change over the years. As a kid in Lagunitas, I wrote New Year's resolutions: "Starting tomorrow, no candy. Brush teeth after every meal. Look up all unfamiliar words."

I loved my lists. Looking at them, suddenly, I was no longer a lazy kid addicted to Big Hunks, but a transformed being, with shining teeth and dictionary in hand.

In my teens, I lost the sense that I could improve myself, and instead took to cataloging everything that was gravely, irretrievably wrong with me, starting with the unsightly congenital bunions on my feet and working up past my knock-knees to a rib cage that stuck out, to an ugly forehead, small beady eyes and unruly brown hair.

Then I'd stare at the list, waiting for despair to descend. But it didn't look so bad. Written down like that, all my flaws were mere tracks on a white page.

In my early twenties, feeling optimistic again, I recorded the skills I had acquired, countries and states visited (two hours in the Dallas airport while changing planes counted as "visited Texas"), men slept with. "Type. Speak French. Drive a stick shift," one chart began.

In my thirties, going through that divorce, I took a few minutes every night to write down the ten times that day when I had felt happiest.

It was a deliberate attempt to cheer myself up, and it worked. I recorded such moments as joking with somebody at a garage sale, making tuna-fish sandwiches with the kids, getting work done, talking to my sister on the phone. I was surprised, looking at my list, to learn how often I'd been happy during a bleak time.

Now, at 41, I've given up most of my lists, along with the dream of brushing my teeth after every meal and looking up all unfamiliar words.

I've stopped making resolutions: Now I tell what I'm going to do by seeing what I'm doing. I've stopped obsessing over my real and imagined flaws, stopped keeping score.

My mother always said the forties are the best years of your life, and she's right. You need so many fewer lists.

But I'm still making them, of course, because they still give me the illusion that I am handling things. These days I make To Do lists on bits of scratch paper.

I write down only those things I don't particularly feel like doing, so today, for example, my list reads: "Buy new tires, call about Versatel card, pick up dry-cleaning, give the dog a bath."

The minute after I send the wet dog out to shake himself off in the back yard, I cross that item out with a thick felt pen, the mere motion of the pen giving me proof that I'm moving briskly through my life.

I like crossing things out so much that sometimes, to my horror, I find myself adding to the list something I've already done.

I'll call the plumber, then, realizing I can't cross it off if it isn't written down, scrawl "Call plumber," and draw a heavy line through it, smartly.

I should worry about this, I suppose. It's not the only odd little quirk I have. Just yesterday as we were leaving I waved to the dog in the window. Maybe I should make a list of my more disquieting habits.

I bet they won't look so weird, written down.

Speaking Freely About Abortion

BILL AND I were sitting on a bench outside the San Francisco Coffee Company on 24th Street, drinking our lattes and reading the paper. I hadn't been following the whole abortion thing very closely, but that wasn't the reason I was having trouble understanding it.

"I don't get it," I said. "What does it mean, that family planning clinics can't mention abortion to their clients? I thought abortion was legal."

"It is," he said. Bill is a voracious newspaper reader: He knows everything.

"Then why can't they mention it?"

"Because they get federal money. The Supreme Court ruled that the government is entitled to decide what it wants to spend its money on, and that its decision to forbid federally funded family planning clinics from speaking freely about abortion doesn't violate the right of free speech."

"You can get an abortion legally, but it's illegal to be told about them?"

"Right."

The sidewalk was crowded with young couples — and not-so-young couples — and their babies. Next to us, a father trapped a giggling toddler in the circle of his feet.

I turned back to the article, feeling sad.

Simon says to take a big step backward.

I knew a Marin County high school girl who got pregnant when she was seventeen. I remember how scared she was when she discovered, after a visit to the doctor, that Johnny had sneaked up the back steps to her room once too often.

She stood in the bright sun of the doctor's parking lot, too dazed to get into the car right away. What was she going to do? Have the baby and then give it up? She knew she didn't have that kind of courage.

She wasn't even seeing Johnny anymore, but she decided she'd marry him — that's what she'd do. He was 17 and had a good job as a box boy at a grocery store. She could probably keep working at the Orange Julius for a while, then get baby-sitting jobs. They could live with his mother.

Johnny would have to forget about engineering school, of course. She thought maybe she could finish high school, if she could endure walking around the school pregnant, but college and her hopes for a career in journalism were on hold, maybe permanently.

Johnny and she sat out in his car and talked about it, bleakly, not looking at each other. Then they began asking around about illegal abortions. People said you could get them in Tijuana.

Then it happened. Just as her choices — and his — had narrowed to a teenage marriage or a back-alley abortion, a family friend told her about a new law just passed.

If you knew how to do it, you could get a legal abortion in Marin County in 1969. All you had to do was convince three sympathetic shrinks that you were unhinged enough by the pregnancy to present a danger to yourself. The friend gave her the names of three she could go see.

And that was it. She checked into Ross Valley Hospital, and by the next morning it was over. She had her life back. She and Johnny parted with relief, and she went back to school, happy to put to rest the ridiculous rumor that Adair Daly, who never did anything wrong, had got herself knocked up.

I thought of that story as I sat in the sun, 22 years later, still grateful to that friend who gave me information that changed my life, and read with growing sadness about a new ruling that insists, under penalty of law, that the flow of information from those who have it to those who need it must stop.

Time Zones Are a Trip

WHAT'S AMAZING about me is that I don't suffer from jet lag. I get a little tired, sure, but that's it. I just throw it off. The kind of people who get jet lag are one, older, and two, people of settled habits. So that clearly leaves me out.

So I wasn't worried on my account that we were flying through ten time zones to Athens.

Bill's another matter. He's eight months older, and thus more subject to maladies of all kinds. Before we went to Italy two years ago with my sister Adrian, I read up on jet lag, to help him out. On the plane, we did everything to mime going to bed, short of getting into pajamas and asking each other crossly if the cat was out or in.

Then when we got to Rome, we did as they say to do: walked around with our sunglasses off, talked to people, ate breakfast. I marched right into a bar and ordered a latte in Italian, and I was proud even when they set a glass of milk in front of me. We were, as advised, persuading our weary flesh that it was a brisk morning on Italian summer time, and not as our airplane-dented bodies thought, the middle of the night, time for California dreaming.

Despite all our precautions, Bill and Adrian were wrecks. Bill looked blankly at the Colosseum, and saw only a giant pillow. When we stopped for lunch, Adrian had a tiny nap next to her untouched pasta. We went to bed when the clock said it was bedtime — and then lay there awake most of the night, listening to the gentle cacophony of the Italian night — street noise, bursts of applause, cats, the whine of motor scooters.

I slept more than they did, naturally. I did have some sort of weird Italian flu for the first three days, but that couldn't have been jet lag, which, as I have said, I am too young for.

This year I arrived at Athens feeling fine. While Bill dozed against a post, I marched into the invigorating Athenian sunshine and found an air-conditioned limousine that was, amazingly, just as cheap as the taxis that the other passengers had lined up to take (we've been told that a cab from the airport would be $5 or so).

When our hotel appeared through the haze of heat and smog in downtown Athens, I shook Bill, since he was holding the Greek money."Eleven thousand drachmas?" he said, snapping awake. "That's $50!"

That was not jet lag. That was a simple error in calculation that could happen to anybody.

When we came home last Thursday, we woke up the next morning at 4:30. The second morning, 4:50. Bill was taking about an hour to finish his sentences, and I remember looking at a pile of messages and thinking, "Yeah, right."

But that was normal post-trip incredulity at being expected to return to work, not actual jet lag. Actual jet lag is like when Adrian came back from Italy, got up at 4:30 and went grocery shopping at Safeway.

"How're you feeling?" the clerk asked.

"Fine."

He looked at her basket. "I asked because it's illegal to buy beer before 6 a.m. Register won't even read it." She went to work and said to her boss, "I don't know what you're talking about." Then she went home to take a little nap, and woke up the next day.

But then Adrian's older than I am, and can be expected to suffer from an ailment that worsens as you age. Here I am already at work, after a trip from Istanbul that took us to four airports over 23 hours and four passport checks.

True, I am typing this at 3 a.m. after having paid the bills and having a bowl of Raisin Bran, but that's simply because I like to get an early start on the day. I couldn't stay in bed anyway, because Bill is washing the sheets — for the second time. He couldn't remember if he had put soap in the first time.

It must be hard, being so susceptible to a simple change of time zones. I'd better go help him. But first I'm just going to put my head on the keyboard for the tiniest of minutes, and then I'llllllll. .

The Eyes Don't Have It Anymore

IN A DRUGSTORE yesterday, I had to ask the counterman to tell me the number on my strip of photo negatives. I had never asked anybody to read something for me before. I was the one to whom other people handed their packages to ask what the directions said. I was one of those people who are always offering to read distant signs for you, whether you wanted to know what they said or not.

I can still read those signs, but that's about it. I've lost my keen eyesight. If you dropped me into a desert with only a guidebook in eight-point type, I would die. I can hardly make out the kids as they leave for school these days: For all I know, they could be wearing scuba tanks. I sign anything they put in front of me.

At first I didn't realize my sight was dimming. I spent a whole year, for example, being annoyed about the light in our house. We bought an expensive new fixture for the kitchen and new lamps for the bedroom. I was thinking of knocking off the roof next, just to get some light in this cave we live in. Which is, of course, actually a corner house flooded with sunlight.

Then I started getting mad at the prescription bottles. How could anybody read those tiny warnings? I'd squint at a bottle, and for all I knew, it said, "Take all of these with a fifth of whiskey and then dance the Virginia reel."

I started wearing occasional reading glasses in June, right after I rubbed the shampoo from our hotel bathroom all over my arms, then went to a party that way, bringing a strangely pungent odor with me. The very next day, I took two Teen Vitamins instead of the aspirin I thought I had picked up. I had an inexplicable desire to wear baggy clothes, play the Dogg Pound CD and get my eyebrows pierced.

Now, I knew this was coming. I read that no one gets to 50 without needing glasses. But Bill, 44 to my much more youthful 43, doesn't need them yet. On our trip to Europe, nothing impeded his view of me reading the guidebooks through an old pair of Morgan's glasses. "No, really, you look very cute," he laughed as I gripped my book, my very posture daring him to utter even one word.

I don't have my own glasses yet, except for a pair I bought at Price Club. I had lunch with a friend who showed me how his trifocals work, and it seemed like a bad joke, something out of a science fiction movie, that you would have to direct your eyes to a different tiny section of glass when you wanted to look at a book, a face or a movie.

It's not the first time I've worn glasses. When I was two and cross-eyed, I had huge horn-rimmed spectacles. The doctors said I would need them forever, but I kept losing them in the driveway, where cars ran over them, and in the midst of everything else there was to worry about, the idea of my wearing glasses got lost. My eyes got better, and that was that.

Now I have to look for my stupid glasses everywhere (yes, I can see to find my glasses, smart aleck), but I don't think I will have that kind of luck twice. I'm going to have crummy eyesight until the day the Grim Reaper comes for me (and has to clear his throat so I'll know which corner he's standing in).

I am less fit for survival now, and that is a fact I'm not blind to.

This is unfair because nowadays we can fight off practically every other sign of aging, with everything from pills to jogging to surgery to hair dye to Wonderbras. But we don't get better eyesight no matter how much we work at it. Contacts work, but you still know you can't see well.

So failing eyesight threatens to make me do that most un-American of things: accept my age. (Well, failing eyesight and the recent humiliation of being turned down for the focus group on vodka because they wanted people younger than forty.) It forces me to make my peace with the gentle decline of the body.

And it threatens to force Bill to accept his own age: If he's curious to know what the fates have in store, he has only to cast his own aging peepers over to my side of the bed, where I feebly grope around for my specs.

The Natural History Of the City Street

MY BROTHER Sean didn't want to go for a walk, I could tell, but I dragged him out anyway. Here on a visit, Sean, 48, lives in a cabin he built himself on ten acres of forest on a mountain in Washington state, near the Canadian border. He hauls his water in by the bucketload from a well, runs his lights off a generator, milks his five goats and sells goat cheese to his neighbors. He rarely comes home, but when he does, what he wants to know is why I would want to live in a city.

And I want to explain it to him, but first I have to take my walk, and since he's here, he has to come along. Out we go, into what James Hillman called "that erotic flush in the city street." After skirting the neighbor's construction signs where a new sidewalk is going in, we descend into the Castro, which always seems to be either recovering from a party or about to throw one. I give a dollar to the sweet-faced woman who always sits in the same place outside the florist, holding a cup. "Thank you," she says as if I have handed her a cup of tea.

I'm still trying to think of a good answer to Sean's question. I imagine that life on his mountaintop is tranquil, full of natural rhythms and views of forest and sky, full of silences. But my thinking is interrupted by the movie on the outdoor monitor at the "Hello, Gorgeous!!" Barbra Streisand museum, actually an alley and a tiny store. As we stop to watch, people pet my sheltie. Everybody in San Francisco had a sheltie when they were little, memories that flood them when they see Cody standing there looking like an exact miniature of Lassie.

Once over the Castro Street hill, our sweatshirts tied around our waists now, we start running into people I know on 24th Street: Ernie with the twin daughters we've watched go from bundled toddlers to lively girls, Sarah with two-year-old Conor, who likes to stamp on Bill's shoes and today has to settle for mine.

Along the way we hear snatches of dramas we never hear the end of. "What are you doing this weekend?" a man calls to a friend he spots across the street. "Remodeling the kitchen," a guy on the other side yells back, and his friend calls, "Hot!"

We watch two babies earnestly talking to each other in baby talk, and suddenly they both burst out laughing.

As we head back home over the Noe hill, Sean is breathing hard, but I'm used to the hills. Every night Bill and I take this walk, using the hour to tell each other the day's accumulated stories.

When we miss our walk, for days afterward I think of things I forgot to tell him, and I bang on the bathroom door, which he hates. We walk to restaurants, to North Beach to meet a painter, to the Marina to see a movie. The street draws us more and more, until we get into our cars only to move them on street cleaning day.

I feel as if I'm claiming the city when I walk, like a squire riding over his domain. It's all mine, somehow, though I'm pleased to let other people live here too — I like a crowded party. Sean and I walk on, looking east at the city skyline. Lit by the setting sun, it rears up like a theme park billboard: You Are Here.

At Market and Noe, Sean exclaims at the traffic rushing by, but I'm watching a golden retriever pass us, a bouquet in his mouth, his owner far behind. Several of us have stopped to smile at the dog, our eyes meeting in that way they do in a city.

Sean perks up on the home stretch up Noe, past the new coffee store that the neighbors complained about and now swarm to, past the hospital where Morgan had an emergency earring-ectomy when she was small, and back up our steps, the dog pausing as usual on the fourth step up to have his leash unsnapped.

After Sean went back to his mountain cabin, I found, shining in the wet concrete of the neighbor's new sidewalk, the word "Sean" followed by a sketch of a dove. While I was at work, he'd been out taking walks. And who could blame him?

The Old Woman We Want to Be

YOU COULDN'T SEE this woman in the fading light and feel afraid of getting old. She was just an old woman getting into a canoe, as my sisters and Morgan and I sat on the gravelly shore and watched. I was up at Blue Lake in Mendocino County, where my sister Robin had taken a cabin for four days.

Although her hair shone silver in the fading light, and her face was lined, the woman looked strong and slim in her red one-piece racing suit. She must have been at least seventy, but she drew the eye with an almost erotic charge. The toned muscles of her thighs tensed as she bent to lift a little boy into the boat, then clambered in herself.

I stared, taking a mental snapshot, wanting to remember this.

I grew up thinking of old people as an oddly afflicted species who live in dark, sour-smelling houses with doilies on everything and old cakes moldering under covers. Old women had humped necks and wore nylons that bagged at the ankle. Old men had flapping clothes and freckled pates. Old age seemed a far worse calamity than death, a time when women grew whiskers on their faces and bodies grew sick and slow.

An old woman I knew confirmed this. "Never get old," she whispered to me sadly, and took her own life.

The woman was rowing now, her biceps catching the fading light. A man on the shore — her son? — shouted to her that they were about to eat, and asked if she wanted a hamburger.

No, she said, they had just decided to row to China and back. Well, she wouldn't want one, I thought, watching. You don't look like that at that age from eating hamburgers.

Nothing about her suggested vanity, or dieting; it seemed to be all about strength. You looked at her and thought about the good food she'd been eating, not the food she'd gone without.

I imagined her life. She swam for an hour every morning, and always ate lightly, but with such huge enjoyment that juices ran down her face. She always felt good, underneath her ordinary clothes; she felt strong.

"That's what I want to look like when I'm old," I told my sisters and Morgan, and they looked over, and fell silent themselves, as we imagined ourselves steadily getting not only older but also stronger, taking more pleasure in our bodies, until we were seventy ourselves, and as strong and straight as the woman in the rowboat. As Robin joked, she'd be our row model.

We'd been out in a boat that day, too, and I'd had to struggle to haul myself into it, bruising a leg in the process. I doubt I can do even twenty girls' push-ups. We'd been in bathing suits all day, too, staring down at our white legs, straining to see ourselves in the streaked mirror of the lakeside bathroom, sneaking glances at one another, assessing.

You spend a lifetime doing this. How many minutes spent assessing and despairing at your body, and how many minutes frankly enjoying, even admiring?

I thought of Morgan at age twelve, proudly carrying me around the living room on her back, tottering only slightly, showing off her strength. She's only eighteen now, but it's been years since she told me how strong she is.

Later we saw the woman standing by a campfire, smoking a cigarette. My sisters nudged me, but I decided not to care. It was only a Merit Light, I decided, and she allowed herself them only while at Blue Lake with her son and his family.

Later that evening the kids and I left, and I passed the woman on the road. Automatically, I smiled and waved. It startled her, but it felt natural to me. I knew her. I hoped to see her again, when I'm seventy, in the mirror.

Packing the Khakis For Indonesia

I NEVER PACK my own suitcase when I'm getting ready for a trip. I pack for somebody else entirely. The person I pack for is someone I hardly recognize, but I can tell from what she's taking that she's somebody I'd like to be.

We are going to Indonesia for three weeks, and I just threw in a khaki wraparound skirt for the warm afternoons. That's how I know I am somehow packing for someone else: I wear skirts to my own weddings, and that's pretty much it. I'm like my sister Adrian, who did consent to get married in a dress, but had a rolled-up pair of jeans in her purse for afterward.

I own several skirts, though, and the person I am packing for appears to be taking those, even the black "kicky" skirt that is perhaps a tiny bit wrong for the equator, and a long black dress. She even tossed in a baggie containing a sparkly necklace with matching dangly earrings.

I envy her that — I've always wanted to be able to wear those eye-catching, shoulder-grazing earrings that other women do, rather than my training-wheel versions, tiny little I'm-not-really-wearing-earrings stubs of color.

And she is chic: I can tell from this pair of tiny strapless sandals I'm putting in that she strides across the world's surfaces in pretty shoes. I myself go everywhere in the same pair of battered green hiking sandals or risk a pair of weepy feet.

She's also taking a cute red belt, instead of leaving her tops hanging loose. And — aha! — this filmy night stuff. I have some identical to it, that Bill bought me, but I'm waiting to feel right about my body before I wear it for him. This woman has no such problems with body image. There the stuff is, bold as brass.

But then she appears to be considerably thinner than I am, able to wear the shorts and little tops that make me want to suck my stomach in constantly. She appears to be a girl of the type I've always wanted to be, wearing heels and tight skirts and able to not only buy eyeliner but, presumably, put it on.

She is a serious reader, eagerly seeking new information. Here's a copy of *Tristram Shandy,* and one called *Flaubert's Parrot* and several guidebooks. She won't be needing any novels, the kind you collapse with on the upper deck, with the sun on your legs and a drink in your hand.

She prefers to put her vacation time to better use than that. It's clear from these guidebooks under the lingerie that she takes an alert interest in her surroundings. I myself have trouble keeping my mind on those dense little paragraphs packed with dates. My own idea of getting ready for a destination is to steep myself in novels set there. My notion of getting ready to visit Indonesia, for example, was to read Joseph Conrad's *Outcast of the Islands* and Charles Corn's enthralling *Distant Islands,* not the *Lonely Planet* guide.

I've always packed like this, not only for trips, but for moves. When I started college, I imagined myself living in a little room in the Sunset, reading poetry down by the beach. This was far from how I usually spent my time, but I would be different, living in the city and going to school.

When I went to live in Paris I brought along a stiff leather coat that reached to my calves and cost half the money I had made working as a banquet waitress at Dominic's Restaurant. I thought that walking Parisian boulevards would turn me into the kind of person who would wear that coat.

Somehow it never turns out like that. I never wore that unwieldy coat once. And I have an idea that when I get to Indonesia, I'll rummage through this strangely packed suitcase, searching desperately for my Nike sandals, for my storybooks and jeans. Halfway across the world, and I keep running into myself.

The First Sunday of The Rest of Your Life

S ATURDAYS ARE great. Saturdays are like the first half of your life. You're young, time stretches out ahead of you, you have an endless list of things to do and plenty of time to do them in. You can watch the game, go to the lamp store, get that poster dry-mounted, get a beef stew simmering on the stove, make love, find out why the car is making that scraping sound, go to the movies. Or you can lie in your back yard with the newspapers on your face. There's always Sunday.

But Sundays. Sundays are like the second half of your life. On Sundays you are Andrew Marvell, always hearing time's winged chariot hurrying near. You haven't even gotten up yet, and already time is running out. You can't do it all anymore. You can go to the art exhibition, or see a matinee, or visit your dad, but then what about that project you wanted to spend a couple of hours working on?

Sunday is a slipstream, bearing you downward toward the black hole of Sunday night. When Patrick was a little boy, Sundays would drive him mad.

"The weekend's almost gone and I haven't done anything!" he would wail over his pancakes on Sunday morning.

Now Patrick is eighteen, which means for him it's still just 10 a.m. Saturday morning. He has time. But I'm 46, and it's early Sunday morning for me. The whole day stretches ahead of me, but after that the weekend is over. Monday looms — Monday, and the grave.

That's why I sold my tennis racket in our garage sale last week. "Why are you selling that?" Patrick wanted to know. He was astonished when I said I had tried, even meeting a coach at the Mission High School tennis courts for lessons once a week, advertising in the *Noe Valley Voice* for a partner, and then buying this $140 racket at a store on Sacramento Street, but had finally concluded that I'd never been any good at tennis and should just stop playing it.

A guy on a bike bought the racket, slinging it across his back and

pedaling away. With him he took all those days I had spent practicing against the backboard back in my Drake High School days,
trying to hit the white line painted on the board, all the games I
played with my brother at the San Anselmo courts, all the lessons I
took at Club Med. And with it he took all the time it would take
from other things, if I kept trying to play a game I'm no good at.

At eighteen, all the doors are open. You can still grow up to be a
firefighter, hike the Andes, live in a commune, live in Manhattan,
sing in nightclubs. Patrick sold his fishing rod in the garage sale, but
he could buy one again, if he ever felt like fishing.

But for the first time in my life I find myself crossing some things
out. I don't suppose, really, that I will ever live for a year in
Manhattan.

Bill sold his racquetball racket at the same garage sale, so I guess
that's over for him. I never saw him play. One of his bachelor
amusements. Nowadays his interest is cooking. He undertook it
with reluctance, when he understood the choice of it or Wheaties
for dinner every night, but now he spends evenings paging through
cookbooks, and serves me scallops when I have said I don't like scallops.

So it's not a narrowing down, necessarily, my giving up my tennis
racket. New interests crowd in. Traveling, writing, biking, hiking
and eating Tamed Pork Vindaloo with Spinach and Potatoes at my
own kitchen table on a Monday night.

Still it surprises me, that I can say it: I will never play tennis again.
I guess it seems stark because it means I will someday die. With the
promise of immortality, you can say, "Let me hang onto that thing,
you never know." I have only forty years left. On Sundays, you have
to make choices.

I am hanging onto the camera tripod at the back of my closet,
though. Sundays can be long and satisfying, and I may still take
that series of black and white city photographs I've been thinking
about for so long.

When
Children
Turn
Into
Cats

The Muted Joys of Childbirth

THE DAY OF my son's birth was a brilliantly sunny Saturday. Everybody was bustling about in a very annoying way, plumping pillows, chattering away about centimeters of dilation and how strong the baby's heartbeat sounded. Nobody seemed to have any interest in my heartbeat, and nobody, but nobody, was getting the picture here. I was not having a good time.

Just as I was about to bring this up, I was wracked by a pain so great that it felt as if a giant were squeezing me out like a sponge. "Little twinge, hmmm?" said Dr. Warner, absently. He was making one of his infrequent appearances at my bedside, in between listening to the football game on an office radio. I had arrived at nine in the morning, and it was now eleven.

What was I doing here anyway? I wasn't the kind of person someone would hand a baby to. I always was the one who stepped high over the tots on my way to the drink table.

I was, in short, cut out to be a maiden aunt, someone who arrives from some exotic junket in a cloud of perfume, carrying armfuls of presents and having to take a wild stab at the names of her nieces and nephews.

How a glamorous maiden aunt had come to be lying for the second time in a badly decorated room in the alternative birth center was an old story — you meet a guy, you like the cut of his jib, and bang, you're a pawn in nature's scheme to cover every inch of the Earth with humans.

The first time around, I was into the birthing experience. I walked for miles every day, attended childbirth classes, made long lists of names. When Morgan was born, "Chorus Line" was playing on the stereo and I was thirty points ahead of Jim in Scrabble. I was sure that only professional ethics kept the doctor from commenting on Morgan's unearthly beauty and the intelligent glint in her eye.

This time I had done nothing. I had heard that second births were easy — you practically just dropped by the hospital and picked up your baby. Besides, I knew all about childbirth, having been through it one whole time. I skipped the walking and left the birth books on the shelf. I even had the occasional glass of wine, though I couldn't help visualizing the baby swinging tipsily from lamp shades in the womb when I did.

I also had forgotten the pain, but that first contraction was a way of bringing it all back to you. While I was hanging half on and half off the bed, with my nose touching the floor — the only position I felt comfortable in — the giant hand squeezed again. I was supposed to be doing my Lamaze panting, of course, but I had forgotten how.

All similarities between us and those happy Lamaze parents in the birthing pamphlets had disappeared long ago. Lamaze couples race-walk to the hospital after a hearty granola and yogurt breakfast, do their rapid breathing number while reading poetry to one another and the select few dozen friends they've invited to watch the birth, and ten fun-filled minutes later notice the arrival of a rosy, fit and alert Lamaze infant, ready to be fitted into a backpack and borne off to a Save the Whales march.

As for me, I was going to give the doctor one more chance to give me drugs, and then I was going to try to get somebody with real connections, like a screenwriter.

Dr. Warner loomed up, six feet of starched unconcern. His every movement said, "This is a man who wants to get back to the game."

"Pain killers?" he said, looking at me as if trying to remember what they were. "They would only relax you between contractions, and you already look relaxed."

I looked relaxed? How would I look if I were in pain?

"You said," I ground out between one of my relaxing contractions, "that you would give me something if I asked for it."

"Believe me," he said, fastidiously flicking my sweat off his sleeve, "you don't need it."

I waved him away. This man could whistle for his fee.

The actual moment of birth is moving. You take off all your clothes — this is after nine months of eating enough not for two, but for a small country — assume the most unflattering position imaginable, and do what the books euphemistically call "bearing down."

"It's a boy!"

A boy? A boy?

Oh God, I wanted a boy.

My baby was the color of a plum and the size of a small van. His father, Jim, his hand trembling in a way that alarmed even blase Dr. Warner, scissored carefully through the cord.

"Come meet your mom," he said through tears, and settled the baby in the crook of my arm before kissing us both.

The doctor said, "I want to be here when they weigh that sucker," and went back to the game. Jim rushed off to call his ninety relatives in the Midwest with the news.

Then it was just me and the baby, with the May sunlight streaming in on us both. He lolled on my arm, all, as it turned out, nine pounds fourteen ounces of him, and stared very seriously at me with dark blue eyes. He was gradually becoming a softer decorator color, more of a mauve. On him it looked good.

I couldn't take my eyes off him. Feeling only a little silly, I told him who he was, and how fast I was falling for him, and that he had an eighteen-month-old sister at home who was probably at that very moment working out a way to make his death look accidental.

I decided it would be all too easy to spoil him.

"So," I said, just before we both nodded off. "When are you planning to get a job?"

Patrick with turtle

Patrick and
Morgan

When Children Turn Into Cats

I JUST REALIZED that while children are dogs, loyal and affection-ate, teenagers are cats. It's so easy to be the owner of a dog. You feed it, train it, boss it around, and it puts its head on your knee and gazes at you as if you were a Rembrandt painting. It follows you around, chews the dust covers off the Great Literature series if you stay too long at the party and bounds inside with enthusiasm when you call it in from the yard.

Then, one day around age thirteen, your adoring little puppy turns into a big old cat. When you tell it to come inside, it looks amazed, as if wondering who died and made you emperor.

Instead of dogging your footsteps, it disappears. You won't see it again until it gets hungry, when it pauses on its sprint through the kitchen long enough to turn its nose up at whatever you're serving. It sometimes conks out right after breakfast. When you reach out to ruffle its head, in that old affectionate gesture, it twists away from you, then gives you a blank stare, as if trying to remember where it has seen you before.

It might steel itself to the communication necessary to get the back door opened or the car keys handed to it, but it finds even that amount of dependence disagreeable.

Stunned, more than a little hurt, you have two choices. The first — and the one chosen by many parents — is that you can contin-ue to behave like a dog owner. After all, your heart still swells when you look at your dog, you still want its company, and naturally when you tell it to stop digging up the rose bushes, you still expect it to obey you, pronto.

It pays no attention now, of course, being a cat. So you toss it onto the back porch, telling it it can stay there and think about things, Mister. It glares at you, not deigning to reply. It wants you to recognize that it has a new nature now, and it must feel inde-pendent or it will die.

You, not realizing that the dog is now a cat, think something must be desperately wrong with it. It seems so anti-social, so distant, so sort of depressed. It won't go on family outings.

Since you're the one who raised it, taught it to fetch and stay and sit on command, naturally you assume that whatever is wrong with it is something you did, or left undone. Flooded with guilt and fear, you redouble your efforts to make your pet behave.

Only now, you're dealing with a cat, so everything that worked before produces exactly the opposite of the desired result. Call it, and it runs away. Tell it to sit, and it jumps on the counter. The more you go toward it, wringing your hands, the more it moves away.

Your second choice is to do the necessary reading, and learn to behave like a cat owner. Put a dish of food near the door, and let it come to you. If you must issue commands, find out what it wants to do, and command it to do it.

But remember that a cat needs affection, too, and your help. Sit still, and it will come, seeking that warm, comforting lap it has not entirely forgotten. Be there to open the door for it.

Realize that all dog owners go through this, and few find it easy. My glance used to travel from my cat Mike looking regal and aloof on the fence to a foolish German shepherd on the sidewalk across the street, jumping for joy simply because he was getting to go outside. I miss the little boy who insisted I watch "Full House" with him, and who has now sealed himself into a bedroom with a stereo and TV. The little girl who wrote me mash notes is now peeling rubber in the driveway.

The only consolation is that if you do it right, let them go, be cool as a cat yourself, one day they will walk into the kitchen and give you a big kiss and say, you've been on your feet all day, let me get those dishes for you — and you'll realize they're dogs again.

There's No Time Like the First Time

WELL, IT WAS bound to happen. My only son asked a girl over yesterday for the very first time. I had heard a lot about her — Oona this, Oona that — and then the doorbell rang and there she was, standing mute on my doorstep. What could I do? I asked her in.

She was pretty enough, I suppose, with her big brown eyes and long brown hair, tangled in a way that suggested she could attract boys without any overzealous attention to toilette. But where had she been when I was tucking him in at night, finding his stuffed brontosaurus behind the couch, teaching him to step into his swing? Had I done all that just to lose him to the first skirt to come his way?

Of course, I knew what Patrick saw in her. He didn't want to tell me, but I coaxed it out of him one night over cups of hot chocolate: She can snap her toes better than anybody else in the second grade.

A cheap accomplishment, you say. But yours is not the heart of a six-year-old boy. To him, a really gifted toe snapper is right up there with the angels. This is it for him.

I know it is, because I have plumbed the depths of his *affaires du coeur* before. Last year, in kindergarten, he met a girl who never went outside the lines when she colored. This absolutely floored him, and he scotch-taped her drawings to his bedroom wall.

That blew over harmlessly enough before anything could come of it — she was transferred out — but Oona was different. For the half hour before her arrival, he simply sat on the couch, arms tightly folded at his sides. He was just waiting.

When she arrived, the toe snapper, Patrick, his sister Morgan and I took an assortment of balls and went over to the local junior high school. It was Sunday, the sun was shining, Patrick's hopes were high.

It had taken him since Christmas break just to get her phone number, and then he had lost more time dialing wrong numbers, but he had persisted and now she was here. She had come to his house! — and therefore could no longer be regarded as totally impervious to his charms.

That was at noon. By one o'clock, after the egg salad sandwiches and grocery store sodas, she had torn his heart to bits. She played only with his sister, she refused a ride on his skateboard, she didn't even look his way when he proposed a game of toss.

Patrick hunched at my side on the playground all afternoon, 58 pounds of sheer male misery.

I could feel no sense of triumph as I helped him blow his nose, brushed the blond hair back from his brow. Love had brought him only pain.

I said, "She's shy and only knows how to play with girls." He said, bitterly, that he wished he were a girl, then. I whispered back that I didn't think that was the answer.

In time, he'll get over it. It might take an hour, but life's joys — the warmth of the sun on his face, the solid thump of a rubber ball against our neighbor's wall — will once more have meaning. There will be other Oonas — some hussy who knows the multiplication tables by heart, another whose handwriting is heartbreakingly symmetrical.

Never again, though, will it be the first time. Never again will he give his heart as freely. Oona is gone now — she just blithely skipped off to her piano lesson. She will never know what she has done.

When Your Home Is a Landlord's Castle

M Y LANDLORD and I are locked in mortal combat. He, with the blood of the owners singing in his veins, is trying to do as little as he can, while I, obeying the ancient law of the tenant, am trying to get away with as much as possible.

Sometimes the tide of battle goes his way. At these times the hallway stays dark, the toilet runs, the horrible '50s linoleum in my bedroom snaps at my heels, and the wheezing fridge has little accidents in the night that have to be wiped up in the morning. While this is happening, my landlord leads his life placidly elsewhere, buffeted from life's unpleasantness by the third of my income I mail to his house every month.

Sometimes I seem to be winning. While he's out spending my money, I stay happily at home, trying to figure how which part of the walls will take a nail by trying different places. I drag my desk heavily across the wood floor of the living room, then decide I liked it better where it was, and drag it heavily back.

I carry mountain bikes in and out, their pedals raking the walls. I keep company with men who rip smoke alarms out of the ceiling instead of just turning them off. Then I call up and complain the smoke alarm isn't working.

At night I tiptoe into two little rooms, kissing two children good night. It says on the lease I have only one. I simply miscounted; it could happen to anyone.

And now that I look around, I seem to have a cat. How did that get in here?

Given these tiny irregularities, I naturally don't like to bother the landlord with my little problems. He, naturally, would prefer not to be bothered. We had been in complete harmony on this point for the 16 months of my residence.

Then the water heater lost all heart. It couldn't go on without its old friend the fridge. It started weeping brown tears, tears that became a sea in the little room it shares with Patrick.

I had to write a little note.

My landlord knows that into every landlord's life a little note must fall. He let the usual six months go by, then arrived unannounced last Saturday with a crew of workmen in a truck. One guy shouldered a roll of carpeting and headed for my room. It looked an awful lot like the flat black carpeting in the outside hall, but that was my fault. I hadn't thought to specify indoor carpeting.

When two more workmen wheeled in a new fridge, missing only a few unimportant shelves on the door and a couple of wire racks, I was so abjectly grateful that it was a minute or two before I remembered this was the *landlord*.

I gave Patrick five bucks and told him to beat it. Then I noticed Mike, the cat, licking his fur in the middle of the rug. You would have thought he lived there.

"What are you doing here?" I yelled loudly. "Shoo! Scat! Go home!"

Astonished, Mike slunk out, following Morgan as she carried out his litter box to hide it.

I thanked the landlord for my industrial carpeting and my new shelf-less refrigerator. "It was the least I could do," he said graciously.

I agreed. The very least. He had forgotten the hall light, the toilet, the water heater, and the knob that sticks on Morgan's door.

I didn't care. He hadn't noticed the cat, either. As I went out to get Mike, who was glowering at me from the fence, it occurred to me it's a shame to have this nice yard, not to mention this nice ten-year-old boy, without some sort of dog to go with them.

We'll need a pet door of course. And those hedges will have to go, and . . .

The Ballad Of Calvin and Hobbes

I T WAS PATRICK who found him curled up in a ball in his tank. "Mom, Hobbes is dead!" he called. I came out and together we stared at the turtle. Ants were crawling on his tightly shut eyes.

"What happened to him?" Patrick asked, balling his fists in pain and bafflement.

I was still standing there, shocked. It was dusk, the sky a dark blue above the wooden fence of our yard.

I opened my mouth, and a lie came out.

"Maybe he went into early hibernation," I said, looking at the clearly dead turtle. A friend told me she buries her land turtles in fall and unearths them in the spring.

Patrick seemed to hold his breath. Then he nodded. We buried the turtle under a sign that said "Dig Up Hobbes April, 1991."

All summer our back yard has been filling with graves. All summer, it seems, I have been trying to explain to Patrick why things happen.

When our newt died, Patrick and I sat on my bed and talked. "Far more creepy-crawlies are born than were meant to live," I said. "Nature planned it that way. The only thing nature did not plan," I babbled on, "was for a ten-year-old boy to care so much about them."

Patrick stared at his hands. I couldn't think of what else to say. I didn't know why the newts had died, although my putting them on the deck during a heat wave might have had something to do with it.

Two weeks later the tadpoles that had been swimming in a bowl in Patrick's room got their back legs and sailed into what must have looked like a pond to them, the blue rug below. "It's just one of those things," I said to my son.

When Patrick got the first turtle, I relaxed. Turtles are the Maytag washers of the reptile world. I figured Patrick's turtles would still be here, staring about them in wonder, when our apartment building had crumbled into dust.

On one of his trips to the turtle store, Patrick fell in love with a tiny African frog. Our book said that it and the turtle could live in the same tank.

As we buried what was left of the frog, I should have been delivering some sage comment on what a turtle-eat-frog world we live in, but I didn't feel like it. I liked that little frog.

To our relief, the turtles seemed to thrive. By the end of August my back yard was transformed into a turtle Hooverville littered with tanks, plastic pumps and colored gravel.

Then Hobbes stopped eating. All one week, Patrick held out cherry tomatoes to tempt him, but he turned his head away.

After we buried Hobbes, I overheard Patrick explaining to his sister that he was pretty sure Hobbes was dead. "Mom thinks he's hibernating," he said.

He *is* hibernating. My interest in facing facts, where the creepy-crawlies are concerned, is at an all-time low.

The very next night, Patrick went outside to find that Calvin, the other turtle, had disappeared from the wading pool we'd put him in. Wet tracks led up the walk — wet raccoon-like tracks.

Patrick and I gazed at the wading pool in the gathering shadows.

"Look," I whispered, "he got his wings."

Patrick tore his glance from those obvious tracks. "Yep," he said.

Some nights, when it's very still outside, we think we hear Calvin out there, flying unsteadily around the rose bush on his new wings, while below him Hobbes sleeps, dreaming of spring.

Mom Gets Cold Feet At the Rink

THERE'S AN ice skating rink out on 48th Avenue, near the ocean. It's been there forever, on a quiet street in a residential neighborhood, but school kids have lately rediscovered it as a place to see and be seen, especially during Christmas vacation.

My kids, who at nine and eleven realize they have to find partners pretty soon, before their looks go, begged me to take them.

And they wanted me to skate, too. "You never play with us, Mom," Patrick grouched. "You're always reading."

"I am not," I said absently, looking up from my page.

Always reading, indeed. No one was going to accuse me of setting that kind of example for my kids. I'd show them.

So I had never ice-skated before. How hard could it be?

The rink is a huge icy barn of a room, with faded snow scenes on the brick walls and "skate at your own risk" signs everywhere.

Patrick charged right out and had already been around once when Morgan was still trying to pry my hands off the railing.

"It's easy, Mom," she said. "Watch this." And then she, too, was a blur in the circling throng.

Left to myself, I watched the crowd of kids for hints. They careened around corners, deliberately crashed into one another, spun around in circles and tried going backward before they knew how to go forward. When they wanted to stop, they just slammed full speed into the nearest wall, then got up and kind of reassembled themselves, like the evil Toon in "Who Framed Roger Rabbit?"

It was like trying to get exercise tips from a bunch of rag dolls. Besides, as you get older you kind of lose that falling-down, picking-yourself-up-and-trying-again stuff. You get into falling down and staying there, waiting for the paramedics.

My plan was to go very, very slowly. I would not fall at all. As I let go of the railing and started out, my fragile 37-year-old knees wobbled, my ankles were Jell-O, and I was dimly aware of a fleet of toddlers streaking smugly past my knees, their tiny skates flashing, their bottoms damp. But I didn't fall. I was cool.

After a half-hour of so, the kids led me to the log cabin snack bar. While I was there, fighting with some sodden tots for space at the stand-up heater, I overheard Patrick tell Morgan there was a girl he wanted to meet.

While Morgan dived into the throng, I scanned the roomful of schoolgirls for someone good enough for my only son. There was no one.

Then Morgan reappeared, dragging a little girl wearing a long black T-shirt who seemed determined to look anywhere but at Patrick.

"She says she might like you, but she isn't sure," Morgan whispered in Patrick's left ear.

"Why don't you talk to her yourself?" I whispered in his right ear.

"Oh, Mom," he said, dismayed to find that he not only still had a mother but also that she was hovering at his elbow, listening eagerly. "You have to go away. This is kids' business."

OK, fine. I'm not one of your suffocating moms. With a great show of picking up my purse and coat and newspaper, I got up and moved about six inches away. I sat down again, very inconspicuously, and buried myself in the classified ads.

"Mom."

"Ummm?" I said, looking up with an air of abstraction.

"You have to go farther away. Maybe you could go out to the car and read your book."

Going to the Country For a Christmas Tree

S O MY NEW FRIEND, Bill, had this idea to take the kids out to the country to chop down a Christmas tree. He saw the four of us getting a nice early start, then riding through the crisp countryside, exclaiming over the brilliantly colored leaves, singing Christmas songs, enjoying a day in the outdoors.

If I had any doubts, based on experience, about the bucolic perfection of a day in the car with the kids, or for that matter of the successful carrying out of any plan involving my kids, I kept them to myself.

Some things people should find out for themselves.

Sunday dawned. Morgan, twelve, announced that she was totally up for going, as long as she could bring her friend Rachel, and we stopped at this pottery sale first. By one p.m. we were humming north on Highway 101, with Morgan's rap tape throbbing from the speakers.

I couldn't tell if "Rigor Mortis" by Heavy D and the Boyz was helping to make this day everything Bill had dreamed it would be, or if he always gripped the wheel that way. "You will tell me if the music starts to get to you, won't you?" I said, and he nodded, and drove.

There was a tiny delay in Petaluma, no more than an hour, to pick up Patrick, ten, who had stayed overnight with his friend Dusty O'Brien, so it was nearly three by the time we got on the road again, now with four kids squashed in the backseat, because Dusty wanted to come along, too.

"This is one of the prettiest drives I know of," Bill remarked when we turned onto Highway 12 heading east through the Sonoma hills. The sun was by now slanting low across the landscape as we slid through a magical countryside, the silence broken only by the heavy beat of "Mo' Jerk Out" and by Morgan and Patrick's bitter dispute about who slugged whom in the back seat, and by my hissing at them to knock it off or else, and Morgan saying sweetly to Dusty, "If you loved me, you wouldn't wear those pants," and my attempt to distract them by opening Juice Squeezes and handing them back without realizing you had to shake them up first.

By the time we finished the mopping up, we were there.

Christmas trees marched up a slope, lit by the setting sun.

"I thought we were going to a real forest," Patrick said, with the resigned air of a boy who had been tricked again, and he and Dusty stalked off to find their own tree.

Despite the failing night, we found a bushy six-foot fir tree we liked, and using my leather jacket as a ground cloth, the kids sawed it down. It fell on Patrick, answering the old question, if a tree falls on a boy in the forest and he laughs, did it really happen?

Bill cut down his own fir in one or two strokes. As we were dragging both trees to the car, I caught Patrick and Dusty just as they were about to saw down a ten-incher with Dusty's Swiss knife (all the trees were $30, regardless of size).

While the sun slid behind the hill and the kids played in a nearby rusty junkyard, Bill figured out how to tie two large trees to the top of a Dodge Colt.

In no time we were on our way home through the now sleeping countryside, with the girls making up new words to Christmas songs, "In the evenings we'll perspire, as we steam by the fire."

Patrick still wanted to know why we had to drive all the way out here to get a tree when they're for sale at Safeway, and Bill slapped his forehead and said, "They sell trees in the city? God, I am so dumb."

Missing Patrick — The Very Idea

I T WAS Patrick's own idea to take off a week in the middle of winter and go, all by himself, to Minnesota, where his Uncle Bob has a fishing resort. "It would be very educational," he argued.

He has been away from me many times, on trips with his dad, but this was his first deliberate departure. His dad sewed a fur collar on his black jacket, his sister gave him $5, and then he was getting on the plane.

"Will you miss me, Mom?" he asked, putting his arms around me.

Would I miss him? The idea is preposterous. After all, I'm a busy grown-up, with a life of my own in one of the world's most interesting cities.

What's the company of a ten-year-old to that?

Ten-year-olds always want to do something inconvenient, like drive twenty miles to look for crawdads, or go swimming in January. They're a liability at parties, being short and not old enough to drink and not having read the *Times Book Review*. They order meals in restaurants and then don't eat them, they want to see horrible movies, and at home they make banana shakes in the blender and leave the peels all over the counter.

So when a ten-year-old leaves for a week, it's really a blessing.

You have this nice clean counter, and nobody grouching at you for forgetting to wash his overalls or buying the wrong kind of Popsicles. You can go out and watch French movies with subtitles, and stand around gassing at cocktail parties to your heart's content.

Miss Patrick? Not likely. No more than I missed his sister, Morgan, that same week, when she spent a lot of time over at her friend's, making brief appearances at home to pick up more clothes.

I ducked into her room one morning to watch her get dressed.

"I thought you were with Bill last night," she said. "I would have come home if I'd known you were all alone."

"Oh, Ta," I said. "I like being alone."

What goes for a ten-year-old boy goes double for a twelve-year-old girl: They can't go to bars, they never show up with hot tickets to a play, and their idea of quality time with you is to go through your clothes like a police sweep and make off with the few things that look good on you.

If a person like this starts spending time away from home, what of it? And if her brother prefers snowy Minnesota to the warm bed you have provided for him, what of that?

It simply leaves more time with the squeeze, and for the delicious reading of books, and the viewing of difficult but rewarding movies, and the having of grown-up conversations.

Miss them now, when they leave on short sorties, their glances straying doorward even as they kiss you good-by? Or later, in that time coming fast, when they're grown and hardly come home at all?

Not a chance. When that happens I'll have even more time for myself, and for doing all those things that children interfere with — none of which I can remember right now, because Patrick's on the line.

"I can't wait to see you and Dad," he says, his voice sounding very far away, "but would it be all right for me to stay an extra week?"

His cousin has taken him hunting, ice-fishing and snow sledding. "I go right to sleep here," he adds, cruelly.

"I wish you could stay longer," I lie. "I'm glad you're having fun."

And I hang up the phone, and sit still for a moment, new fears crowding me like shadows.

Miss Patrick? What an idea.

My Kingdom For a Jellybean

IT'S MORNING, and Morgan and Patrick are trying, in their quiet, civil way, to divide a sack of jellybeans. I had bought them the day before in a fit of indulgence.

"I hate every inch of your body. I'd like to tear your little neck off," Morgan tells her brother. "But I'm a reasonable person, so I'm going to explain my plan to you one more time, so you can understand it perfectly."

"You're so stupid, Morgan," Patrick says mildly. He's lying on his bed, waving his legs idly in the air.

"I say we separate them into piles of each kind of jellybean," Morgan continued as if he hadn't spoken, "then divide the piles equally in half, with all the leftovers going in another pile. Then we divide the leftover pile, and give the extra jellybean to Mom, if there is one."

I'm at my desk, half listening to this, which has been going on for a while. I hid the jellybeans and told the kids they could not have them back until they figured out a way of peacefully dividing them. If they couldn't agree, I announced, they could not have the jellybeans at all.

Half of me wants the kids to find a way to agree on a way of dividing the jellybeans, and thus learn from the experience, and half of me wants the negotiations to break down completely, so I won't have to produce the bag.

I got up early and ate rather a lot of the jellybeans while reading the paper.

So I'm not being particularly helpful. "Do what the king did when he had one kingdom to divide between two sons," I suggest. "One of you divides the jellybeans, and the other takes his pick."

"Yeah, Morgan," Patrick says, kicking her.

My plan is to let the yelling go on a little longer, then get mad and confiscate the jellybeans.

"Why do you have to divide them exactly that way?" Patrick asks Morgan. "Why not do what I want to do, and take turns choosing until they're all gone?"

"Because this is the way Rachel and Cleo divided their jelly-beans," Morgan said fiercely. "I want to divide them the way they did."

So I was not the only one in the room with a secret agenda. Wars are lost, nations betrayed, vital talks sabotaged because a key player has a deeply held, secret idea about the way jellybeans should be divided — or a hidden reason for wanting to sabotage the whole process.

"Why didn't you tell us that in the beginning?" I ask Morgan.

She bursts into tears. "Why should I say so? Why can't you just do it my way? I'm a generous person. I let people have sips of my drinks," she rages, irrelevantly.

"You're crying, so I'll give in to your stupid plan," Patrick says in disgust.

Reluctantly, I go get the paper sack of jellybeans from the top of the bookshelf.

"There were more! Where are the rest?" Morgan cries.

"Oh, were there?" I say, and wander vaguely off to look for them, as if they might have strayed from the sack. This worked when they were littler, and forgot things quickly.

"Mom, there were five blacks, eight white ones and three of these splotched ones. You ate a whole lot!" Morgan says when I come back.

"I may have had one or two," I allow.

Their heads are bent over the coffee table in total harmony now.

"Mom ate all the burgundy."

"She ate all the blues. The blues are the best."

The Secret Of My Success

MORGAN INFORMED ME the other day that other mothers — mothers who care about their kids — pack food in lunches in the order it's to be eaten. Sandwich, then chips, then an apple — like that.

I paused in wrapping up cold pizza from the night before and said, "What's the difference? You and Patrick always leave your lunches sitting at the top of the stairs anyway."

Then she wounded me to the quick. "I hate to tell you this, Mom, but Dad makes much better lunches than you do." Her dad lives about ten blocks from me, and has the kids half the time.

I already knew that, about his lunches. I find them still in the kids' knapsacks days later, and guilt floods me as I open the bags to see carrot sticks, ham and cheese sandwiches with lettuce, salt-free chips and miniature cans of orange juice.

I can't deny it: The lunches he makes the kids — lunches that they leave squashed for days under geography textbooks and balled-up sweaters — are much more nutritious than the lunches I make that they forget on the stairs.

The Lunch Gap is widening.

The only bright spot in this bleak landscape is that while the kids are out bumming money from their friends to buy a burrito on the corner, I tend to wind up with all the lunches. Tossing the ones I made into the trash, I settle down to enjoy Jim's, the delicious whole wheat sandwich and the cunningly sliced carrots still fresh in his careful wrappings.

I've been trying to think of a way to get him to use less mayonnaise and to switch from salt-free chips, but I suppose even Jim would balk at having to add making my lunch to everything else he does.

Still, you never know. He's the kind who does more than his share. He fell off the backyard fence and broke his leg, and three days after he came home from the hospital I caught him in his station wagon, trying to work the clutch with his cast so he could drive Morgan to dance class. "I think I can drive all right," he said, and it took three of us to put him back in the house.

Which brings me to a confession. For years now, I've been prettily accepting compliments for managing a career and children at the same time. "You must be very well-organized," people said admiringly as I climbed the masthead at two magazines, not a hair out of place. "That's so wonderful."

And I *was* wonderful, during those years. I never annoyed my employers by staying home with a sick kid, going on field trips to the state capital, or running off to the school with a tray of homemade cupcakes just because my eleven-year-old was having a birthday. Jim did all those things.

If Morgan had the vapors in arithmetic class, or Patrick fell off the bars and chipped his tooth, Jim went down to get them. He worked at home, so he could, but that wasn't all of it. He just did it, because they're his kids.

I got to go on merrily at work, a stirring example to every woman who wants to juggle kids and a job. I never even had to call home, except to catch up on the news, because every moment the kids weren't with me they were with someone equally crazy about them, and one who had a better working knowledge of the food groups.

Not that Jim's perfect. He yields, helplessly, to Morgan's wish to have crutches for an imaginary bruise on her toe. He keeps buying the kids moderately priced off-brand clothes they wouldn't be caught dead in, and lets them stay up too late, and of course he puts those salt-free chips in their school lunches, when he must realize by now that I prefer the other kind.

Mothers and Sons — And Homework

I F YOU HAVE ever dreamed of having a child, then you have dreamed of helping that child with his homework. The light of comprehension dawning on his little face, the child smiles up at you as you offer a lucid explanation of long division — yes, he sees. He excitedly scribbles the correct answer. "Gee, thanks, Mom."

And this is exactly how it is, in real life, when you're helping one or the other of your children with his homework.

The only difference is that it's nine p.m., and the two of you are staring at each other with loathing.

"Just start over, and show me the steps," you say, thinking with anticipation of the book waiting for you on your bed. "Pretend that I know nothing about long division."

But the child is not fooled. He's kicking his chair.

You'd like to kick his chair, too, but you're the Mom. "Hmm," you say. "378 into 12,908. Shouldn't be too hard." Turning away slightly and coughing, you run the problem through the calculator hidden in your palm. "There's your answer," you say briskly, writing it down for him. "I'm supposed to show my work," the child grumbles. "How did you get that remainder?"

What on earth was a remainder? You knew that once, back in the Eisenhower administration. It's unfair to have to be doing subtraction now that you are all grown up and driving a car.

The child now remembers that he has to get a book on sea turtles for his report, assigned six weeks ago and due tomorrow. This is the first you've heard of it, you say, but the child is sure he told you all about it. Also, somebody stole the sheet of paper with the social studies questions on it out of his locker at the rec center. If he goes to school without it the teacher won't let him go on the fifth-grade camping trip.

"The library is closed," you point out.

The child buries his head in his arms. He hates you. You should have sensed his need to get to the library tonight, and helped him remember his report earlier. You should never have made him go to that stupid school.

Now that the child thinks of it, you never take him and his sister out of state on vacation, and you don't do the wash often enough. He grabs the arithmetic paper.

"Thanks anyway, Mom, I'll do it myself," he growls.

You return happily to your book. Minutes later, just as you are getting to the exciting part, a drawn-out scream suggests that the child has changed his mind about wanting help.

When you huff downstairs, all warm and hopeful again at the idea that you are needed, he says, bitterly, "I'm supposed to figure out the distance between Yosemite and Yellowstone parks."

"Great," you say, relieved it's not long division again. He shoots you a doubtful look but tries to explain how to use the graph to calculate the distance. "Oh, I see," you say. But then there's a silence, and after a minute it's clear to him that you don't see anything. He's at a loss to understand how you keep your job.

You squint at his paper again, muttering to yourself about the base ingratitude of children and wondering who would want to go straight to another park anyway. The child sighs, clearly resigned to flunking out of the fifth grade.

If someone were to come into the room, he would see a touching sight: a mother standing over a child who is sitting, their faces alight in the circle of lamplight, bending together over a sheet of paper.

Death Comes To Dinner

IT WAS DINNERTIME, and we were talking about this and that when Patrick said that his new philosophy was that we should all live for today. "No, Patrick, you cannot have a dirt bike," I said automatically. We all got to talking, and somebody happened to remark, "After all, you only have one life."

Something about that made Patrick put down his fork. "What was death?" he wanted to know.

Bill gave it a try. "You know, there was a time, a time your Mom and I and even Morgan can remember, when there was no Patrick. Death is like that — there will once again be a time when there is no Patrick."

You could see that sinking in. No Patrick?

I suppose we can all — or all of us raised without the consolation of religion — remember this moment of knowing that you will stop but the world will go on. I recall sitting on a swing when a neighbor kid squatted down and buried a sowbug in the soft dirt. "It's dead as a doornail," he said. I must not have looked adequately shocked, for he added, "You're going to die, too, and be buried in the dirt like a sowbug, with the worms eating your eyes."

Like that moment, years later, when someone first explained sex to me: It was repulsive, shocking, and it instantly made sense. For days after I found out about death, I wondered why anybody bothered to go to school, or read anything, or struggled through long division. Why not just lie in bed and wait for it to come?

Then it receded, that terrifying discovery, to a kind of distant rumor. In a way, I stopped believing it.

I guess that had been Patrick's moment, because a few days later he brought it up again, at bedtime. I was bustling around, turning out lights, but he just sat there. "You made me die," he said, when all I was doing was trying to get him to brush his teeth. "I gave you life," I answered. "Yes," he answered bitterly, "so I can die."

So the three of us talked. Morgan told Patrick that he should be worrying about something important, such as were we going to buy him a car when he was sixteen. Then she started coughing loudly — she has that flu that's going around — and I asked her to stop. She fell off the couch and lay on the floor, still coughing. "Don't let me interrupt your little moment, Mom," she said, wryly.

By now I was babbling. I told Patrick that I had read that as you get older, the cells that make you worry begin to die off, and as you get closer to death you worry about it less and less. I told him he would be a very old man when he died, and would leave children behind him to remember him, and perhaps his own good works. The time when there is again no Patrick would not be exactly like the time when there never had been.

Finally, he stopped worrying about it. The cloud passed. But I thought of it again the other day. Patrick had been caught with his bike after dark, and I had followed him home in my car. As I drove, I watched his T-shirt billowing up over his back as he ostentatiously slowed down at intersections, turning to grin at me.

The sight of that bare back made me wonder what good it was supposed to do, my following him. If another car darted out of a side street and walloped him I could do nothing but watch.

The thing is, we both already know that I can't keep him safe. He knows he can ride through the streets just as easily without me. Still, it made sense to him, that I shepherd him home through the dark with my car. He must already know that it's the little moments like that, strung like lights on a welcoming porch, that hold back the darkness.

Tenancy in Common: Uncommonly Nice

FINALLY, AFTER all the carrying on, the agonizing about leaving the city, the sinking feelings when we looked at the houses we could afford, Bill and I own something.

It's a flat, not a house, but who cares? We're tenants in common with the kids' dad, upstairs, and of course we all have a lot in common. There's a garden apartment downstairs that a snotty friend archly suggests we should reserve for Bill's ex-wife.

Tenants-in-common deals are notoriously risky. If we don't pay the mortgage, Jim will have to toss the mother of his children into the street. If I don't like the noise upstairs, I can have those pesky kids arrested. Of course, I'd have to bail them out immediately, because they're mine.

According to the agreement, we are co-tenants. We can't erect awnings, or get a horse, take out any walls, have more than two four-legged pets, or walk on the roof without each other's permission.

Other than that, Bill and I are landowners, with absolute dominion over an undivided 34 percent of all that we survey. When the escrow closed, we invited Jim over to celebrate with a bottle of champagne. He had good luck with the traffic — there was nobody on the back stairs at all — and was down in fifteen seconds.

Generally, those stairs are more crowded. Jim came down and watched television with the cat while Bill and I were in Cape Cod this summer. When Bill overwatered his cactus pot, he sent Patrick upstairs to ask Jim for a turkey baster to drain the pot. Jim promptly sent a message back with Patrick saying that if Bill was making turkey, he had some peppers and green beans that would go well with it.

We have sent things upstairs: rice, a wicker bookshelf, Morgan once or twice. We tried to send up two leftover pea pods, those mushroom-like chairs you sink into. But Jim refused to have them.

"I have to draw the line somewhere," he said with uncharacteristic firmness, "and I'm drawing it at the pod chairs."

In a fit of housekeeping, I threw out a huge ball of unmated socks. "Oh, I know you did," Jim said when I mentioned it weeks later. "I found it in the trash and took it upstairs. Turns out I had most of the mates."

It isn't an extended family, exactly, and in another way it is. Bill, reading the paper over breakfast, is sometimes surprised to hear Jim's voice in the kids' rooms, telling them to hurry and get ready for school.

Jim showed no surprise when he came upon me in his kitchen, stealing a tomato, and I somehow wasn't startled when his brother-in-law from Indiana materialized in my kitchen as I was making myself a solitary cup of tea.

Morgan and Patrick think it's one big house. I heard Morgan tell somebody on the phone, "All of my parents are going out. Can you come over?"

It isn't easy to have a glass of champagne, though, not with Morgan at the same table bolting soup before a dance and trying to put a baseball cap and oversized shirt on me so that I would look cool when I dropped her off, and Patrick asking for a T-shirt from upstairs.

Morgan was furious when she discovered that after the champagne we were all going to drive her, in Jim's station wagon, on the way to the movies. She said her life would be ruined if her friends saw her climbing out of a Volvo with all her parents in it.

Our agreement doesn't say which co-tenant's car should be used to take the kids to dances, but I think it's only fair that Jim do 66 percent of driving the kids.

The Parental Illusion That We Matter

WHEN I LOOK BACK at the past sixteen years, I could laugh at how seriously I took my role as a mom. All those hours on the floor playing Monopoly while the dinner burned, all the earnest lectures on why the sunglasses removed from the store by mistake must be returned, all the hours in the car learning the lyrics to "American Pie" — in fact everything I've ever done or said — turns out to have been a waste of time.

I've just finished reading a magazine article that assures all of us moms everywhere that nothing we do — not early toilet training, not expensive piano lessons, quality time, swimming lessons or long sweet talks over bowls of hot soup while the rain falls outside — is going to make one bit of difference in who our children turn out to be. They are born entirely themselves.

Environmentalists have long believed that people are born fundamentally alike, then are made different by their families, by traumas, by schooling.

But studies show that identical twins separated at birth and then reunited in middle age turn out to be in many respects the same person, with the same beliefs, the same way of dressing and the same character — despite different upbringings and different parents. It's as if nothing that happened along the way made a bit of difference in who they were going to turn out to be.

Even all attempts to improve intelligence — all that playing Mozart to them in the womb and reading Dickens to them at 3 — ultimately fail. Adopted kids turn out to resemble the biological parents they've never met, rather than their adoptive parents whom they've lived with every day of their lives.

Truly wretched parents can harm a child, but so-so parents turn out to be just as good as good parents. "This suggests that life is somehow a charade," laments the article.

And so it does, but it nevertheless comes as something of a relief to me. It hasn't been easy being a mom, constantly being told over and over it's up to me whether they grow up to shoot up shopping malls or win the Nobel Prize.

I haven't liked knowing that if Morgan finds a cure for cancer, it's because I read *Treasure Island* to her at bedtime, but if she winds up dining out of dumpsters, it's because I would not let her be in "A Christmas Carol" at A.C.T. when she was ten, just because I didn't want to do all the driving it took to get her to rehearsals.

According to this article, I give them life, bus fare and clean socks, and the rest is predetermined. I can whisper in Patrick's ear, telling him to become a doctor, and he will go ahead and do whatever his genes have programmed him to do — at the moment, he's sure it's becoming one of the first professional snowboarders.

I could march into their bedrooms right this minute and tell them we are joining the Young Nazi League, or moving to Seoul, Korea, to finish out their high school years, and it wouldn't make a bit of difference.

Bill's parents raised him to be a priest and got an ardent nonbeliever instead. My sister Mickey, encouraged to be a nurse, became a bartender. My twin and I, raised by the same parents in the suburbs, split for small towns and big city lights, respectively. I have grown up with a passion for reading and a taste for yard sales and the beach that could only have come from my parents' example, but am otherwise entirely myself.

Morgan just called needing a ride. Hell, I'm thinking, she'll grow up to be exactly the same person whether I give her a ride or not. It would suit me better to go on working, or even to head out to the park with the dog and a book.

And I would do just that, except for something the article fails to mention: that weird congested feeling parents get in the chest when they look at their little bundles of genes, that inconvenient feeling that, despite all the studies, what we do and say does matter.

I'm looking for my keys.

Driving Mom Around the Bend

PATRICK drove me to school today. I don't go to school, of course, being too old and not fitting so well behind those tiny desks anymore, so I had to turn around and come right back home again.

At fifteen he has to have someone older than 25 in the car with him, and as it happens I am a few months older than 25. And, of course, I supply the car.

Since Patrick got his learner's permit, I have become like one of those inflatable plastic men you stick in an armchair or the passenger seat of your car to discourage intruders. When he wants to drive, he sticks me under his arm and props me up in the passenger seat.

I need propping up, because riding with a raw teenage driver is like being on the Haunted House ride, careening with no brakes and no steering wheel toward light poles, fences and other cars, then veering away as new horrors pop up in the form of merging traffic, people throwing their car doors open on the traffic side and pedestrians recklessly creeping past car hoods with their heads barely showing.

Now we're whipping around the corner to find a pileup of cars at the red light. I stomp on the brakes as hard as I can, though my brakes are mysteriously absent, and then brace myself for the crash. Instead of ramming the car in front of us, Patrick brakes smoothly, and I can't for the life of me see how he does it, how he knows to put on the brakes like that. How'd he get so good at this, so fast?

I would be calmer, I think, if I had not given birth to the driver. When he was 5 years old, I raced along behind him as he headed his Big Wheels down the slope behind Duboce Park, straight for the curb. It and Patrick flew headfirst onto the curb, knocking out both his front teeth. A few years later, I saw him hit a pothole, then dive headfirst over his bike, which cartwheeled over to hit him in the back of the head. Now I'm watching again as he steers a ton of machinery — my five-speed Toyota — down the hill toward school.

It's also true that the driver, possibly, would be calmer if the passenger had not given him birth. He needs an actual plastic Mom doll to drive around, not this breathing bundle with hastily brushed hair and perhaps one too many cups of coffee, sucking in her breath every time a car merges in front of him. I know how he feels because when I drive my own mother around, her frightened yelps raise my consciousness of driving to such a pitch that I find myself plunging right into oncoming traffic, more or less for the hell of it.

Patrick always forgets to signal. I make a chopping motion with my left hand, which means "put your signal on," but it also means "slow down," so he gets confused. Also, this slight chopping motion may not be visible to the cars behind us, which have no idea that we are going left — NOW.

"Bill says when he got his license it only increased the number of ways he could be put to work," I say conversationally when the signal is finally ticking away. "You've told me that about 40 times," Patrick says, downshifting into second, concentrating on the road.

As I did with his sister, I take deep pleasure in teaching him to drive. Parents used to teach their kids to sew, cook, run a tractor, plant green beans. Now the world moves so fast that most of our knowledge is irrelevant by the time they need it.

But you still need to let the clutch out slightly as you give it a little gas, same as in my day. I am leading my duckling to water, where he will swim for himself.

I read about a mother who would let her son drive only to school and back, despite his protests. "I'd rather have him be mad at me and have to work it out on the couch later, than dead," she said.

She sounded to me like a sensible woman. But of course it won't work. He's just going to have to go out and take his chances in traffic along with the rest.

Along the way he may pass my mother and me, sweat running down both our faces, as we zip past the Wrong Way sign and onto Highway 101.

Gifts for Mom: The Teen Years

I WAS SITTING at the pool at my mother's complex, feeling pretty good. For Mother's Day, I gave Mom a very nice voice-activated tape recorder, a box of popular songs on cassette, a bag of croissants, two slightly battered eight-track tapes and a green baseball cap.

Then my brother Shannon, that show-off, arrived with a present he had to borrow a truck to deliver: a new pingpong table that he set up in the carport. This from the same kid who gave mother an electric carving knife about five years after she had last cooked anything. She made him take it right back to the store.

I don't think she'll make him take the pingpong table back.

"So, what'd you get?" Mother asked me, brushing a leaf off her new pingpong table.

Well, if you must know, I said, my presents are all still at school, drying. Much too big to be moved. Or so I'm told.

Patrick had stayed over at a friend's, but when I woke up on Mother's Day I still had one child left to fake a little gratitude for all those years of care and comfort. I had heard Morgan indignantly scolding her friend Steve on the phone that morning, "But it's Mother's Day! Aren't you going to spend it with your mother?" (This from a girl who the night before had said to the same boy, "No, I'm home all by myself tonight. Well, Bill and my mom are home.")

So I guess I was the tiniest bit let down when there was nothing actually on the table when I came down in the morning, ready to go wild over my cards and school-made flower vases. Not that I remotely cared about getting presents, of course. Honestly, it's enough, the satisfaction of having raised a pair of lazy, good-for-nothing, ungrateful . . .

I stomped upstairs to find Morgan luxuriating on her bed in a pool of sunlight. "Clean up this mess," I said, by way of good morning. "But it's Mother's Day," she protested, not moving.

"Oh, is it?" I said. I went downstairs to sulk on the back porch. I stared out the window at the cherry tree, my heart as shrunken and hard and disappointed as the fruit on that neglected tree.

"Where are you, Mom?" she called.

"Here," I said. My voice was thin and bitter. I had no idea I liked those paper vases, those cards with ribbons glued in them, the table decorated with weeds before I came down to breakfast. Two years ago I was wakened at six when the kids brought in a cake and made me eat a slice on the spot, before I even got up.

Morgan came up. She was wearing my white tank top. I would have to pitchfork through the piles on her floor to get it back. "Did you do your room?" I said.

She ignored that. She sat down, unruffled. "Look," she said. She showed me a plaster relic in a shoe box. It was a model of the red shorts we have been hiding in each other's stuff all during this difficult spring, a spring of surly answers, sneaking out of the house and sideways looks.

And that was just me. She was worse.

"See where it broke?" she said. "I've been trying to glue them back all week." She had, too. Bill found his tube of glue, open, down by the door to the laundry room. "And I have a painting of the shorts at school, all different sizes, all colors of red. I couldn't bring it home because we had class outside and I couldn't get back in."

"That would have been good," I said, still sulky. But I liked it, the idea of a ceramic of the red shorts, and the painting. It's almost as good as cake at dawn.

When we got in the car to go to my mother's, there were the red shorts, stretched out on the steering wheel.

Mom's Invisible Virtues

I MET PATRICK at school with the car, to give him driving practice by letting him drive all his buddies home (he only has a permit, so I must be stuffed into the car somehow). Although it was midafternoon, and I had deadlines, it didn't seem strange to either of us that I would interrupt my work to do this. I am, after all, his mom.

Will he remember that I took him driving, or will he, like most of us, suffer from momnesia, and remember only that I am refusing to buy him a car for his sixteenth birthday?

Momnesia is the inability to remember that when you were inside having your piano lessons, your mother was outside in the car, doing last week's crossword puzzle.

When the person waiting is a mom, it seems normal that one person would wait in the car so that another person can learn to play the piano. It's so unremarkable that it's the kind of thing you forget all about until, thirty years later, you have three drinks at a dinner party and sit right down and play "Claire de Lune" by heart on the host's dusty old Steinway. Or, even more likely, you find yourself flipping through an old magazine outside a suburban bungalow, waiting while your child inside stumbles through "Camptown Races."

We all seem to go through a period of dwelling not on what Mom did for us, but on what she did wrong, or left undone. I have no trouble remembering that my mother hated to come to school on open house night and that she let me wear stupid-looking wrinkled boy's shirts to school in the sixth grade, but I forget that she took me to the county clinic for braces when she had the flu and that she typed my English papers, correcting as she went along.

When I recall going to Disneyland when I was seventeen, all I remember is pining all the way down in the car, delicately picking at grapefruit in the coffee shops, mooning about this boy I had just met, Mike Lara.

What I wonder only now is how Mother, struggling to raise us single-handedly, managed to pay for all those meals, for the motels we stayed in, the entrance fees to Disneyland and Knott's Berry Farm. My sister Adrian says that when we were teenagers Mother used to let her take the '67 blue Camaro out for a spin every afternoon at five o'clock. Adrian still remembers how exciting it felt to say, "I'm going for a buzz, Mom," then get in that Camaro.

"She knew I was using the car to drive past the house of a boy named Dave Carroll in Sleepy Hollow, and never said anything about that either." On one jaunt Adrian rear-ended another car while fiddling with the radio. "Mother never said anything except, 'Are you all right?'"

A kid's memory can be weirdly selective. For years I remembered how sunburned I got on a summer trip to the Sacramento River because no one remembered to put sun lotion on me. Only now do I realize what it must have been like, taking seven kids to camp on the river, with no money and a husband who had never changed a diaper.

When we have children ourselves, our momnesia sometimes magically clears up. A friend of mine was going to move to a tiny apartment in Albany so she could pay the $13,000 a year to keep her son at the University of California at Santa Cruz. Neither of them found it curious that she would uproot herself so that he could go to the college of his choice. But when her son sends his own child off to college, taking an extra job to pay the tuition, he may remember his mother's apartment.

I just walked Morgan the three miles uphill to her school because she wants to get in shape for the senior prom. It did not occur to either of us that once I had delivered her, the dog and I would have to walk back the three miles.

It slipped our attention because it was such a pleasure to take the walk together. And I had time, on the long way back, to think about all this, and remember what I am in constant danger of forgetting, which is all my mother did for me.

Investing for The Long Haul

WHEN YOUR KIDS are little, you are like an investor in a bull market: You can do nothing wrong. The investor buys the wrong stocks, sells them at the wrong time, screws around and still his stocks go up.

Same with the parent of little kids: You can forget to wash their school shirt and stand scrubbing at the spots one minute before it's time to leave, and they'll still spend class time writing you a note with lots of hearts on it.

You can force them to eat liver and onions, forget to pick them up at school and actually cook their pet newts by putting their smelly tank out in the garden, and they'll still wail if they don't get to sit next to you in front of the TV.

You can sing "Tie a Yellow Ribbon 'Round the Old Oak Tree" in the car while driving them and their "date" to the matinee. You can have boyfriends eating Cheerios in the morning who weren't there when they went to sleep. Through it all, they are fine.

They are cheerful and funny. You live in an endless, satisfying present, playing Legos and walking down the street with a small blond child by each hand.

Then they hit their teens. One day your child is crawling into bed with you and bringing birthday cake at 6 a.m., the next he's smoking in the garage with his buddies while you're upstairs trying to figure out where the birthday boy went.

Suddenly you find yourself like an investor in a bear market. You are doing exactly what you always did, buying the right stocks and holding on to them, but now they plummet.

Same with teens.

Everything you do is wrong. Your jokes are dumb, your mild rules drive them wild and the fact that you exist at all humiliates them. Your daughter bursts into tears when you say hiring a hall for her birthday is out of the question. Your son says he was going to do his homework, but you ruined it by telling him to.

You have done your reading. As an investor, you read *Smart Money* and *Kiplinger's*. As a parent, it's *Get Out of My Life, But First Could You Drive Me and Cheryl to the Mall?*

You know you're supposed to be patient, wait for the market to go back up. With teens, you are supposed to walk away, mirror feelings, use humor, be patient.

Instead, panicked, you find yourself dumping stocks, buying others. You find yourself turning off the TV and standing in front of your child — who is collapsed on the couch, spooning in Froot Loops — interrupting her view of "Mighty Morphin Power Rangers" and delivering impassioned infomercials about how it felt to find your good sweater crumpled up on her floor.

You try not to listen to your feelings. You try not to panic. You want to show her love when she needs it most, even when she is crying and hurling defiance at you, and instead you blow up and blow it.

I know parents who retreated altogether, who said to the aliens who had taken over their children's bodies: I don't know what to do with you anymore. I'm going to clothe you and feed you and that's it. Some sent them to special schools in other states. Parent confidence plunges, and the kid goes down and will stay down, if parent confidence doesn't reassert itself.

So you do what you're supposed to do when the market plunges: Ride it out. Don't throw up your hands and sell. You have to look at the fundamentals. You were a good mother once. And somewhere beneath the baggy clothes and pierced lips and slammed doors is the kid you had, who was pretty good herself.

That kind of stock can only go up in the long run.

I'm Not Missing Her at All

I ALWAYS FEEL ridiculous when in the grip of some common social malaise, some well-documented phase of life — this time dutifully falling apart because a child has left the nest.

It isn't as if Morgan didn't try to prepare me, back when she was eleven. She made me refer to her room as her "apartment" and told her sixth-grade teacher that she'd return her missing math book when she moved into her own place.

He should be getting that book in the mail any time because she has her own place now, or close enough to it. She got herself a room with a family down in Santa Cruz. She's got her own wheels, her own bank account, her own baby-sitting job, trips by her own self over to the Safeway for cornflakes and yogurt and Mountain Dew. She has a full-time schedule of classes at Cabrillo College.

We have dusty rectangles where our furniture used to be. I was not losing a daughter — I was losing half of our stuff. She talked me into taking her wrecked old boom box and giving her my nice new one. She made off with towels, blankets, lamps, an armchair, a futon, some bookshelves. A scavenger hunt through the house netted her an additional microwave oven, a toaster, all our cans of tuna and every last bottle of shampoo.

Her dad and I rented a U-Haul and moved her down to Santa Cruz. I hugged her and gave her some parting advice about being quiet and not eating the family's food. She stood there on the sidewalk for just a second looking a little lost, and then we drove back to the city.

Her room is empty. We cut down the little paper stars she had hanging from her light fixture, peeled the snow-boarding decals off the closet doors and put the bed back on its frame. (Morgan had never liked sleeping on a frame, a fact I had never bothered to argue with. I was just happy she wasn't sticking the head of the bed into the open closet anymore.)

When I go into her room, I try to remember how often she was irritating to live with, how it felt to be cleaning up her spills of rice milk on the kitchen counter while she roared with laughter at the Brady Bunch movie, or forking through the clothes on her floor to find my good black bra, or trying to work while she perched on the chair next to me and argued until I conceded that, yes, the absences on her class attendance record could be computer errors.

But those memories are already slipping away, and instead I remember dancing with her in the kitchen to Blondie's "Heart of Glass," and going out to breakfast at Spaghetti Western, a neighborhood cafe, she in a ball gown and red bowling shoes.

Despite my most brisk efforts to the contrary, I have felt bereft all month in this looted house, in the throes of what an onlooker might be tempted to call — hateful phrase — empty-nest syndrome.

But it's not. We don't live in a nest, and anyway I refuse to go through anything so wearily predictable, at least not while Morgan's brother is still home. Though Patrick technically lives upstairs, his father unfairly not giving him back when the one I had harbored left, I probably see him as much as his dad does. His rap music comes down through the ceiling of our bedroom, and he's around a lot, watching HBO when he is supposed to be doing a four-page paper comparing the speeches of General Patton and JFK.

No, I have just gone about my business, thinking about sponge-painting the spare bedroom, helping Patrick figure out how to sell his snow board so he can buy a new one, hardly even remembering from one minute to the next that I have a daughter somewhere. Most of the time I have no idea where she is or what she's up to. (That part, I have to say, can be wonderful.)

I page her only when I have something I urgently need to ask her, like how her philosophy exam went, or if she wants that lamp she left on the porch, or if she thinks we'll have an early winter this year.

Dances With Snowboards

THE NICE MAN in the Kirkwood staff jacket picked me up at the bottom of the chairlift ramp and lugged me out of the way of the skiers coming down after me.

I was on a snowboard and had fallen off the lift for the fourth straight time. "Appreciate the help," I said to the liftie, one snowboarder to another. "Kind of a steep ramp you have there."

I gestured to where toddlers were coasting down off the lift, chatting with one another as they did so.

"I just think it's so great that you come out here," he answered.

Meaning, At Your Age.

For a second I saw myself through his eyes. Our car became an Oldsmobile, its glovebox packed with Gelusil and hemorrhoid medicine and flyers from the bingo parlor.

Just then my twenty-year-old snowboarding instructor returned to claim me. Wearing a green helmet and a brightly colored Kirkwood jacket, balancing effortlessly on her snowboard, she held out her hands and pulled me to my feet.

"There you go, Mom," she said, her staff badge glinting: "Morgan, San Francisco." She is taking the second quarter of school off to recharge in Tahoe, with my blessings.

Squinting down the slope through my goggles, I saw Bill, the codger I had come with. A struggling figure in red pants, his feet strapped to a board like mine, he would stand for a second, then pitch back into the snow. Patrick was off somewhere in the heights on his own snowboard. He and Morgan had a bet about how soon Bill would stomp off cursing to the lodge, and Bill was determined not to give them the satisfaction.

I've been watching the kids fly gracefully down hills on their snowboards for years, while I foundered after them on my old skis, dropped my poles off lifts and listened to them yell, "Come on, Mom!" from the bottom. I wanted to try snowboarding myself. It is, like, way cooler than skiing now, and not just because you have a lot more contact with the snow.

Aside from having a little trouble with my dismounts from the chairlift, I did not need help. Morgan had assured the other instructor for our group lesson, Andy, that I was a skateboarder — I had made it down two blocks on the flat part of Waller Street when she and I went out to breakfast together last summer — and so would have no trouble making the transition to this alpine form of that sport.

"Oh, do you surf, too?" Andy asked. I said no, in a way that implied I really hadn't found time to take that up.

I learned from Andy and Morgan that riding a snowboard is sort of like riding a skateboard, except that you can jump off a skateboard when it gets going too fast. You can jump off a snowboard, too, but the snowboard tags along. Your feet are stuck to it in a way that reminds me of those tiny green Army men we used to play with. Imagine one of them in the snow, with its little green standing platform sticking out of a snowdrift, its head buried, and you have an idea of what happened when I sailed past Bill, who was just getting to his feet again. I shouted "Look at me!" and pitched forward into the drift of snow beside the run.

Morgan came over. "That was better, Mom," she said. She pulled me up; we were doing the Snowboard Dance, where the instructor floats along in front of you on her own board, keeping you upright by holding your arms.

We have danced so often, she and I, since the days when I used to bounce her around the living room to "The Beer Barrel Polka" when she was three months old to cure her colic.

This was just another kind of dance, only now she was leading.

"Relax, Mom," she said, "I won't let you go."

And she didn't. We danced off across the snow.

You Have to Let Them Go

I WAS WATCHING at Glen Alpine Falls in Tahoe as two kids about seven and ten forded a steeply down-rushing waterfall. A single misstep and they would be hurtling down the falls, their tender bodies slamming onto the jagged rock below.

Or so it seemed to me as I watched from below, unable to chew my tuna sandwich. Above, their mother watched, barely visible in a red tank top. I could not see her expression, but I knew from her frozen stance what she was feeling: that she had to trust them, had to let them climb around the falls.

People think that being a parent is a way to express one's natural feelings. I've found that being a mother means getting up every single day and doing exactly the opposite of what comes naturally. You let them cross streets, walk to school by themselves, get on bikes, drive away in 3,000-pound automobiles. There's nothing natural about that.

Your heart is lodged permanently in your throat, and yet you are supposed to smile and wave and say, as I do to Morgan as she hits the road, "Drive recklessly, sweetie. Try to tailgate as much as you can, and exceed the speed limit whenever possible." Trying to make a joke of it, because what else can you do?

Now Patrick, nineteen, has just gone off to New York to attend Hunter College. His dad is a wreck. "Patrick's idea of life in New York is based on 'Friends,'" Jim says. "Mine is based on 'NYPD Blue.'"

"Why does he have to go, anyway?" he asked, looking at me as if to say, "This is your fault. You encouraged him. You took him to that place and made him fall in love with it."

I remembered going to New York with Patrick when he was fifteen. He loved even the fact that the deli man was rude to him. I remember, though, watching him trip down the subway steps at 42nd Street as he went off by himself to find a coffeehouse in Greenwich Village to write in after declining to come to a play with me. And I had to just let him.

Patrick himself accuses me of wanting him to go to a nearby junior college, living at home where I can see him every day, Hi, Mama," in that tender way of his, where I can tell from the way he's spooning his Honey Nut Cheerios that something's on his mind. We wait until everybody else is gone to talk.

"I don't want you to be gone," I say, "but I want you to go."

He smiles. I tell him about going to Paris when I was twenty, deliberately sending myself to a place where something could happen to me. I remember standing at the bow of the ship taking me across the English Channel, the spray hitting my face, and feeling exultant, as if I could see the whole world spread out in front of me. For the first time in my life, no one knew where I was.

I was not thinking about my mother, who had had no say in the matter of whether I could take myself off to Paris or not. I was just going, and that was all.

I remember being twenty, and scared — I cried all the way to the airport, my sister and her boyfriend looking at me curiously — and how my tears stopped the moment they left me alone. That was 27 years ago, but that girl in her ridiculous long leather coat and her heavy red corduroy suitcase looks at me from across the table and says, "Don't you have some frequent-flier miles he can use?"

So he went. I couldn't think of what else to say in the airport, so I reminded him to always look behind him when he was about to leave a car or a room, to see if he was leaving anything behind. We had to break it to him that we won't be setting him up in an apartment of his own on the Upper East Side. He has a couch in Queens for a week, and then it's up to him to find a place to live.

And all this is fine with me. I'm glad he went. Really.

My thoughts returned to the woman watching as her two children played on the rocks amid the steeply down-rushing falls. I realize it only looked that dangerous from where I stood on the rocks below. The mother watching had done what mothers do, assessing the pleasure and adventure against the risk, and let them go.

The Days
of
My Life

Go Ahead and Scold, I'm Used to It

I T WAS IN the paper a few days ago: Some joggers drove to Ross, a wealthy town in Marin, chatted loudly and played the radio while preparing for their early-morning run, and came back to find a deep scratch running the length of their car. A note warned the joggers to be more considerate next time.

This is a good example of the two kinds of people there seem to be in the world: the scolders and the scoldees.

I'm a natural-born scoldee, the kind of person who will reach for any drink that happens to be near her or absent-mindedly cut you off in traffic and then wonder what you're honking about. A scold-ee will drive blithely into the parking space you're waiting for and never even see you. If scoldees spot the sandwich you made for yourself for lunch in the fridge, they'd just eat it, and never ask themselves how it got there. Scoldees sail right up to the cashier without noticing there's a line.

As a scoldee, I'm always bumping up against the other kind, the scolder. Scolders never drink other people's drinks or park in people's driveways, and they don't want you to, either.

Scolders seem to spot me even when I'm not doing anything wrong at the moment. I was sitting on the curb on 18th Street, waiting for Bill to come out of the cactus store, when a woman and a man came by.

"Is that yours?" the woman said sharply. A Twinkies package fluttered on the pavement at my feet. "No," I said. "Well, do you want to grab it and put it in the trash?" the woman asked.

I don't litter, but I'm a scoldee, and I look like one.

Scolders are always watching scoldees. I once bent down to pick a flower on a deserted block early Sunday morning, and a scolder burst out her house like a rifle shot, screen door banging, to bellow, "Put that flower down!"

Somehow the two kinds always seem to get on each other's nerves most when it comes to cars, and to extensions of cars, such as driveways and streets and neighborhoods.

A scoldee I know returned to her car one hot afternoon to find an enraged woman standing by it. "How long have you been gone? Your dog might have died in there!" The driver of the car felt terrible (the shade had moved), but her apologies did nothing to deflect the other's rage.

It was as if all the sorrows of her world, every wrong ever done her, had been poured into this moment, as if she were that overheated spaniel, and finally the second woman actually hit the side of the car with the flat of her hand.

A few years ago, when I wasn't used to street parking, I'd circle the block endlessly, looking for a place big enough for my car. Sometimes I would look up to see curtains twitching, as the garage owners (natural-born scolders) watched me from their living rooms.

One morning I found someone had crumpled one of my windshield wipers as a warning not to block his driveway again. I had left him room to get out: I thought that was the idea, for him to get out. That's how a scoldee thinks. That's why we give scolders nervous breakdowns.

Scolders are different. We don't care if you sit on our car, and we sit on yours without dreaming that you'd mind. You can park in our driveway if you leave a note to say where you are.

But the scolder is easily annoyed when his own rights are violated, and when he retaliates, he retaliates against property. He crumples a windshield wiper or scratches a car. You are hurting him by hurting his property, and he thinks this is the way he should hurt you. It never occurs to him that he might let the air out of the tires of that car owned by noisy joggers, to trade inconvenience for inconvenience.

Piddling Around Is Good for the Soul

IT WAS Saturday. "If you don't mind, I'd just like to piddle around here for a while," I said to Bill when he proposed a bike ride in the park.

I had a lot of important stuff to do. I had to collect the pennies from the bottom of my purse and put them into the huge Alhambra bottle marked "College Fund." I had to read last week's New Yorker and mutter to myself about the new perfume strips and celebrity stories, then admit it was getting livelier. I had to drift into the bedroom to refold the T-shirts the kids messed up in my drawer.

Meanwhile, Bill's brisk weekend warrior stride had taken him out of the room, and I could hear banging and whistling as he fixed things around the house. As I was browsing through my junk mail, I heard the whirr of the vacuum cleaner.

Fifteen minutes later, he was back. "If you're not doing anything in particular," he said, watching me clean out the keys on my computer keyboard, "we could take that ride we were talking about."

I was doing something in particular.

I was piddling.

I realize this is not one of your heroic human activities. No great poems have been written about it. No one goes on talk shows to confess her husband piddled around one hectic Sunday until she finally stabbed him with a pitchfork. Piddling impresses no one: If your office mate asks what you did last weekend, and you say, "Oh, just piddled around," he thinks, "Couldn't get a date, huh?"

I don't care. Piddling refresheth the soul. Today, for example, I had quite cheerfully hiked over the hill to Noe Valley with Bill to get coffee. In my book, this meant I had bought an hour or so of just fooling around at home before I could be considered ready for another social event, even one as minimal as a bike ride.

I just seem to need it. The world is too much with us, sometimes, and we need a break, time to quietly assimilate all the information that has flooded in. For me, piddling is to larger life events what the white spaces in between are to printed words: without importance, but crucial nonetheless. If my life were a TV show, piddling would be the commercial breaks.

I doubt I'm the only one: The history books may not record it, but I'll bet that before the attack at Waterloo, Napoleon had to spend a good 45 minutes futzing around in his tent, going through his pens and throwing out the ones that didn't work, practicing writing with his left hand, matching up his socks, before he was ready to re-enter the fray.

That was how I felt about going to the park on our bikes. I was game, but first I had a few pressing things to do, like plucking the dead petals off the roses on the table.

When I had finished, though, I was eager to go out and do something. I looked out the window. What a glorious day for a ride!

I went to tell Bill I was finally ready. I found him in the living room, repotting his cactus collection, watering them, experimenting with putting them on different tables.

"What do you think about putting this guy here, and that one over by the chair?" he said, pointing to two of his spiny plants.

"I thought you wanted to go out," I said impatiently.

"I do," he said, eyes on the cactus, "but I'd like to fool around here for a while longer first, if you don't mind."

If I hadn't known that he is a weekend warrior, determined to spend every minute charging from one event to the next, I would have sworn he was just happily piddling around.

Hello, It's Me . . . And Who Are You?

H I, ADAIR!" "Hi! So glad you could make it. The drinks are over there." Lisa? Debbie? Paula? I didn't know the name of the woman who had just come in, nor of the woman I had been talking to for 15 minutes.

Someone greeted her. Lisa. I have the name now, but which face was it? That one there, 40s, slender, short hair? Or over by the fridge, 20s, blond hair, black hat?

Holiday parties are exciting or draining in direct relation to the number of people you don't remember but are supposed to know.

The less of a clue you have about the name, the more energy and delight you are obliged to put into the greeting — "God! You look great!" — and subsequent small talk, as you try to discover who they are before they realize you have no idea. I don't know about you, but after five or six of these encounters, I'm ready to take to my bed.

I've always had a terrible memory. I leave messages on my own voice mail, feel my toothbrush to see if I've brushed my teeth yet, write notes on my hand.

But names are hardest. I'm so busy trying to respond to an introduction that the actual name goes out the window, leaving me to flail about at the next chance meeting.

Of course, often enough the person I'm talking to can't place me either. The two of us stand there, exchanging bright remarks about the decor, while we each desperately cudgel our brains, trying to figure out who on earth this is. I'm tempted to say something like, "You don't happen to remember your name, do you?"

If Bill's around, he might, while pretending to tidy my hairdo, whisper, "Joanne. Debbie's friend. Graphic designer. You've met."

Or we might wreck things for each other completely. There I am, cheerfully exchanging remarks with whoever it is, when he appears at my elbow, smiling. I can say, "This is Bill," and then tie my shoe, but then the jig's up.

I have revealed not only that I don't know her name, but also that I haven't known it for the past 10 minutes, when I was asking how she's been, and exclaiming that we must get together more.

The worst time is when you know her name perfectly — you grew up together — but the brain cell her name was precariously perched on is not responding to frantic signals from you.

You can't, you just can't, ask someone who lived next door to you for seven years for her name. Here an alert partner will note the glassy look in your eye and either bolt for the drinks table, or else hurriedly introduce himself, forcing your childhood friend to tell you who she is.

People want to be remembered. It's a deep human need, represented in its full terribleness by fear of a blank tombstone. The very fact that we have a cultural horror of name tags suggests that we attach meaning to remembering without the use of prompts.

Only the very mature among us don't wait to see if you remember them. They politely say their whole names and where you met as they shake your hand. "Shirley Murdock. We met at Donna Levin's book party. I'm a friend of Ray's."

This is, of course, wonderful when it happens to me, but also slightly insulting, as if it can be assumed that my memory is a sieve. I'm always obliged to interrupt such a person just as I get the gist of it, saying hurriedly, "Don't be silly, I remember you perfectly well!" because, of course, I do.

Now.

Simple Directions For Simple Folks

BILL'S FRIEND Antonia invited us to her house in St. Helena, in the Napa Valley. We had never been there before, so she sent directions.

As we came into St. Helena, we unfolded them with the usual sinking feeling. I expected to read on the faintly gray Xerox the usual terse remarks: "Just past St. Helena, go left opposite the winery. You can't miss it."

Such directions, while clear to some, would have left us peering anxiously at every left, wondering if that was the one we were supposed to take. When we got to the winery, we'd see two lefts and take the one that dead-ended 20 miles later in an abandoned mining camp.

Yet we hate getting lost. It makes us feel as if we are losing ground. For us, a gifted giver of directions is up there, along with the right turn on red, French bread and the Bill of Rights, as one of the hallmarks of civilization.

Bill was driving, and I was reading to him. Ordinarily, we would have already panicked, because Highway 29 had disappeared and we were wandering down something called Main Street. Most directions would not bother to tell you when a street changes its name. They don't care if you are now sitting up nervously, peering out the window, mourning the disappearance of Highway 29, because they assume you will continue straight until told otherwise.

But this isn't always what you do. You slow down, argue, finally hail a passer-by who doesn't know what you're talking about but hates to let you down: "Tell you what, I'm just here visiting my sister, but I'd say go back three, maybe four blocks, turn left at the 76 station."

Not this time. "At this point," I read to Bill as we sped into St. Helena, "Highway 29 north becomes Main Street. Continue on

Main Street, passing Beringer vineyards on your left at 2000 Main Street."

Thrillingly, the vineyard appears as promised. There's little room for confusion, but just in case we completely lose our minds and wonder if it's the right Beringer vineyard, there's the address.

"You'll go through a `tunnel' of Dutch elm," I read aloud next. Sure enough, we were now speeding underneath a canopy of trees. The wonderful thing is that we haven't even made any turns yet. These remarks, pointing the sights along the way, are purely to reassure us.

I rattle the sheet with a confidence I have never felt while looking for someone's house. A seasoned pathfinder leading the endangered caravan unerringly over the passes to California, I snap out the next direction: "Continue north two-tenths of a mile past winery complex and turn left just opposite a stand of mailboxes."

You'd have to be in a coma to miss both the mailboxes and the two-tenths thing, but Antonia, bless her, assumes you are. The sheet continues: "You're on the right road if: (1) You're climbing a hill; (2) there is a six-foot board fence on your right."

A fence. A hill. God, this is great. Columbus could have used this woman, 500 years ago. "You know you're on your way to India if your way is completely blocked by a large continent." If Antonia had sent Moses a map, he'd have been in the promised land not in forty years, but in time for cocktails.

We all lose our way now and then. We're likely to wonder if "Not a Through Street" really does go through, to take the next left just for the heck of it, or to yield, crazily, to the temptation of a freeway on-ramp when we're just going around the corner. All we ask for is a guide that assumes we're human, and fallible, and that we will find a way to screw up the simplest of directions.

91

Noticing Is in the Eye Of the Beholder

I AM A NON-NOTICER, what the men in white coats call a person low on "sensation function." I am the kind of person for whom life is full of small surprises. My attention goes on little vacations, and I find myself brushing my teeth with No. 15 sun screen, or absentmindedly tossing the dry-cleaning into the washer. When I was a teenager, I sat on our new living room furniture for six months before the day when I looked around and said, "Hey! This stuff is new!" I'm not completely oblivious — I will notice that you're jittery about something — but I won't be able to figure out it's because you shaved off your beard.

This is OK because it also means I'm immune to life's small annoyances. I can keep walking with an untied shoelace, and I don't mind if the tag sticks out of your sweater. It's fine with me if the faucet drips, if an alarm buzzes endlessly in another room, if the toilet roll is on upside down.

The only problem for me in the somewhat vague but untroubled world I live in is the noticers. Noticers are keenly aware of their world. They can tell if you moved the green chair inches nearer the cactus, and can be driven mad by a lash on your cheek. They feel a sharp joy at a clean, harmoniously arranged room, the taste of good black coffee, music coming through expensive speakers.

When a non-noticer marries a noticer, cultural differences are bound to arise.

There I am, happily curled on the couch in a blanket watching TV with the yellow number 003 blinking in one corner of the screen. Bill comes in on his way to the living room with a book.

"How can you stand that?"

"Stand what?"

"The TV like that."

"Like what?"

"That blinking 003."

"What? — Oh."

Snapped out of my happy blur, I now see the blinking 003.

It's all I see, now. I do understand. It's normal for Bill, a noticer, to yearn to share his world with me, a non-noticer. Noticers want to train your hearing until you can enjoy only the finest CDs, educate your palate, lead you into a world of non-blown-out speakers, freshly brewed coffee, dishes stacked in the dishwasher according to some logical plan, couch pillows arranged zipper side down, blinking 003s turned off.

It sounds like a nice place, that world of rarefied sensibilities. Full of aesthetic pleasures, subtle flavors, pleasing sounds. Being capable of such aesthetic judgments is part of what makes Bill good at his job as a book editor.

I would willingly be led into his world, if only it didn't require that I wouldn't be able to sleep through the mosquito. The same night Bill pointed out the blinking 003 to me, I woke to find him swatting at the shadows in our bedroom with a rolled-up New Yorker.

"How can you sleep through that?" he said, bashing at the wall next to my lamp.

"Sleep through what?"

"That mosquito."

"What mosquito?"

Then I heard it, faintly, the whine of a mosquito coming from over by the closet. Now it was my turn to try to lead Bill gently into my fuzzy but serene world, the world of the non-noticer. "Go to sleep," I mumbled into my pillow. "Pay no attention to it." After one more lunge in the direction of the closet, Bill came to bed and lay down rigidly, eyes wide open, magazine clenched in a fist.

When he gets up tomorrow, his coffee will still have a more subtle taste than mine and music will sound better. If his car starts making a funny sound, he'll notice before it's too late.

But he'll be very, very tired.

Fear Of Not Flying

B ILL AND I were leaving San Francisco for a flight to New York. I was nervous, as usual, about missing the plane, and he was nervous, as usual, about getting to the airport too early. (He's what the airlines call a "runner" — one of those people who like to run to the gate at the last minute to catch their flight.)

He's so scared of getting there early that he asked me to call Supershuttle and tell them our flight was at ten, instead of its actual time, nine, so we could cut it as close as possible.

As everybody knows, I am a compliant wife, so I called the shuttle and lied, as he asked. Only I said our flight left at eight.

Well, I'm sorry, but I worry. I'd like to be a "runner," dashing through the airport at the last minute, with twelve outfits cunningly packed into an overnight bag, then sweep through the gate in a cloud of Chanel No. 5, tossing a boarding pass over my shoulder to the attendant.

But it's not me. If I were that late I'd be sweating and worrying, with my purse slipping down my arm and my bags banging against my ankles, looking as if I'd been chased into SFO by a hostile mob.

Bill was still in the shower when the shuttle driver rang the doorbell. I was ready, two suitcases and a garment bag waiting by the door. We were going for only a week, but when I travel, I like to be prepared for a freak snowstorm, a power outage, an invitation to the White House, anything. Bill, of course, had everything in one carry-on garment bag, ready for that last-minute swan dive into the 747 as it pulled away from the gate.

"What?" he said when I pounded on the door and said the shuttle was here.

"The clock must be slow," I said brightly. "Anyway, they're here, so could you hurry up?"

As we sped toward the airport, I kept an eye on the shuttle driver to make sure he made no more than the three stops he's allowed. I was sure this would be the day a truck full of leghorn chickens would overturn on the freeway.

Bill, his hair still damp, gaped at his watch in disbelief when we arrived at SFO. "We have over an hour to wait!" he gasped.

"I know," I said worriedly. "It's not that much time. And I still have to check my bags."

When we got to the gate with 55 minutes to spare, I relaxed for the first time. I had time to browse the airport shops, have a cup of coffee and use the rest room near the gate instead of standing in line fighting with two-year-olds over the tiny one on the plane.

"At least we know we won't miss the plane," I said to Bill. Secretly I'm sure that if you don't make your flight they clap a dunce cap on you, with a sign saying, "This idiotic couple missed their plane."

"We could have missed our plane and caught the next one in the time we're sitting here," he grumbled, sitting down. I could tell by his face that he was sorry he hadn't suggested we say good-by to each other in the kitchen and meet at Rockefeller Center, by the ice skating rink.

He paced, he sat, he read. Finally, as they finally began to board our flight, he announced that he was going to the bathroom.

"You're going to the bathroom now?" I said.

"There's plenty of time," he said. "They never leave on time, and it's stuffy sitting on the plane."

He took the tickets with him. And I waited, his garment bag and my purse slung over my shoulder, while they called the passengers for first class, then the rest of us, row by row. As I heard "Last call for flight 809 to New York," calm descended on me. We were going to get the dunce cap after all.

The last passenger had disappeared into the jet way, and the last airline attendant was wheeling her little suitcase aboard when Bill flew by me. "Come on!" he yelled. And we sprinted for the plane, getting on at the last minute, just as he wanted.

Martha Stencils For Our Sins

A WHILE BACK I caught Martha Stewart on Oprah Winfrey, which I had to watch because I was folding the laundry. As everybody knows, Martha bones her own Cornish game hens, built a replica of her house out of gingerbread, scrubs her copper pans with lemon and salt, sponge-paints brown paper to make her own gift wrap, grows her own herbs and uses a hot glue gun the way the rest of us use hair dryers.

I was impatiently stuffing the whites in with the colors, trying to make up for the time lost watching daytime TV, when I found I was imagining that Martha had come over to my house.

"I was in the neighborhood," she said in a friendly way when I opened the door in surprise. "Can I come in?"

"The place is a mess," I protested, trying to hide a chewed dog bone with one foot and a cereal bowl with the other. I finish breakfast at my desk, and put the bowl down for the dog and cat. Sometimes I forget to pick it up again.

I removed a pile of junk mail from my office chair and asked Martha to sit down. I know from reading the monthly calendar she publishes in her magazine that she must be tired, having aerated, top-dressed and reseeded her lawns (and she has seven houses), sowed spinach and chard, and vacuumed all the grates.

I have pursued my own regular May schedule of ignoring the yard completely, asking Morgan to pitchfork through her room until she uncovers the plum sweater she borrowed and the Cheech and Chong video the store has been calling about, and trying to get the kitten to see reason about keeping her gravel in the litter box.

Martha and I chatted — she looks fabulous for 54, by the way — and after a little while she said she had to run — something about building egg topiaries. After she left, I felt not a sense of guilt at not having done anything about egg topiaries myself, but a strange contentment.

We women read Martha Stewart and sigh over the lovely pictures of how to make wild strawberry jam after a berrying party or how to set a table that will gladden the hearts of our guests.

Then we close the magazine, or turn off the show, and make instant popovers and dial in a pizza or wet the kid's hair to suggest that he's been bathed. If anyone looks at us askance, we say, laughing, "Well, I'm no Martha Stewart."

There's an odd relief in that idea. It is easy not to be her: Anybody can do it.

The trouble with most other standards we consciously or unconsciously set for ourselves is they are, however distantly, attainable. It is possible for us to once again weigh 123 pounds, to get through our kids' teen years without becoming raging alcoholics or running away, to read Proust in the original, to quit our jobs and start that small airline, to be as good a cook or housekeeper as Mom was.

But it is not possible to be Martha Stewart. Martha has had the civility, the delicacy, the Christlike resolution, to set an impossible standard.

You can't be her, and once you are not Martha Stewart, it doesn't matter by how much you fall short. It doesn't matter whether you merely forgot to treat your autumn leaves with glycerin in preparation for holiday wreath-making, or whether you forgot the holiday entirely and took the family out to the local Squat and Gobble.

You are free to be whoever you are, using paper towels for napkins, letting crumbs drop unheeded into the silverware drawer, leaving the driveway unstenciled, letting the linen spill out of the bathroom shelves. It is freeing, not being Martha Stewart. Until she came along, we did not have this feeling.

We make fun of her, but we owe Martha Stewart our gratitude. She assumes the burden. She is Martha Stewart, so we don't have to be.

Are You Out of Your Mind?

AFTER RESISTING for years, I now have e-mail. I like it, but I can't get over the difference between how the machine thinks I am and how I think I am.

For example, after I hit the button for "Send Message," it asks, "Really send message?" Then, when I hit the button for quit, it asks, "Really quit?"

The e-mail system seem like a fretful mother, knitting its eyebrows, asking if I'm sure, trying to force coat and galoshes on me. It worries I'll send a message I'll regret, as when my friend Jill accidentally sent a message to her whole office, including her boss, Mike, saying she wished Mike would get off his fat duff and read the galleys.

I feel the tiniest bit impatient during all this hand-wringing. Yes, really quit! Really delete messages from inbox! Yes, I really want to go out of the house looking like this! Just do what you're told and let me live with the consequences. I'm up to it, I really am. Or am I?

Should I be worried about what I said in this message I'm about to send? Am I making a big mistake by quitting the e-mail system?

Just when I've started to feel I was really grown up, really over the worst of my insecurities and able to make good decisions, self-doubt steals in again. I realize that not only do I need these reminders in my e-mail system, but I also could use them in my life.

I could have used them, for example, back when Nick and I moved in together, mutinous offspring and all. I signed a year's lease with him after a vacation from hell together, and after he had asked me, in a voice that said he just wanted to know, whether I was going to throw rubber bands on the floor for the rest of our lives.

I would have liked a program then that asked, "Move in with Nick? Really move in with Nick? Have you forgotten that he became hysterical when you used his stupid markers? Are you out of your mind?"

Or when I bought my black Toyota — a Toyota Corolla Sport, twin cam, fuel-injected, five-speed, electric sun roof, cruise control, for $3,000 more than it was worth, and then let them heap on life insurance ("Just think! The whole car is paid off if you die!"), an extended warranty, a $7,000 down payment and an interest rate three points over prime. "Really buy this car? Why not fling the money out an open window instead?"

When I absentmindedly ask my computer to delete all files, it asks, "Are you sure?" But there's no program to ask me this when I blithely get on a chairlift to the Black Diamond run at the top of the ski slopes in a snowstorm, then spend a half hour bitterly regretting it as I try to find someone to guide me back down. Quitting e-mail takes three keystrokes, with the machine clinging to your ankle at every step, trying to get you to reconsider.

It slows you down, but maybe that's the point.

I wish I'd had it several years ago when I threw over a job I loved on a local magazine. On my first day, a copy editor wandered around the editorial room asking everybody — interns, editors, passing writers — how to spell "olallieberry." No one knew, but everyone seemed mesmerized by the question. On one wall of the copy room was a sheet marked Department of Repetitions, Redundancies and Repetitions Department, on which the copy staff thumbtacked stuff they had overlooked in copy. I was surrounded on every hand by English majors unfit for jobs in the real world. I felt the way I've always imagined my sheepdog, Cody, would feel if he ever saw a flock of sheep: He would know instantly, in his gamboling feet, what he was for. I was home.

Two years later, sulking, I was offered a job on another magazine, and I took it.

I wish I'd had those e-mail prompts then. Really quit the job you love? Why?

Quit? Really quit? Are you sure? Omit deleted experiences from future memory? Y/N?

What Price Price Club?

MY FRIEND MARJANNE called on a Thursday morning and mentioned that she was going to the Price Club and was willing to take me.

"I have much too much work to do," I told her. "I can't go out shopping, just like that."

"I do, too," she said. "I'm way behind on my November invoices. Should we take my car? It holds more."

I had begun to have a disturbing feeling that everybody in the Bay Area belonged to the Price Club but me. While I am out at the No-Price-2-Hi store, paying full retail, they're out there in their mini-vans, loading up on cassette tapes and frozen asparagus.

I had the further unhappy feeling that at least one person has to pay full price so others can skip merrily home with discounts, and I feared that person was me.

Today, however, that was going to change.

When we arrived at the huge windowless warehouse, I looked around, riveted, at the stereos, cookware, film, watches, jewelry, liquor gift sets, razor blades, tires, socks, sheets, stationery.

Hardly noticing when Marjanne disappeared, I grabbed an over-sized orange cart and headed into the crowd. Some people were pushing industrial pallets, piling toilet paper and pancake mix and cases of Kahlua on them as if it had been announced that all buying everywhere in the world would cease in fifteen minutes.

I began to throw things into my cart, at first slowly, then faster and faster. My list forgotten, I lobbed in everything I saw that I have ever used: a 24-pack of film, a lifetime supply of tampons, a hundred plastic tumblers, champagne, couch throws, Christmas wrap, Reeboks I didn't even try on.

Everybody I saw was doing the same thing. It was as if we were all Scarlett O'Hara in "Gone With the Wind," whispering, "As God is my witness, I'll never pay retail for toilet paper again."

Veterans say it's dangerous to let people go to the Price Club alone the first time out.

"A gallon jug of maple syrup," the novice thinks. "What a good idea. Why not a case of gallon jugs of maple syrup — an even better idea!"

For everything I grabbed, I had to leave scores of other things behind, including a huge box of the Eggo frozen waffles the kids like. If I cleared everything else out of my fridge, including the ice trays, I could fit the waffles in. If I moved the kids out of their rooms, I could take advantage of these terrific bargains in paper towels. If I moved out myself . . .

I calmed down, but not before I bought about 30,000 granola bars. The kids will polish them off by the time they start college, I figure, and can start on the frozen pepperoni pizzas.

I handed over $337 to the cashier my first time out, which is about the average for a first-timer, they say. The Price Club is so cheap that you end up spending a fortune.

But I suppose I saved money in the long run, and I suppose I'll go back — I'd be a sucker to pass up these bargains, wouldn't I?

Wouldn't I?

In truth, the place gave me the creeps. So much consuming, at such dreadful speed, and in such dreadful quantities. They even have food stalls with samples at the ends of aisles, so you can get started on your consuming right away.

It reminds me of the time when I was about four, and an enterprising neighbor girl decided, while her parents were out, to sell everything in their house for one or two cents apiece. I got some good deals that day too, but as I was lugging it all home in my wagon, I felt something was wrong. At four I couldn't put my finger on it.

At 37, I still can't.

It *Is* Whether You Win or Lose

A WHILE BACK, I read that the University of Connecticut had issued a proclamation banning "inappropriately directed laughter" and "conspicuous exclusion of students from conversations."

And when students at Madison, Wis., proposed an alcohol-free Halloween party, the student senate rose in protest, saying that masked students might take advantage of anonymity to inflict "poking, pinching and rude comments" on women and minorities. And the mother of a little girl teased by boys on the school bus sued the school board.

All of this suggests that modern parents — and sometimes the kids themselves — are doing their best to shield our young from life's little unpleasantnesses. Take for example, the game of T-ball, which a man named Jack described to me at a recent party in Napa. His 6-year-old daughter, Emily, plays T-ball.

Nothing bad ever happens in T-ball. It's life as it should be: Losers are applauded, no one ever gets out, everybody bats.

The game has three innings, and everybody on the team — often as many as sixteen first-graders — gets to bat in every inning. There are outs, but they don't count.

Kids do run the bases, and plays are made, but if a player is thrown out, he gets more applause as he walks off the field than he would if he'd made it on base. You know the inning is over when every kid has batted.

All sixteen players take the field at the same time. Once, Jack says, the third baseman got confused when the ball was hit, and he ran and slid into home, glove and all. The crowd of parents cheered him loudly, and the coach told him it was a good run and a terrific slide. Then he mentioned that the third baseman, generally speaking, does not run home.

No one ever strikes out in T-ball because you get as many strikes as it takes to finally hit the ball. The kids hit the ball off a kind of stiff upright hose — the T.

The coach shows each kid how to bat as he or she comes up to

102

the plate. At first, Jack says, the parents approved of this, but when a kid was on his 20th swing, and the members of the other team were sprawled on their bases with their gloves off, the parents started muttering things like, "If that son of a bitch talks to one more kid . . ."

Jack thinks T-ball is the revenge of all the parents who, back in grade school, found themselves squirming on the playground while everybody argued about who had to take them. "I took Paulie, so you have to take Mary . . ."

T-ball may well be the right way to introduce little tykes to a demanding sport. Jack appreciates the gentle approach, but worries about the day he'll take Emily to a Giants' game. "But this is all wrong!" she'll say when the runner is thrown out at first, then jeered off the field by fans who are openly keeping score. In real baseball, you are not only instantly penalized for a mistake, but also your entire career of hits and errors flashes on the scoreboard.

In the meantime, though, Emily has T-ball, where there is no such thing as mistakes, consequences, regrets — or, by extension, excellence, triumph, skill or winning; where you can throw out twelve players (as one little troublemaking hotshot named Jose did, said Jack) and still not get up to bat any faster. Where you never experience the joy of winning or the sting of defeat, only three innings of a scoreless game, followed by snacks, during which no one is excluded from the conversation, and no one is teased.

Political correctness is like T-ball: a strenuous effort to make life painless and fair, doomed to make it only ludicrous — and pointless.

The rules of T-ball, or rather the lack of them, reminds Jack of the son of a friend of his who was told in high school to wear a jock strap. He did as he was told, but couldn't see the reason for the straps that hung down, so he cut them off. Then, Jack says, "He found out what they were for."

"This is like cutting off the straps," says Jack. "You take away the rules, then you find out what the rules were for."

We'll Never Grow Out of Our Jeans

M Y FRIEND ERIC mentioned that he had just bought his first pair of jeans since high school. "Wait a minute," I said. "What do you hang around the house in?"

"Oh, old wool slacks," he answered. His whole life, Eric says, has been devoting to resisting trends. He believes that except for medical advances, our civilization should have stopped at 1956.

"I'm pretty much as I was then," he says. "I went through that fattie thing once and then said the hell with it."

This is the kind of statement that reminds you that thousands of miles of uncrossable, barren terrain lie between you and other human beings.

How could someone you talk to every day not own a pair of jeans? The whole world is wearing jeans — pegged jeans, loose jeans, stone-washed and original blue. We have our old jeans, our new jeans. We split into hostile camps on the zipper vs. button question, on the agonizing loose fit vs. classic fit decision, on whether jeans should hit the top of the foot or just reach the ankle bone, on whether designer jeans are either merely uncool or actually geek wear. Now we have to decide if we want Miracle Boost jeans to lift and shape our sagging baby boomer butts.

Back in high school, we put them on in the shower to shrink them, and refused to wear them until Mom had time to get out the sewing machine and peg them. We bleached them in strategic places, cut them off so the dark pockets stuck out. When stringy holes appeared in them, we whiled away algebra classes pulling on the strings, then drawing on our knees through the holes with ballpoint pens.

I come from a generation whose lovemaking begins not with the rustle of silk, but with the clank of jeans hitting the floor, a generation whose standard of thinness is whether your length size is greater than your waist size. We girls all have Three Bears pants: Papa's (for fat days), Mama's (regular days) and Baby's (after a five-day flu).   We put our toddlers into tiny jeans with tiny pockets so they'll look cool and have a place to keep their rattles.

A friend of mine once remarked that you can tell how a woman feels about herself by how many pairs of black pants hang in her closet. I would say you can tell how either sex feels by the number of pairs and kinds of jeans they own. We measure our age by our progress from 501s to loose fit.

Only teenagers today don't care much about jeans, because kids today wear their pants several sizes too big, and for that chinos and cords work just fine. Jeans have to hug the backside. Jeans are for showing off what you got, not for covering it up. Jeans that sag three inches below the top of the boxer shorts work, but barely.

When my dad knows I'm coming over, he gets into what he must think of as his good clothes, some slacks and a shirt he got hold of somewhere. So I don't tell him I'm coming anymore: I want to catch him looking like my dad, in the jeans he's always worn, not in his geezer wear.

People get to be over seventy and act as if it's the law they can't wear jeans anymore. It's Polyester Time. Former cool dressers let their wives put them in apricot play suits, matching shorts and shirt. Yet old people look the coolest of all in hard clothes like jeans.

Eric confessed that he had bought his after he went walking with a woman down at Baker Beach, the two strolling hand in hand along the shore, with the sea tugging at the cuffs of his wool slacks, and she suggested he get himself a pair of jeans.

When Eric told me that, I knew the woman at Baker Beach wanted to sleep with him. When a woman herds a man into a pair of jeans, it's like a man buying his girlfriend a red teddy at Victoria's Secret: The woman has something on her mind. This spring Bill had a few beers in San Antonio and bought himself a silver belt. Then he said he was waiting until he gets a pair of black jeans to wear with it, and I got impatient and went out and got him some, because a woman can wait only so long.

Survival Guide For New Grads

I T'S JUNE, and everybody's spilling out onto the sidewalk at Civic
Auditorium in their gowns and mortarboards — including
Patrick, graduating this morning from Lowell High School. It's
been 28 years since I did the same, crashing out of the Drake High
gym, through with books and teachers' dirty looks, at least until
college started in the fall.

What would I tell the new grads as they grab the keys of those
new cars and head into the future?

If you must err on one side or the other, buy your pants slightly
too long.

Do things you don't want to do, then remember to pat yourself
on the back, maybe even buy yourself a little present, a packet of
bubble bath or a Miata.

Never hate anybody you've loved.

Return smiles.

Live outside the lines.

Never go to the movies on Friday night and expect to be able to
go right in.

Never carry highlighting pens in your purse.

Everybody has 25 words they misspell. Learn your 25.

It pays to be sensitive to the needs of the IRS.

Never leave a place where you are having a good time to go somewhere else where you only think you'll have a better time.

Shop like a Marine: Buy a few good clothes, and wear them all
the time.

If you said you would bring the birthday cake, bring the birthday
cake. Do what you say you are going to do. Be the sort of person of
whom people say, "Oh, I asked Shirley. She said she would, and she
always does what she says she'll do."

Don't buy white linoleum, unless you want to spend the next
twenty years mopping the kitchen floor.

Don't buy a car on the same day you fall in love with it. Make yourself wait a day. Above all, never buy a Ford Tempo in San Rafael on a rainy Sunday, or a brand new Toyota sports car just because you're mad at a guy who went to a party without you.

Read seriously. Keep a list of the books you've read, starting now.

To shy types, the kind I was: Get over yourself. Nobody is watching you.

Go to parties and resolve to speak to the first person wearing yellow. Tell the man in the green jacket that you think he's the handsomest man in the room.

Buy old furniture and new computer equipment.

Drive the speed limit.

Don't hurt people.

If you want to give the impression you've done your share of the housecleaning, make a neat pile of something — items on the kitchen table, say. Then spray some Lemon Pledge in the air.

Save time by defrosting the chicken in the shower water.

Figure out where you want to live, and go live there — everything else will fall into place later.

Pay your credit card bills in full the day they arrive.

When you get stuck, just do the next thing.

Take plenty of days off.

Get a pet. You can make jokes about them, and they don't even know what you're saying.

Collect interesting mistakes.

Explore the stock market by losing a little money.

Learn about cars by getting burned on one or wrecking one.

Go out with all the wrong people.

Be nice. Don't fight.

And, finally, as my dad says, "Talk straight, be a little chaste now and then to increase the enjoyment of the blowouts, and watch for the humor."

I Already Have Friends

THE OTHER DAY, while out running errands, trying to get everything done before it started raining again, I stopped in at the bank to deposit some checks.

"Hi!" I was disconcerted to see that the teller, young, moon-faced, with neatly slicked-back hair, was beaming at me. He barely glanced at the pile of paperwork I had handed him. "Some weather, isn't it?" I agreed it was some weather.

"So, you don't have to work today?" he asked. When I muttered that I worked at home, he wanted to know what kind of work I did, uh — a glance down at my check — Miss Lara? Oh, a writer? What kinds of things did I write? Every time he spoke, his hands grew still. The transaction slowed.

I had a horrible suspicion that the bank had put him up to this.

"Chat with the customers," it must have said. "Shoot the breeze a little. Call them by name."

Morgan said it took her an hour and a half to open a new account at her bank because they were just so nice. She was late to her cultural anthropology class. Later she got a handwritten note in the mail from the teller. "Keep me informed about your snowboarding!" it said cheerily.

And Safeway. Time was when you could dash in there, pick up a small chicken and a pound of broccoli and be back in your car without having to swap commonplaces with a single human being. Now the clerks don't tell you the hoisin sauce is on Aisle 9 and go back to stacking cans. They escort you there, while you wonder whether you're supposed to make conversation or just walk with them to Aisle 9 in silence.

It's the new personal touch. It says this is not a crass, businesslike transaction we're having here, your dollars for our broccoli. This is a warm social exchange. To reinforce that, they read your name off the receipt. "Plastic or paper, Ms. Lara?"

But here's the thing: I'm just not that lonely. I already have friends, other people who call me by name. I don't go to Safeway to socialize, but to buy groceries. I go to the bank with the sole objective of conducting my business with all due speed, not telling a 21-year-old teller how I got started writing.

Nor do I especially want to bond with the people at directory assistance. But bond I must.

Last year, I called a catalog company just to tell it not to send the tropical microfiber blazer now. "The blazer will arrive about a week after I've left on my trip," I explained.

"Oh, where are you going?" the man who had identified himself as David exclaimed. "Paris? Oh, you have to try the old wooden subway cars. It's much better than the regular Metro."

And when I called the phone company to get the number for Bizou, a restaurant on Harrison, the operator said, "Oh, Bizou! I haven't been there yet. Have you tried Fringale? I was there just last night. I heard Bizou was more intense about the food, and I'd like to compare them. . . . Oh, here's your number."

I yearn for the old days, when phone operators were all business: "What city, please?"

The trouble with all this friendliness is that it makes me the curmudgeon. It makes me stand in the bank thinking grouchy thoughts like, "Say, could you just add up those checks a little faster?" when the poor teller is just trying to be friendly, and probably doesn't care all that much how I got started writing anyway.

It's like the day I went into a store in a little town in South Carolina and the owner was affronted that I apparently planned to just buy my Coke and leave. He wanted to chat, and I just wanted a cold Coke. He got to be cuddly and cozy while I, the hurried Northerner, had grown horns, claws and a tail.

Now I live in that little town.

The Right Way To Do Halloween

I T'S HALLOWEEN AGAIN. In an effort to do my part to safeguard the precious traditions of this holiday, I have come up with a few simple rules for tonight.

➤ Rule No. One. No hiding in the dark and not answering the doorbell because you forgot to buy candy (or ate it all). Go to the store. Taking off before the trick-or-treating and leaving your house dark is not allowed either. Some blocks in San Francisco on Halloween look like London after the blitz.

Ever watch a three-year-old in a ball gown and wings, tripping in high heels down a darkened block, trying to find a house with a porch light on? The kids are all done by seven or so — you can stay home that long.

➤ Two. No grilling the little guys about what they're supposed to be before you drop in their candy. Nobody likes being cross-examined, especially when his mother has pinned leaves all over him and he has no idea why. If you don't know what he is, he's a ghost.

➤ Three. Anybody who wants to can trick or treat. One of the most stinging memories in everybody's life is the moment when some jerk of a neighbor says, "Hey, you, the big kid at the back. Aren't you a little old to be out here?" Let them trick or treat until they're ninety if they want to.

➤ Four. The first rule for parents is no giving out apples. No granola. No nuts, no raisins, no homemade cookies. Giving kids nutritious snacks on Halloween is like passing off underwear as a present at Christmas. (Not to mention that these are the treats most easily tampered with). Also, no school supplies, and no money, unless you'd like them to become comfortable with panhandling. (Collecting for UNICEF is different). It's only once a year, so give them candy, already.

➤ Five. The other rule for parents is no neighborhood hopping. Year after year I've watched cars fill up and head for Pacific Heights, where the pickings are supposedly better. Halloween is a neighborhood event. Besides, how do you know in a strange neighborhood which houses have people who eat children, who gives out the best junk, who very thoughtfully offers hot brandy to the adults?

And, kids? Hoarding candy is not allowed. When I was little, there'd always be some kid, usually a girl, who'd slide out her bottom drawer in March, show us her bowl of Halloween candy, and primly reach in and take out her one piece for the day. These children grow up to give out five-grain crackers on Halloween.

The proper way to behave is to let Mom inspect your booty for tampering and give her the candy of her choice as a reward. Then jettison anything with actual food value.

Trade what's left with other kids until you have exactly what you want, then eat candy for 24 hours straight, until you wonder what you ever liked about it.

This brings up a question: Can parents take away some of the candy? Absolutely. Do it as long as you can get away with it, which in my experience is up to about age four.

Finally, everybody should wear a costume on Halloween, except those for whom it would be redundant. Even if you're a gray-haired accountant staying home to watch Nightly Business Report, wrap a dishrag around your head or do a little something to your eyebrows.

Nobody should be quite himself or herself on Halloween. This night is so much about make-believe, madness and the kindness of strangers (not to mention an orgy of cross-dressing) that it seems to embody a uniquely San Francisco spirit.

And it's most of all about breaking rules, so feel free to ignore the above and do whatever you like.

Heard Any Good Books Lately?

AFTER A LONG dry part, my book (Colleen McCullough's *Fortune's Favorites*) had finally gotten good. An irate consul was going to decimate (kill every man in ten) a quailing Roman legion, the drums were beating, the men in line were counting off . . .

All of a sudden I was back at my garage. I shut off the car, and my book on tape stopped.

I went upstairs and tried to work, but I kept thinking about that Roman legion. Of course, I had other books to read upstairs, but the one in my head was the one in the car. Deciding I had to drive across town that minute to take back some camera gear, I took the longest route I could, listening happily to my book.

I've gone from being a bookworm, carrying a book around with me and pulling it out at stop signals and bank lines, to being a book-on-tape worm.

When I try to share my enthusiasm for book tapes with other people, especially those who commute long distances, they tell me they enjoy listening to their own thoughts. I always take this as a hostile remark. What do they mean they enjoy their own thoughts? If their thoughts are like my thoughts, they're thinking: I wonder if I can get home on the gas I have? Did I throw my backpack in the trunk of the car, or leave it in the parking lot after I got a dollar out for the bridge toll? Was that car honking at me?

I can do without my own thoughts a lot of the time. As someone said, God gave me a wonderful brain, but then he put my mind in there, too. I appreciate the brief respite of hearing other people's thoughts — in other words, books.

Numerous magazine articles insist, rightly, that we're supposed to live in the moment, be present in our own lives. But sometimes I want to be transported out of the moment. I want to be taken entirely away from the ugly sound walls on the Bayshore Freeway on a gray Friday and plunked down in *Remains of the Day*, where an aging butler is trying to learn the sort of impish humor he believes is expected by his new American employer.

Bill and I have a wonderful memory of driving down the coast highway in Sonoma in a thick fog, trying but not very hard to find the road that cut back inland, while listening to Jane Austen's *Emma* read to us by an Englishwoman who pronounces the language beautifully. It might have been an irritating afternoon, what with the fog and being lost, but now the landscape outside our windows looked vaguely English in the mist, and some of the most savagely witty writing in English was massaging our eardrums.

On ski trips I force the kids to agree, before we ever get in the car, that I can listen to a book on the four-hour ride home. If they fight in the car, I swerve to the side of the road and stop. When that doesn't work, I have a tape of 19th century English poetry that I quite enjoy. The mere mention of my poetry tape often brings harmony even to two siblings battling bitterly over which of them is more stupid.

I always assume I am listening to the book by myself, but they surprise me. When they were little, the three of us drove to Los Angeles, then barreled back on Highway 5. I had saved Russell Baker's *Growing Up* for this, knowing they'd be asleep. I listened raptly for hours, then pulled off the highway for gas.

When I shut off the ignition, the car erupted in howls. "Don't turn it off!" both kids cried. I had to leave the radio on while I pumped the gas, then quiz them on what I had missed.

I'm like Bill now. Standing at the kitchen window on the phone, I sometimes see him arrive home, park under the oak tree and then just go on sitting in the car. I wonder if he's gathering his nerve to re-enter the domestic fray, then realize he's just listening spellbound to KALW. Now I arrive at places and then just sit there. I probably look as if I'm planning to burgle your place, but really I'm just trying to hear the last few pages of Mark Childress's *Crazy in Alabama*.

When Correcting Errors Is a Mistake

S O OFTEN, when we had you back in high school, you were inspirational. You were like Michael James, the English man who taught my humanities class in my senior year at Drake High School and told a fellow student that her prose was like clear spring water, or like Mardys Whiteman, who had so much confidence in me that she let me grade multiple-choice quizzes.

You were like the teacher at Lowell who read Patrick's paper on Holden Caulfield last year, underlined the statements he liked and wrote "Nice!" in the margin. Sometimes, after we'd spent time in your classroom, we left with a sense of having found out what we could do, not what we could not do.

Some of you, though, hardworking and well-intentioned as you are, still regard it as your main job to find and correct errors. You circle the word "this" and write "ambiguous" in the margin. You circle spelling errors, call attention to faulty logic, mark run-on sentences.

And you do this in *red ink*. Red ink directs the student's attention to what he's doing wrong. When he sees all the mistakes he has made, he crumples up the paper in embarrassment and slouches lower in his seat. You've seen him; most of us have been him.

Yet if we uncrumple that paper, the one with all the spelling errors and run-on sentences, what do we see? A boy writing about a fishing trip with his dad, his language so vivid we can see the two of them out on the lake, the trout flashing in the sunlight, the boy leaning forward earnestly as his father talks.

I had a teacher who used to highlight in yellow those passages in each paper that he found felicitous. When the papers were turned back, each of us had something — a paragraph or two — bathed in yellow, something we would read aloud in thickly embarrassed, pleased voices. He read our papers searching not for mistakes but for passages that pleased him. Because he looked for them, he found them.

I do a little teaching now, and I have found that even adults, long past adolescent sensitivities, become more excited about writing when a teacher shows them what they are already doing well.

Of course you can't send students into the world not knowing how to use a comma before a conjunction in a compound sentence, or how to spell "ingenious." Correctness in language is like table manners, in that all sorts of importance gets attached to whether you use the right salad fork or whether you say "take" when you mean "bring." Neglect that, and future bosses will look up from your student's error-strewn resume and sneer, "Who was your English teacher, anyway?"

So you make it separate. You respond to the writing without regard to the errors, then, in a separate process, show them the mistakes in grammar. I blush to remember my own years as a teaching assistant at College of Marin. I marked my first set of papers with a red pen.

My ex-husband Jim, then my master teacher, said nothing; he just noted to the class, "The essays marked in red ink were done by Adair." And I got it, about the red ink.

I stopped using it, but I went on marking errors. I'd tell a student that his construction wasn't parallel, that he said "that" when he meant "who." I wish I could go back in time and mark, in broad yellow slashes, the parts of those papers that I particularly liked.

Kids come to high school English teachers when they are in the throes of putting together a self, when they are making up their minds what to think of themselves and their abilities. Being teenagers, they want to think the worst.

It's just not a good time of life for people to have their errors circled in red.

Poetry to Their Ears, And Bankbooks

I AM VERY excited today. I got a letter from the National Poetry Forum of New York. I had sent in one of my poems for consideration, and senior editor Aaron Klein sent me a letter saying, "Dear Adair, I am pleased to inform you that your poem, 'My Puppy,' has won an Editors' Choice Award."

The Forum wants to publish my poem in a book called "Passionate Whispers," "a beautiful hard-bound anthology that showcases talented poets of 1998." Because I won an award, I will get a chance to buy this "impressive literary work" at the prepublication price of $27.

I have also been issued a privileged membership to their forum, with the VIP No. 49820813.

I know what you're thinking — that this is a scam, a poetry award offered by an anthology-publishing clip joint whose sole purpose is to prey on the weak-minded. You are probably thinking that there is no National Poetry Forum, that it exists only on paper, as a letterhead.

Envy is an ugly thing.

All I can do, by way of rejoinder, is to share with you the work found meritorious by a "distinguished panel of literary judges":

MY PUPPY

By Adair Lara

My puppy is warm

My puppy is fuzzy

My puppy is warm and fuzzy

but he barks at me

at me.

My friend Susan won, too. Her poem, called "Meat or Flowers — Take Your Pick," was singled out by the National Library of Poetry for its anthology, "A Prism of Thoughts." The poem is about some chicken that went bad in the fridge, with a deft comparison to carnations that last two weeks. It was very moving.

Susan declared herself excited to have won the acclaim of the National Library of Poetry, and announced that she had scrapped her vacation plans and was instead driving across the country to visit Poetry Plaza in Owings Mills, Md. She told the Library how relieved she was to learn that somewhere, in this crass land of sports and beer, resided a community of poets. She wouldn't say when she was arriving, though — she wanted to surprise them.

Of course I am jealous, knowing Susan will be communing with her fellow sensitives at Poetry Plaza while I stew here at home with you philistines, who probably don't even recognize the genius of "My Puppy."

There will be a lot of them, too. I have an ad here that says the National Library of Poetry has published the work of more than 100,000 poets. The deadline for the latest poetry contest was March 15, in case you were thinking of dusting off those odes in your shoe box. Luckily, the next contest began March 16.

"All poets who enter will receive a response concerning their artistry," the ad promised. My feeling is, they are going to like the artistry of your poem a lot, so send it in. Even if your only talent is for writing out checks — for anthologies, say — you are Robert Frost, as far as the poetry library is concerned. "We have a ten-year history of awarding large prizes to talented poets who have never before won any type of writing competition."

Well, that lets me out, now that I have been recognized by the National Poetry Forum. Though I have only a "P.O. Box 381, New York," to go on, I would like to travel to New York and talk to Aaron about my poem, maybe show him some other ones that I have written about my puppy, in case he thinks they could go in the anthology too. I'd like to commune in that rarefied atmosphere with others in the Forum, maybe get to know the people on either side of me, VIP No. 49820812 and VIP No. 49820814.

And I will, as soon as I can find a directory in New York State that lists the National Poetry Forum.

Just Thought You'd Like to See This

I READ THE PIECE in The Chron about a Philosophers Club over at Cesar Chavez Elementary School, so naturally I had to cut it out to send to Morgan.

She's in Tahoe, and I haven't seen her since Christmas. I've had to content myself with the warm bath of her husky young voice on the phone, telling me of avalanche training, hiking in snow, reading her philosophical dictionary, and how she'll tune up her Tracker "soon, Mom."

When I run across an article like this and cut it out, it's as if she's right across the kitchen table from me, and I'm saying, "Hey, take a look at this."

My friend Ronda knows what it's like to be on the receiving end of parental clippings. She was a Brownie thirty years ago, and she still gets articles from her mother every time a Brownie troop's cupcake drive is mentioned in the paper.

When Ronda was pounding out a living as a legal secretary, her mom sent her clippings about getting paid what you're worth. When she worked for a hospice, Mom sent articles about Elizabeth Kubler-Ross's five stages of dying. When she got into the adoption-reform movement, her mom would forward to her touching stories about people who had been reunited.

"Just thought you'd enjoy reading this!" the little yellow Post-It notes on the clippings say. Or "Were you aware of this?"

Neither of them mentions the one-way barrage. It's there, part of their lives.

Jay Schaefer would understand. He went on a trip to Peru in 1976.

"Now every time a bus falls off a cliff in Peru," he says, "I hear about it from my mother."

My friend Mark Sloan, a Santa Rosa pediatrician, says his dad forwarded results from high school track meets in his hometown of

Kankakee, Ill., until Mark's shot- putting and discus-throwing records finally fell. "Now I only get medical articles from him," Mark sighs.

Terry Norton's mom is a regular wire service. "I'll bet you don't know that several drops of bilberry in your morning juice improves eyesight," she tells me after opening one of her mom's dispatches.

Patrick's bedroom is upstairs at his dad's place, so I send things through his mail slot. These include the Harper's Index, which he once mentioned he liked, articles on snowboarding, and recently, one on the new trend for poetry slams among high school and college students. I dropped in a piece I liked — "Examsmanship and the Liberal Arts" by William G. Perry. — on the difference between writing "cow" and "bull" on college exams. ("Bull" is defined as "the cerebrations of a student who has little data at his disposal.")

I get clippings, too. My mother sends me columns cut from other newspapers. "This writer seems very good," she'll say in her strong handwriting. "Have you tried this?"

Bill leaves funny clippings on my office chair — articles on some quirky habits among penguins (the females have sex with other males in return for stones from their nests), and today one on how a Finnish sex fair "hopes to attract older people who still have a twinkle in their eye, and can find enjoyment in each other's arms." (The geezers they're talking about are 45 and older.)

There's a regular blizzard of leafletting out there. I imagine the post office a sea of little yellow Post-Its, each one saying, "I just happened to see this . . ."

Whether arriving through the mail, in e-mail, on chairs or slipped into the pocket of your jacket as it's slung over a chair, this leafletting always carries the same message: I was thinking of you. I want to share this with you.

I carry you around in my head, waking and sleeping.

Kite and Rock

WHEN HIS WIFE, Hillary, died recently, my friend Roger discovered that he didn't even know how much money he made, let alone how to change a furnace filter or file taxes. A chaplain said to him, "You were the kite in this marriage. Hillary was the rock." Roger is now living in a cabin in Vermont, writing.

Kites need rocks to anchor them. My brother-in-law, Rich, is a kite. In the nine years I've known him he's switched careers, from executive at GTE to studying plant biology, which entailed years of night school, pulling down A's in organic chemistry in classes with 22-year-olds. When he was close to a degree, he began writing a horror novel, which is now in the hands of an agent. His wife, Monica, works steadily, takes care of their daughter and enthusiastically applauds him in his new adventures.

Jim, my ex upstairs, is a rock. He's lived in the same house since long before the kids were born, and will always live in it. Everything about him is permanent, from the antiques in his house to the close friends he's had since he was young.

He's the best sort of rock. He's the one you call when you're in trouble, because you know he will come. The summer I moved in with him, I didn't even have an address but was moving from place to place, house-sitting. "Sleeping around," he called it. I needed a rock, and there he was.

Rocks can be very indulgent of kites.

My friend Stacy's mother had the kind of husband willing to allow her to be the Artiste. He got the kids up and off to school while his wife opened the antique store of her dreams and showed the kids how to find four-leaf clovers.

My parents can tell you what happens to a marriage when one is all kite, the other all rock. While my mother sat over her figures, trying to save money to build a house, Dad would stare out the window at the dark night.

"Let's move to Alaska," he'd say suddenly to Mother. "You can live on practically nothing there." I'd listen wide-eyed, and go around for a week imagining us all huddled in an igloo, coloring in our coloring books while the Arctic gales howled outside.

Instead of building a house, he set the one we lived in on fire to get the insurance money. Already the breeze was tugging at him.

Finally, when I was eleven, he fluttered away. He never got his chance to be a rock. Nothing ever anchored him again, after her, and he drifted with the wind, to the desert and back again. And she had seven children by then.

She never got her chance to be a kite.

My friend Marie did, though. "In my marriage," she says, "I was usually the rock. I was in charge of investing in the stock market, paying bills, scheduling appointments and completing applications. I had to keep telling him he couldn't quit his job and move to Hawaii to surf and swim while he developed some accounting software. I selected and bought most of my husband's clothes, and said no to him when he came up with improvements like turning our son's closet into a two-story playhouse complete with slide into the bedroom, or using the entire backyard for a tennis court."

When they divorced, Marie finally had a chance to be a kite. Now she was the one who wanted to do something with the backyard. "I went out and bought two boulders that together weighed a ton. "When they were delivered, left on crates on the side of my driveway, I panicked. The supplier said they weren't returnable. Finally, after a day of grunting and cussing, five men managed to move the rocks into the backyard. I pulled a huge sheet of plywood from the garage and coached the angry, pessimistic men along.

"It cost a thousand dollars, a hundred more than the rocks themselves cost. But they look great, and I read my book out there, lying on my sunny rock."

Marie, in a strange twist, became a kite by buying rocks.

The Book Club Has A Mind of Its Own

YOUR BOOK CLUB is 0 for 2," Bill remarked in the kitchen. "*Charming Billy* won the National Book Award, and *God of Small Things* won the Booker Prize."

"Who are you going to believe?" I said. "Us? Or some be-nighted committee?"

We in my book club are not amused by reviews or awards that say a book is good when a book is not good, such as *Charming Billy*, by Alice McDermott, a wan little narrative about the Irish working class. Nor were we much impressed by the "Look at me! I'm writing!" style of *The God of Small Things*, by Arundhati Roy, Booker Prize or no.

We think what we think. That's the great thing about a book club.

The not-so-good thing about a book club is feeling guilty. For weeks I've been devouring this wonderful book on the French revolution, called *A Place of Greater Safety*, when I'm supposed to be reading the book club book, called *The Professor and the Madman*, about the making of the Oxford English Dictionary. It sits there on my bedside table, unread, and the book club meets Tuesday.

I took it to Costco and read it in line, then to the plumbing store with Bill, when he let me stay in the car, but I'm still only 75 pages into it. How can I read it, with Danton's large scarred head coming ever nearer the blood-soaked sawdust awaiting it under the guillotine?

Book clubs are not about reading the books you want to read. No one needs a club for that. They're about reading the books you would probably not read if left to yourself because of your natural sloth and apathy. If left to yourself, you would just read the Oprah selections and let it go at that.

I am sort of the den mother for the book club. They come to me with their pathetic excuses for not showing up or for not being able to find the book. Only two people were able to find *Three by Flannery O'Connor* last month, copies of which are, I believe, stacked by the dozen in every used bookstore.

People sometimes get mad at other people in the club over who can and cannot invite new members in and who did not show or even call, and factions form. I love that because then I feel as if I am a little girl again, only this time in a club.

It's all I wanted when I was a pathetic little thing with my hacked-off bangs and dusty jeans, mooning down by the road, piling stones together for a "clubhouse" for the club I planned to be the president of, when I formed it. But no club appeared — that plan went the way of my plan to have a neighborhood circus, an event for which I spent an entire week in the living room trying to learn to stand on my head so I could be the clown, and of my plan to be an explorer.

Some thirty years went by, during which I formed no clubs and was invited to join no clubs. In fact I had to start this book club, along with my friend Janice, in order to be allowed to join it, but it was worth it.

We are all women. Men are not drawn to this communal way of reading. Maybe they already know what they think and are satisfied with that. Joan arrived for the latest meeting armed with three bottles of wine from her new winery job in a little town in Sonoma, wiped out from the freeway, but happy to be, as she said, among sentient beings again.

Then Donna, a novelist, came rushing in from her son's school open house, which featured the Earth's layers made out of peanut butter. And then Janice, a banker, right off a plane, and Monique, who came from her law firm, and Cecille, who works for a non-profit foundation, and Veronique, who does investment banking, followed by Maria, a food writer, and Wendy, a free-lance writer.

Sure, it makes us feel very big to sit around eating pizza and trashing Booker Prize winners, but our books don't have to stand the test of time; they only have to stand the Test of Nine.

Books: Don't Leave Home Without Them

T DINNER at their house the other night, our friends Ann and Robert Cromey said they were flying to Puerto Vallarta for a week to read. They don't even leave their hotel room much, they said, they just read from ten in the morning until bedtime, with breaks for meals.

"Why don't you just stay home and turn up the heat?" I asked.

But, of course, I understood. Most of our friends go off for weekends or camping trips that are thinly veiled reading trips. They sit in expensive bed and breakfasts, putting up with chattering hosts and lumpy beds and odd fellow guests, just for the privilege of having nothing else to do but stretch out on the porch and read. It's a lot of trouble to go to when you can just as well read at home, but it's hard to read at home.

First, you keep thinking of other things to do. I love to read, yet almost as soon as I pick up a book, I switch to doing something else. I switch on the TV, power up the computer, do the wash.

Second, you could be reading *The Iliad* in the original Greek and you still look as if you're killing time. Anybody who walks by and sees you lying there on the couch with your legs sticking out from the bottom of your book naturally starts thinking of other things for you to do.

Wives who watch their husbands sunk in that sorry old recliner can suddenly almost hear the old coat of Sherwin-Williams peeling off the long-unpainted outside of the house. They remember you promised to put up the bulletin board. Or the sight of you stretched out horizontally will remind your mate that the two of you used to have sex, and how nice that used to be.

If you're a parent, the sight of you reading will remind kids of all the loose cash in your purse, and how the right sequence of arguments can sometimes persuade you to part with a little of it. Or it will make them realize there's no reason why you shouldn't drive them to the mall, since you aren't doing anything.

Even the dog, seeing you reading, will hook his long face, with his lovely brown eyes and horrible breath, over your knee and look at you, and kind of shiver in excitement, pretending that the movement you made to turn the page is the precursor of a romp.

A house: not a good place to read. So now whenever I go out, I stuff my purse with magazines and books. I stagger to my hair appointments with a backpack of books, and the poor lonely hairstylist, facing forty minutes of cutting my hair with no one to talk to, stares at them with dismay.

"You sure read a lot," she says, reproachfully.

I carry a book even when we go bike riding because you never know: Bill might let me guard the bikes while he goes into the Safeway deli to buy turkey sandwiches, and I'll be able to get in a quick two pages of Annie Lamott's new book.

A friend of mine copies several pages of his book to read at graduation ceremonies ("Your kid is only on stage for thirty seconds," he says defensively). For large business meetings he punches holes in the copies and fits them into his Day Planner.

And of course longer trips work well, too. Instead of trying to read at home, we're all using our Visa cards to pile up the frequent flier miles — even though the trips keep getting longer (according to my frequent flier plan New York is now 25,000 miles away) — and endure months of planning, and stack up books, just so we can sit down and flip the pages over in peace.

And then, of course, your mate turns to you after two hours of blissful reading while the tropical breeze plays over you, snaps his book shut and says, "We didn't come halfway around the world to read, did we? There's a tour in ten minutes . . ."

Breaking Green Eggs To Get an Omelet

W E WERE HAVING several of our rooms painted by a company that specializes in faux finishes. My dour blue wallpaper walls, the legacy of a former tenant, were being turned into Italian walls the color of sunlight on old stone, and Morgan's room was going from blue-green to rosy earth tones.

We wanted the bedroom painted French country yellow, with the old color — a stenciling of pink leaves on white — covered up. Yellow is a morning color, the color of sunlight hitting the front steps, of butter, of lemons, of the highlighted sentences I get back from my writing partner. I wanted a yellow bedroom.

Then the painter arrived. Hank was a lean, serious man about my age, wearing jeans and a sweatshirt.

Hank came up with the idea of putting a yellow wash over the old paint, with the textured pink stenciling showing through. He put a sample of this on the wall. He and Bill both looked at it, and then, as a formality, they called me in.

I didn't like it. It wasn't French country yellow; it was pink and yellow. I said I didn't think those two colors looked good together, and Hank said yes, they did, they were both spring colors.

When I said that well, I guessed I still didn't like it, he invited me to squint through my cupped hands to get a better idea of it. He said it's hard to visualize the whole room from looking at a sample, by which he meant that I would like it when I saw the whole room done like that. He kept talking, and, a little surprised at his insistence, I repeated that I didn't like it.

Hank blinked at me. "Let's give it a couple of days, and maybe you'll change your mind."

Finally, in despair, I blurted out, "You know, I really hate that color."

One thing about being 45 and a quarter: By this age, you have the pleasure — and it *is* a pleasure — of knowing what you like and what you don't like. When you're younger, what you are supposed to like gets in there and confuses you. For instance, because black is a color associated with being cool, you think that you must actually like dressing like a witness to a hanging.

These days, though, I'm letting my real taste, or lack of it, whatever, show through. These days, I look at the sample that the painter who knows so much about color is saying looks wonderful, and I think, "Well, no, not wonderful, not to me."

We left the sample on the wall, and went on to less dangerous ground, the soft earth tones for Morgan's room. All afternoon Hank and I were careful with each other, nice. But I was still puzzled.

Hank called the next morning, surprisingly upset, to say that maybe we shouldn't work together, as there was evidently no pleasing me. "I am an artist, a colorist," he kept saying. Samples take time, he said — he really couldn't do more than one. One was usually all that was needed.

I listened, stunned. It was as if I had looked at and rejected fifty samples, not one. A business relationship — you paint my walls, I give you money — had somehow become something else. It shook me. Was he that mad, or was I that maddening?

My sister Adrian called afterward and said, "Just tell him you do not like green eggs and ham. That you could not, would not, not in a train or a plane or in a boat or on a goat, not in a house or on a mouse — like the pink and yellow."

In the end, the company sent over Rita. Rita is the one they send over when a client is being very difficult. Rita can work with anybody. A wonderful Aussie, she painted tirelessly and sneaked cigarettes and gave us four such wonderful Italian rooms, including a bedroom like an afternoon in sunny Siena, that I have to conclude that Hank was wrong. There is so much that pleases me that I hardly know where to begin, some days. I just don't like green eggs and ham.

If You're So Smart,
Why Are You So Stupid?

IN THE MOVIE "Forrest Gump," the hero (played by Tom Hanks) has an IQ of 75 and still manages to become a football star, war hero and self-made millionaire. The rest of the time, he kind of fakes it as he goes along. When somebody asks him if he's "stupid or something," he looks at them squarely and says, "My mama always said, 'Stupid is as stupid does.'"

I had just seen the movie, and was remembering it as I waited for my friend Stan outside the Mill Valley Book Depot. He was already a half-hour late. He's a writer type, naturally, as I am. As I tried not to keep glancing at my watch, I wondered why writer types can't arrange to meet for lunch without screwing it up.

Just a couple of weeks ago, I sat fuming in Chevy's in the city because Bonnie, a friend and editor of a local magazine, had evidently blown off our lunch date. I had arrived promptly at 12:30, sat by myself at a table for two drinking coffee, playing with the silverware and reading the paper, and left shortly before one o'clock. Bonnie arrived at one (as, it turned out, we had arranged), only to discover I was a no-show. She waited a half-hour and left.

Meeting for lunch seems like the easiest thing in the world. You decide when, where, what time. You each write it down. Then the day comes around, and one of you gets wrong the time, or the place, or the day, or forgets the lunch entirely.

The simplest things are inexplicably difficult. Jon Carroll and Leah Garchik and I are supposed to work out a schedule so only one of us is gone on vacation at a time. It sounds easy enough, yet the sheet they gave us is so marked up and full of cross-outs that nobody can read it, and both Jon and Leah have claimed the last week of August, which is ridiculous, because I have dibs on that.

Of course we all, not just writers, but all of us, think of ourselves as smart people. We all got good grades in school, or could have if we'd tried. We get Woody Allen's jokes and read the *New Yorker*. Our IQs soar past 100.

Yet very little of this supposed brain wattage shows up in our daily lives. My friend Donna says she'll take the loss of $50 rather than try to figure out the insurance forms. We rent videos we've already seen, run out of gas on country roads, absentmindedly brush our teeth with suntan lotion, get frustrated for hours trying to set up our voice mail.

Bill has a friend named Jack who was waiting for the elevator one day, repeatedly hitting the button, when a group of mentally retarded people passed him on the way to the stairs. Jack was thinking how sad that was, to go through life that way, when the last guy to pass him pointed to the sign above Jack's head: "Elevator Out of Order."

Jack isn't alone. We all go through life like Forrest Gump, knowing how to do some things very well, and the rest of the time kind of faking it as we go along, hoping that if we buy the VCR we'll figure out how to use it, that nobody will notice that our jacket was buttoned up wrong, and that sheer willpower will keep us from getting lost on the way to a friend's country estate.

The other day, Bill and I stopped at a Taco Bell on Van Ness. When our order arrived, Bill handed me my chicken taco. It turned out to be a bean burrito, and I never order burritos, but I ate it.

After a while Bill unwrapped his lunch. Oh, I thought, he got a taco. More time went by, as we read the paper. Then he said, between mouthfuls, "That was my burrito you ate." I said, "You ordered a bean burrito? Why didn't you say anything?"

"I thought it was yours," he said. He gave me the chicken taco and went off to get himself something else.

Meanwhile I'm still at the Mill Valley Book Depot, waiting for my shiftless friend Stan. When I duck inside to call him, there he is coming back from the phone. He said he'd been waiting for 35 minutes. He was inside all the time, and I was outside all the time.

Stupid is as stupid does.

The
Mating
Game

Turtle On The Lam

I DIDN'T MEAN to lose the turtle. It's just that since Neil and I had this fight, I've had to work brooding into an already crowded schedule, and I completely forgot that I put the turtle in the yard.

We just got him last weekend. Seventy bucks for one five-inch turtle with accessories, including a glass aquarium and a dozen feeder goldfish. Despite this largess, the turtle seemed depressed and was spending all day staring moodily through the glass.

Thinking a little constitutional would cheer him up, I plopped him down by the rosebush and went in the house to vacuum the ants out of the freezer and run a speculative finger across the top-soil on the Venetian blinds. Then it was time to brood about Neil for a while. By the time I remembered Todd — short for Todd Turtle — and raced outside, he was gone — a lean, green escaping machine.

I don't think he was justified in taking off. There should be such a thing as commitment, even for turtles. Besides, I liked the little guy. The kids had fallen in love with his fish dinners, giving them names like Spud and Tiny and putting them in cereal bowls, but I had bonded with Todd. He was slow in more ways than one — in a classroom where the seating is by IQ, turtles would sit right in front of salamanders — but he reminded me of Neil. Maybe it was the way he would go into his shell sometimes. At least in Todd's case you could see him doing it — you just glanced over to see if his head was there or not.

Besides, I have money invested here. Todd is worth $15 on the — what? Not hoof. What are turtle feet called? Hold on, I'll look it up. A little turtle research might take my mind off Neil. Patrick asked whether the turtle came with instructions (city kid), so I got this book called "Turtles."

Here it is. How to operate your turtle. But there's nothing on what turtle feet are called.

Wait, here's something else. "Turtles do not pair for life or even for a season. A male finds a female who acts or looks or smells right and he rubs her face with his long claws or bites her legs, and eventually she may become receptive."

"Acts or looks or smells right?" He just nibbles her feet, whatever the hell they're called, and she melts? I had no idea girl turtles were this easy.

This is working. I have pretty much forgotten about what's his name. Still perplexed about Todd, though. Might have to get a plaque out there, dedicated to the Old Turtle, whose fate we shall never know. "He just marched off one morning, without a word to anyone, and the waters of history closed over his little green head."

Either that or he's hiding in the ivy by the brick wall, congratulating himself on his cleverness. and planning the next stage, a sprint into the Nakamuras' yard.

He would do better to just come on back. I can't offer him a goldfish — they are all swimming around in my dinnerware — but we do have that great staple of turtle cuisine, Tetra Repto Min Floating Food Sticks. Todd is the same bilious green as every plant in my garden, and so stands a good chance of being discarded by the teenager who's coming over in a little while to pull weeds. Even the Old Gringo didn't have to go out to face his maker in a brown plastic bag with bits of hedge and rosemary.

Could be worse, though. Listen to this: "If your turtle is sick and past saving, the humane way to kill it is to seal it in a plastic bag and put it in the freezer."

I can just see this. Neil comes over, begging forgiveness for momentarily forgetting how wonderful I am. I manage to pluck his name out of the air and offer to make him dinner. "Honey, what do you feel like eating?" I'll ask. "Oh, I don't know," he'll say. "Why don't you defrost something?"

Shaking Off The Burden of Cool

I WAS SITTING in the Cafe Babar talking to a woman who was thinking about going out with Tom, someone I knew. Apparently his mother knew her mother and thought they should get together.

"What's he like?" she said. I said, "Oh, you'll like him. He's really a nice guy."

A really nice guy. Back in high school, saying a boy was a really nice guy meant he was a loser, the kind of person who ran for junior class treasurer or raised bunny rabbits in his back yard.

The word "but" has always been invisibly present in the sentence, as in, "but he's a really nice guy." Nice guys were eager to please, passionless wimps with clean, pressed pants and neat margins on their typed papers, who stocked shelves at the corner grocery after school.

We didn't want nice guys; we wanted the best-looking boy our own looks would buy, and if he was a brooding sociopath who spent his free afternoons gluing together bombs in the basement, so what? Being a nice guy was nothing anybody would bother with who had a genuine claim to more appealing qualities, like a sullen air of alienation or a Camaro.

In my junior year, a redhaired boy named Blake asked me to the junior prom. He was shorter than I was, got good grades and was obviously a sweet guy. I went with him only because he asked me to, out in front of the pool, where the other kids were watching, and I couldn't say no.

I got my hair done at a friend's cousin's shop in San Rafael. It was piled on top of my head in the shape of a baseball glove, held in place by the contents of a can of Aqua Net. I had had it done a day early and had to sleep with my head propped on three pillows, so it already had a few dents and holes even before Blake walked me three blocks to the high school.

I had wanted to be picked up in a car, and seethed the whole way.

The walk wasn't a bit good for my already dented hair. Also my dress, nothing to write home about in the first place, was riddled with tiny pinholes from our clumsy attempts to pin on the corsage he'd brought me.

We walked onto the floor, spoke to no one and gamely danced, although neither of us knew how. Then he brought me a Coke, and we sat stiffly on folding chairs watching the dancers, desperately waiting for teenagerhood to pass. It was all predictable.

I never saw Blake again after that, except in the hallways, and then at our high school reunion, when he had metamorphosed into a very cool-looking man with a wry, intelligent look — a look that must have been there all along, if only I had had the wit to see it.

Tonight, talking to my friend, it struck me that I was now offering the highest praise possible in saying that Tom was a nice guy.

A nice guy now is not somebody who has nothing else to offer. It's not a guy who has three ex-wives, has done time, has tattooed pecs and now drives the silver Porsche he wanted in high school.

It's a man who will let you choose the movie at least half the time, take the kids for a weekend so you can go to a conference, paint the trim on your windows, vacuum the collie hairs out of the rug and remember your mother's birthday all on his own.

One of the innumerable benefits of no longer being a kid is having the burden of cool lifted from us. We all emerged from adolescence exhausted from the constant effort of a rebellion that called for having hair exactly the correct in-your-face length, the right size surfer stripes on our T-shirts and the right air of jaded detachment. Cool blinded me to Blake's wry humor.

Despite all that jive about us benighted women preferring bad boys, the thirties and forties are the age when nice guys, open, sincere, decent types, guys who lose at badminton and come out smiling, come into their own.

Money Plus Food Equals Disillusionment

I'VE FIGURED OUT why first dates don't work any better than they do. It's because they take place in restaurants. Women are weird and confused and unhappy about food, and men are weird and confused and unhappy about money, yet off they go, the minute they meet, to where you use money to buy food.

Say, for example, that a man and a woman meet "cute," as the expression goes. They've been bumped from the same flight, and are fuming separately in the airport bar, waiting for the next one, when they spot each other. He is craggy and dark, in that way she likes. He's wearing designer jeans but she instantly forgives him.

She is blond and lithe, with the kind of intelligence that shows even in photographs, even in repose. She is paging through a self-help book, but he forgives her.

They fall into conversation, and he says he has a car, why don't they go into town for lunch?

At the back of their heads, the old song starts up: "Oh, I like this one. Could this be the one?"

Then it starts. He parks three blocks away from the restaurant because parking in lots makes him feel like a sucker. He is hunter. He will find parking space in jungle.

She doesn't know he is hunter. She thinks he is cheap.

She wonders, now, if he's going to turn out to be one of those guys who gloats over the deal he got on his Reeboks and never buys himself any new clothes.

She now has reservations, although the restaurant doesn't require them.

They enter the dining room and are shown to a quiet table at the back. They talk. They discover they both like stud poker, hated "Raising Arizona," like to walk down city streets in the rain. When they get mixed up over whose water glass is whose, their hands touch.

The waiter appears, and the man orders a hamburger, medium rare, with home fries.

The woman considers the menu. "I'll have the Greek salad," she says, "with the dressing on the side."

As he watches with horror and fascination, she tears a roll into little bits and then eats the bits. He wonders if she's one of those women who knows what all her clothing weighs. He bets she can list everything she ate yesterday.

She notices his look, and guiltily stops rolling the last bit. "I had a late breakfast," she lies. She is on a diet. She's been on it since she was twelve.

When the bill comes, he is unsure whether he should pay or not, and lets her pay half. But, she is thinking, lunch was his idea. Also, he has pocketed the receipt. He's going to write this off. A flicker of annoyance crosses her face. She really hates his jeans now.

Both of them move their chairs slightly away from the table, hugging their disappointment to their breasts, neither of them aware how contrary they're being.

She wanted him so stupefied with passion at the prospect of lunch with her that he absentmindedly abandons his car to the nearest lot and can't remember his own name, let alone the receipt. Yet she likes it that he has money, and after lunch she wants him instantly to resume his thrifty ways, so they can get a nice split-level.

He wanted her to abandon her habitual pickiness and order the biggest, juiciest hamburger on the menu because a meal with him should be a celebration. But he likes it that she is slender, and would be happy if, right after lunch, she were to resume her lifetime diet, so he can enjoy tracing the line of her adorable jaw.

True Love and the Art of Housekeeping

I DON'T KNOW where this myth comes from, that women are neat and tidy and men are slobs. The men I have known have been, by and large, a fairly prissy bunch, prone to utter such inanities as, "If a thing is worth doing, it's worth doing well."

If it's worth doing well, it's probably a waste of time. I say put off what you can, buy cookies to match the rug, and lie in bed and kiss a lot. You can't go wrong.

You can't go wrong, but you can end up alone this way, if you team up with someone who hates walking on crumbs. But when you fall in love, you shrug off such details. Both of you will change. You will be neater, he will be taller. Love will find a way.

Take Nick, for example. He lived right next door to me, and pretty soon we fell in love — that is, I told him that he would do until someone else came along, and he told me how far from his usual physical type I was, and how interesting that was for him.

With a passion like this, you ignore signs of discord. I used to treasure the memory of how Nick came over after our first night together, silently handed me the earrings I had left on the floor beside the tousled bed, and gone back home.

It wasn't until much later I realized this was Nick's way of saying that I'd left a mess in his bedroom.

But we tried to overcome these differences when we moved in together. I tried to straighten things up whenever I could, and he tried leaving glasses unwashed for minutes at a time. If he did notice that I liked to run the heat full blast and then open the windows to get a breeze, he said nothing.

Gradually, though, we felt comfortable enough to let our true natures emerge. Nick sprinted in to turn off the light whenever I left the living room. I blew up potatoes in the microwave, turned off the stereo without lowering the sound first, sorted the laundry by whose it was rather than by color.

Nick remained outwardly calm. Then one morning I noticed him staring at me. "Are you going to throw rubber bands on the floor every day for the rest of our lives?" he asked.

Looking at him, I thought: This is what leads people to shoot up shopping malls. One rubber band too many.

Many nights found him bending over the dishwasher, restacking all the dishes I had put in. "The water can't get to them if you put them on top of each other," he explained, not noticing that I was searching through the flatware for something to kill him with.

I even grilled Nick's mother about his compulsive housekeeping. "Did you do this to him?" I asked. "No," she said, "it was his father." Nick didn't have to ask my mother anything, as the first time he met her she was setting a coffee mug down in his potted palm.

It started not working. I thought if he loved me he would care that it upset me to watch him restack dishes I had just stacked. He thought if I loved him I would not drive him crazy by stacking them that way in the first place. We couldn't separate love and housekeeping.

We were trying hard, though. He would put his arms around me and say, "Do you think I could ask you to turn the bathroom faucets all the way off?" and then clasp both my hands to add, "Was that all right, the way I said that?"

I got him a black T-shirt with "Don't Sweat the Small Stuff" printed on it.

He ironed it.

Eight Perfect Mates — The Mind Reels

I WAS LYING on the couch in my apartment the other night, flipping through a magazine in search of Calvin Klein ads, when I read something that made me sit up with a start. It said that everyone alive has eight perfect mates somewhere out there, wandering the world.

I let my eyes rest on that line again. I don't believe everything I read, but this had the ring of truth — that is, I needed for it to be true.

The only other occupant of my apartment at that moment was a pet rat who had been staring at me through his glass cage. It was a chilly evening, and he needed something to snuggle up to.

I had just the thing — Neil had left his favorite Hawaiian shirt here when he left on his weekend without me. Torn into strips, it would make a perfect blanket for the rat.

The one in the cage, I mean.

I turned my attention back to the article. I was in heaven. Eight. Perfect? According to Random House, "perfect" means "without any of the flaws or shortcomings that might be present." The mind reels. Eight Ken dolls, correct in every detail.

I glanced across the room at Neil's picture. He was looking at me from his frame with his eyebrows raised, wondering what I was up to this time. But Neil isn't perfect. Failing to appreciate me properly, for example, is certainly a flaw.

I turned back to the article, treasuring its implications. For each of these men, I am the feminine ideal. For them heaven would be a lazy Sunday afternoon at my place, with "Graceland" blasting on the stereo, Morgan dribbling her basketball in the living room, and the dishes piled high in the sink while I, their dream woman, snored prettily on the couch with the *TV Guide* over my face.

I was immensely cheered by this thought until I remembered.

There are seven billion people in the world. Where were my eight? Was one wading through rice paddies in Mongolia, another kicking dogs out of his path on a back street in Madrid?

Were they pining for me, doomed never to know that I am waiting here in a Western city by the sea, thousands of miles from the rice paddy and the sunstroked alleys of Spain?

Then I recalled the word "perfect." How could a guy be perfect for me if he's soaking his well-formed calves in a Mongolian rice paddy and I'm lining a rat cage in San Francisco? Surely being 10,000 miles away would count as a shortcoming? I decided perfection must include proximity — if these eight guys are perfect, then they, too, wouldn't live anywhere but San Francisco.

They're here, and they're looking for me, the perfect woman for them. But how will I find them? Surely the gods wouldn't put eight ideal men in the same city with me and then wait, giggling and slapping one another, as I try to find them among 700,000 people?

Then another, even more chilling thought occurred to me. If each of those guys has seven other perfect mates, that means I have 56 rivals out there — each of them flawless. And only eight of them have to get there ahead of me for me to be left out in the cold.

No wonder I have always found math depressing.

Should I tell Neil he has eight perfect mates here, too? Eight women who, finding he has gone off on a press junket and did not invite them, would only smile forgivingly at him?

No. Wait until he asks.

I had one more thought. If each of my mates has eight mates, and each of those has eight, and so on, that can mean only one thing: all the perfect people are here, in San Francisco.

Love Means Going On Errands Together

BILL AND I were at dinner when I overheard a woman at the next table talking to her girlfriend about some guy she'd just met. "He shows up on my doorstep on Saturday afternoon to return a book he'd borrowed," she said, "and then asks if I wanted to go with him to get his car a smog check-up.

"Why would I want to do that? I had the whole afternoon free. We could easily have gone to a matinee, or for a walk on the beach."

I looked over at Bill. "She doesn't know it yet, but he's smitten."

Ordinarily, errands — post office, dry cleaners, lamp store, taking the videos back — are just little holes in your time. With couples, though, they take on a different meaning. Back when I was dating, I knew a man was going to be one of the serious ones, not when he'd ask me home to meet Mom, but when he'd ask me to come with him to buy his sister a bird cage, or to tag along while he zipped over to get his tires rotated. I knew he was serious when he'd want us to do something very ordinary together, something you do when you're part of someone's life.

Couples just starting out, not yet sure where they want things to go, should probably stay away from stores. A harvest moon and a romantic candle-lit dinner are fine, but unless you're ready to escalate, the last thing you should do is down a couple of margaritas and wander unchaperoned into a futon shop.

Once a man I had known professionally for a long time dropped in, and we went for a walk and found ourselves browsing in a soap boutique. A woman we both knew from work was there, shuffling through the shampoos. She took in the sight of us pawing at the strawberry sachets, giving them to each other to sniff. Aha! her glance said.

Discomfited, we hurriedly dropped the scented soaps and shoved our hands back in our pockets, as if she'd looked in through the curtains of our room at the motel. She knew what we only sensed — that errands, in this quick-to-bed but slow-to-the-altar culture, are more intimate than sex. A woman of modest habits, even I have slept with more men than I've gone shopping with.

One of the latter was a blind date in the towel department of Macy's years ago. I turned when he touched my shoulder, and thought, Nice. We fell to loitering through the stacks of merchandise, running our hands over the stacks of towels, rooting through the bins of pillows. I patted a green-striped couch with wide, soft pillows, then he showed me a row of polished wooden end tables and told me which ones made his heart pound. We sank down four floors to the basement on the escalator, where we went methodically through the dish collections, showing each other what we liked.

Six months later when we broke up, we were surprised to discover we really had little in common. The too-early juxtaposition of romance and shag toilet bowl covers had misled us. If we had met at a restaurant we'd have immediately clashed over the money, the food and the parking and managed to lose each other's telephone numbers.

Later, at the bitter division of the household goods, it's the errands you remember. A T-shirt reminds you of the time you pretended to be picking each other up in the Gap, but stood too close together, tipping off the onlookers.

You pack a bowl, and remember how he stood when he was bargaining for it, how the light came in the dim glass of the shop, and he glanced at you, and smiled. A pile of car parts in a cardboard box takes you back to the hardware store, when she asked the clerk for oil filter Part PB-8A, and you saw how patient she was, and how her eyebrows flew upward when she asked a question.

And then you meet someone new — a guy who asks you along when he gets his car tuned up. You want to say, "I hardly know you, let's just sleep together a few times first," but find yourself saying, "Oh, hell," and getting in his car, adding flirtatiously, "Maybe on the way back we can pick up my printer."

Dancin', Dancin' In the Streets

L AST SATURDAY I heard an odd noise below our kitchen window. When I looked out, I saw that a truck was parked in our driveway, and a strange man, balding with wild blond hair, was bopping around in back of it, loudly singing "Call Me Al" from Paul Simon's "Graceland" album.

He turned out to be the boyfriend of a woman who was storing a china cabinet at Jim's house. I felt a decided liking for him, a man who would let his inner band of musicians run him like that, make him burst out dancing on a residential sidewalk in the middle of a routine errand.

He also looked foolish, of course. Bill looked over my shoulder at the man dancing down there, raised his eyebrows and went back to his newspaper.

Bill and I danced at our wedding, to the Motown sounds provided by a disc jockey who had grilled me about the age of the crowd beforehand. In all the pictures, we're dancing.

And that was it. Dancing went out of my life.

Oh, Bill offers to take me dancing, as in, "Did you want to go dancing? Sure, we can do that . . . if that's what you really want to do." At his own office party, I caught him urging a male co-worker to ask me to dance. He did everything but pay him off.

He has it in his head that he can't dance, and he isn't about to go out there and make an idiot of himself.

What men don't realize is that we don't care how they dance. I know some women like the good dancers, but I am intimidated by a man who does a lot of fancy footwork: I can't follow him, and feel clumsy. In fact for me the worse he is the better because the appealing idea is not the dancing, but the willingness to look foolish, to toss cool away with the jacket that flies to a nearby chair. To be a dancing fool.

A man who dances is a man who lets go, who has joy inside him that can't be contained. It's why all those movie scenes show the characters dancing around their apartments: The movie makers know we can't resist people who dance in their kitchen. The woman always shows up, and that's when she falls for him, as she peeps in his window, watching him mambo with the dust rag.

Once I lived with Nick, who was a dancing man. On Friday nights we'd go to the Rockin' Robin club on Haight. He'd shed his three-piece suit (he had six of them), pull on black jeans and a T-shirt, then dance until the sweat poured off him.

Nick even danced around the house, jacking up the Talking Heads, throwing his head back, shouting with the music as he bebopped across the floor, pushing the vacuum cleaner ahead of him.

It was madness to move in with Nick, for other reasons. (OK, one example: He asked me turn the faucets to the washing machine off between uses to save wear and tear on the machine.) But he loved to dance, and those dangerous, strutting rhythms had turned my head.

The very birds in the trees know this. When the Australian bower bird goes about his courting, he collects bits of bone, shell and flowers, which he then arranges in a neat semicircle on the ground. He steps back, eyeing this collection to see if it pleases his aesthetic sense, then fussily rearranges it until it's exactly right.

Then he conducts his intended to the spot. He steps into the circle to do a ballet intended to wow her, and only when it's over does she consent to whatever less delicate activities he has in mind.

Men have long known that dancing has pretty much the identical effect on the human female, but they have got it in their heads that it's the dancing we like. It isn't. Like the female Australian bower bird, we like the willingness to get out there and do whatever. The less adept he is, the more charmed we are that he does it anyway.

I looked back out the window at the man on the sidewalk below, who was now drumming on the car, his feet shuffling. He happened to look up, and I smiled. He grinned, and went on dancing.

Why Women Nibble on Sweets

AFTER MY FRIEND and I had lunch together in New York, she wanted to stop at a card store to get something for her husband's birthday. I went along, and, when I noticed she bought herself a handful of candy corn, got myself some red licorice.

"Why is it only women eat candy?" I said. "The irritating thing about men is that they have no such bad habits."

"That's not true," she said, offering me some of the candy corn. "Men eat candy."

But they don't. Bill never touches candy. Candy doesn't fit into a man's meal plan because it isn't a meal. I once put a mint into a boyfriend's mouth at 5 p.m., as he was driving us home at twilight, and he actually spit it out into his hand.

Women don't have meal plans; they just have nervous eating fits that occasionally coincide with mealtime.

Women are always nibbling on something. When I worked at a magazine, the associate editor brought in her six-month-old wedding cake, the frosting on it stiff with age, the cake inside cold, and set it on the galleys table.

At the end of an hour it was gone, every stale, sweet bite eaten by women who now stood around the box, scraping the lid with their fingertips. The men were not even tempted. Men don't eat at 3 p.m.: They've had a good lunch at noon, and are looking forward to a good dinner — a dinner that we will just pick at, having had six-month-old wedding cake at 3 p.m.

Men eat desserts, and occasionally fine chocolates, after dinner. Women eat candy.

I did skip the cake, because I don't eat desserts. Because of this, for a long time it pleased Bill to believe that I didn't have a sweet tooth. He went on believing this even as he learned to open a packet and a half of Sweet'n Low into my morning coffee. He doesn't realize that candy and desserts are quite different things.

For me right now, it's Good & Plenty, but candy preferences, like the taste for a fine vintage wine, change over time. When I was pregnant, only M & Ms would do. When I was little, I liked Big Hunks and Looks, because you could wallop them against a door and break them into little pieces.

Eating candy was a dangerous weakness back then. It meant agonizing hours at the dentist. When I was a teenager fretting over my thighs, it meant empty calories. But now I'm past the age of cavities, and most candy (not chocolate, of course) is fat-free, and thus on the list of foods we are currently being commanded to go forth and enjoy.

The nonsense of dieting, I've found, tends to go away in your 30s. None of my women friends is on a diet, and none is overweight. I went to a pool party this summer, and you could see the men hating the idea of taking off their shirts, while the women all went right into the water in their sleek bathing suits. This is the opposite of what happened when we were all teenagers, when the boys took their fine bodies for granted and girls worried endlessly, and nourished new neuroses about food.

Part of our secret at the party now was that we were more attracted to the tin of red licorice whips on top of the fridge than to the bowls of chips the men were devouring.

A lot of us women are coming out of the closet, at least to each other. Annie eats peanut M & Ms. My sister likes Good & Plenty, like me. Donna told me she found herself at Walgreen's with an armload of brightly colored candy: Sweetarts, Sprees, M & Ms, Bubble Yum, dumping it all briskly on the counter, like a mom who likes to get her Halloween shopping done eight months in advance.

It's liberating to discuss candy choices with a connoisseur like Donna. She can actually tell the color of Neccos by tasting them with her eyes closed. She cleanses her palate, then closes her eyes and takes the one I give her. After a pause, she says, "Orange."

It is a pleasure to spend time in the company of a woman like that.

Pillow Talk

I HAVE LOOKED and looked, but I can't find the earrings Bill gave me for Christmas last year. They were a wonderful sort of paper bag color, and I wore them almost every day until they disappeared. Bill says I'm not to have any more expensive earrings.

Then he happened to mention that he still has his pillow from seventh grade. Back then his mom noticed that he was sneezing and gave him a featherless pillow to try out. He's had it ever since.

I could not pick my own pillow out of a lineup. I can identify it only by the United Airlines pillow piled on top of it — I always swipe those little pillows from the plane because they fit my head exactly.

I asked Bill how he even knew what his pillow looked like.

"Did you take it with you to the Navy?" I asked, awed.

"Yes," he said, a tad defensively.

Then he said that it wasn't what I was thinking, that he went lots of places — trips to Europe and New York and Tahoe — without his pillow.

"But you missed it, just a little bit?"

He didn't answer, but I drew my own conclusions.

People who say men and women are essentially the same, with just those anatomical differences, overlook the fact that Bill looks at San Francisco street signs in the same sunglasses through which he gazed at the ivy-covered columns of his college campus 24 years ago. I've never owned a pair of sunglasses longer than three months.

Bill also wore the same pair of green and blue swimming trunks until two of my sisters cornered him by the refrigerator and said that if he didn't get another suit they were going to have to hurt him. When his loafers wear out, he has them resoled. He urges me to get my shoes resoled too, as if that's really what I want, to go on wearing the same pair of shoes forever.

Bill says that when the day comes when he needs reading glasses, he'll probably have just one pair. I have 15 or so pairs, all over the house, in purses, in jacket pockets and under books, and I can never find even one pair when I want to read the PG&E bill. Reading glasses hate me as much as I hate them, and simply self-destruct, so that when I pick up a pair one defiant earpiece stays on the table.

Bill was astonished when he lost his umbrella on the train in London. He talked about it for weeks, even though everybody knows it's in the nature of objects — and most particularly of umbrellas — to get lost or wear out or, if they refuse to do either, to be hurtled into the trash during spring cleaning.

Of course these may not be male-female differences, but our individual idiosyncrasies. But find me the woman who still has her seventh-grade pillow. Many women I know change the objects around them all the time through loss or throwing out or shrinkage or ennui. But then we get change out of our systems, and don't go running off to Tahiti with nineteen-year-olds, like some genders I could name.

But I was discussing the pillow. It went along to Bill's first marriage to a Massachusetts girl, and to their cottage in the Sunset when they came out here.

Unknown to me, it was there lying on his neat bed in his neat apartment when I dropped him off after our drink at the Ramp on our first date, and it came with him in the car heaped with his stuff when we took a house together in Noe Valley. I suppose it will be going with him to the retirement home, when the time comes.

Meanwhile the earrings are gone. I could have kept them for a lifetime, passed them down to my daughter, who could have passed them on to hers. They were bound to weigh me down in the end, those earrings. They had to go.

In Marriage, Every Action Has a Reaction

IN HIS BOOK *Couplehood,* Paul Reiser says that when you're by yourself at home and just sitting there, you're just sitting there. It's fine. But when you live with someone else, and you're just sitting there, "laziness doesn't look like laziness. It looks like Indifference, Presumption, Insensitivity, Hostility."

When Morgan's boots leave black scuff marks on Bill's just-washed kitchen floor, he assumes this is what goes through her mind: "I'll just go ahead and walk all over this floor, leaving marks, and I won't worry about it because I have good old Bill to clean it up for me."

This is what Morgan is actually thinking: "I don't have time for breakfast this morning, so I'll just grab this bagel from the fridge. Where did I leave my keys?"

She doesn't leave her backpack on the floor for him to pick up, or leave wet towels on her floor for me to wash: She just leaves them. There's no connection between her act and anybody else. With a couple, though, there's always an assumed connection. If I'm reading in the sun on the front steps, and Bill is inside vacuuming, both of us have moods assigned to us. I am indifferent, selfish, pleasure-seeking; he is a martyr. Neither of us actually feels these moods consciously, but they're there, like an undercurrent.

If I go outside to pull weeds, and he stays in the living room reading the paper, again we don't have two separate acts. My weeding acts like a magnet on his reading, distracting him, making it an almost defiant act rather than simply reading the paper. He is forced to think about it: Will I go out there and help, or I will keep reading my paper?

When you inhabit a house with someone, even the smallest actions are assumed to be about both of you. If you take a long time in the bathroom, you are holding someone up. If you chew cereal noisily, you are forcing someone to go read the paper elsewhere. If you read in the living room while others are talking in the kitchen, you are being anti-social.

Living with someone is like sitting on a bed he's sitting on: Every motion of yours jounces him a little.

When you're alone in the house, all this goes away. Just now I left the Raisin Bran in the dish drainer, the milk out and my papers spread out on the rug, and no stigma is attached to any of these acts — they have no reverberations, no resonance, no meaning. The fact that I haven't combed my hair doesn't mean I am taking my husband for granted. It is just me, inhabiting space as I see fit.

That's why I have to have the house to myself all day. When Bill or one of the kids stays home sick, I am terribly nice to them, but I want them to get better fast. I need this stretch of hours when it's just me in the world.

In marriage you think of the other as taking up enormous amounts of your time, but it's not the time. It's this psychic drain, everything you do having somehow to do with them. Bill and I live lightly with each other, but no couple escapes it entirely.

I feel this most when we're traveling together, filtering our every impression through the consciousness of the person at our side. I sometimes think I haven't really seen a place until I've seen it alone, wandered the streets, free from conversation, just feeling the cobblestones through my sandals, watching the children playing in the streets. At some point in our trips I have to go off by myself for an afternoon, just to move through air that no one else has disturbed, just to see the colors for myself.

For some people even this is not always enough. My friend Liz is going to drive off into the desert, alone, for two weeks, leaving her kids with their dad. She'll go from motel to motel, ostensibly doing research for a novel, but really soaking up solitude. There are canyons in southern Utah that resonated for her, she says, and she wants to see them again. I think she is really looking for herself, the Liz who is no one's wife and no one's mother. I think you have to be alone to find that person.

Playing Cupid

WE ASKED Annie, a novelist, and Ron, a journalist, to come to our house for dinner on a Friday night. Ron brought the prawns in ginger and peanut sauce that he has learned to make since he became single, and Annie brought her two-year-old son, Sam, who promptly fell asleep on the bed.

It was a blind date. We had taken it into our heads that these two should meet, that each would instantly like in the other one the wit and gentleness that made us so infatuated with them both. They would marry and name their children after us.

We were convinced of this, even though experience suggested that this might not happen, that instead one of them might blurt out, "You thought of that one for *me?* I'm so *flattered!*" And the other one would be timid and feel rejected and hate us forever.

But we couldn't help it. When you've met someone yourself, your mind becomes this hideous soup. First to go in is a gladness that must be shared, and then the most awful smugness, as if, having stumbled across each other, you feel as if you have the secret and can play Cupid to an uncoupled universe.

Third, we want to think that we can make a difference, that it's possible to influence the course of love. We regarded ourselves as key elements in the play about to unfold, enjoying the thought, probably, that these two brilliant people would depend on us to get through this awkward, artificially arranged meeting.

As Bill sauteed the abalone, I got the conversation going. Neither of us knew how to cook it, but we had done some calling around. "I saw 'Dead Man Walking' last week," I volunteered, and I had a lot more to say about that . . . but Annie and Ron were talking about the Giants and their childhoods and the music they liked. They sawed away cheerfully at their overcooked abalone, not noticing that Bill was scraping his and mine into the garbage.

I was about to renew my ice-breaking conversation with a general question about the weather when our guests grabbed their drinks and rushed upstairs, throwing apologies over their shoulders, to watch the baseball game.

When they came back they ate my fruit salad, which was unfortunately still partly frozen, but Annie, who moonlights as a food reviewer, insisted she liked it that way, and she and Ron started to talk about insomnia, which they both suffer from.

Seeing my opening, I began to tell the interesting story of how I had trouble sleeping once, and I discovered that hot milk . . . but they turned on me fiercely. What did I know? I was a *sleeper.* Annie turned back to Ron and asked him what his ten favorite books were.

I shut up and sipped my drink moodily. Didn't anybody want to hear about *my* ten favorite books? *Lonesome Dove? Sex Tips for Girls? Lady's Maid?* I was going to tell Annie that my list included her book, *Rosie,* but apparently she could govern her curiosity.

At 11:30, Annie had to head for Marin, and Ron coincidentally had to leave that same instant. They disappeared down the steps together in a group, sleepy Sam jack-knifed over Annie's shoulder.

I couldn't help noticing that not only were they failing to fall all over me with gratitude for introducing them, but they had forgotten I was alive. Oh, well.

"I think that went well, don't you?" I said to Bill.

"They managed to get over their shyness a little at the end," he said drily, picking up the empty glasses.

Love's Peculiar Censorship

WHEN BILL AND I had a garage sale awhile back, sales went briskly, but he was holding all the money. I was irritated. I sold a laminated redwood tree stump for $19, then a solid oak table for $100, and he held that, too.

I wanted to hold some of the money. I couldn't tell him, naturally. It would have been like showing him a dried-up lake bottom and saying, that's what I really look like inside. It would reveal the pettiness of my nature that I keep from him, the tiny anxieties about money that I would keep even from myself if I could.

The hardest part of being married is when you're not supposed to be mad, but you are. In every relationship, there's a laundry list of things you are not allowed to be annoyed about.

You can't take any notice if he talks to his old girlfriend at the cocktail party, if he eats horrible greasy tortilla chips, if he deserts you to take his brother to the baseball game, or if he breaks the remote moving it to the fireplace mantel when it was perfectly fine on the coffee table.

He, in turn, can't be mad if you empty your purse into your kid's outstretched hands, if you can't go for a walk because you have a cold, or at the way you're loading the dishwasher, or at your annoying habit of leaving the remote on the coffee table. But sometimes you *are* mad. You don't want to be, but you are.

And you want desperately to conceal your unattractive feeling from your mate.

When you're dating, such concealment is easy. When my boyfriend Nick several years back gave me a pair of pink coral earrings for Christmas and nothing else, I thanked him prettily, and then lay awake all night, seething.

Everybody knows that when you are boyfriend and girlfriend, you are supposed to give one big present, and then several little ones. I gave him a jogging suit, and a lot of other little stuff — underwear, books, doodads. I couldn't let Nick know I was mad about the coral earrings. I didn't want him to think of me, a woman supposedly in love, stewing in the bedroom, totting up the presents she got with a chilly counting finger. So I said nothing, and he never knew the difference. (Though when I went to Mexico without him three months later, that was why.)

In marriage, it doesn't work.

Say you are sulking about not getting asked to his after-work office party. You can't say anything: It's on the list of things you can't be mad about, under Things He Does At His Own Office. So you assure him over and over that everything is just fine. That's how you say it, in a really calm voice, "It's fine, really." The trouble is, he knows you now.

He's seen you eat Raisin Bran from the box and lie through your teeth to your mother. He can tell your exact mood from the angle of your head and the tiny swing of your foot, or the icy clink of your coffee spoon in the cup. He doesn't need to see the hacked remains of his wardrobe in the closet to know you're the teensiest bit put out.

But he takes no notice, because he's busy trying not to let you see how mad he is that you gave your kid a ride to work when you swore you wouldn't. He can't be mad about that, because it's on the list, too, under Things She Does With Her Own Kids.

He can't mention it, so he smiles and pats you and rustles his paper, in that way that, since you know him so well, instantly makes you think, uh-oh, he's mad about something.

It is not easy, in marriage, to conceal the pettiness of one's nature or the shortness of one's temper or the length of one's memory. But it can be done, as long as each is willing to put aside trifling annoyances.

I, for example, have forgotten all about how Bill held the money in the garage sale, even though it was my oak table and half my laminated redwood tree stump.

Sometimes It's Better Not to Talk

BILL AND I were walking along, talking intently. I had specific ideas for reforming his character that I was eager to share with him and that he, for some reason, was not eager to hear. As we walked along we talked about what he felt, what I felt, what I remembered saying about a trip to India, how he just as clearly remembered me saying exactly the opposite.

After a while, we noticed that we were feeling worse and worse as we talked, instead of better and better. This is always a surprise: We were all taught that every issue can be wrestled to the floor, every disagreement solved, every aching resentment cured if only we talk to each other about it long enough. It's like the cartoon in the *New Yorker* years ago that showed a couple seated in a living room talking to another couple while a giant furry beast loomed over them. The host couple was saying, "We deal with it by talking about it."

Of course, most of the time, you can reduce the size of the beast in the living room by talking. Talking clears the air, eases hurt feelings, heads off misunderstandings. Talking is the principal way we establish and maintain our romantic relationships. But we were sold a bill of goods when we were told that talking would solve everything.

My friend Susan found this out. She'd been upset for weeks about the fact that the novel she had worked so hard on hadn't sold. As she and her boyfriend, Tom, were out driving, she wanted to talk about it again, but this time the usually patient Tom balked. "I don't know what to say, and everything I do say seems to make it worse," he told her.

Susan was stunned. How could he not want to hear the outpourings of her heart? Furiously, she turned to stare out the window, resolved not to say another word to him on the subject. And didn't. To her surprise, she told me, "Having decided not to talk about my disappointment over the book, I discovered I didn't have to think about it as much. I started to feel a lot better."

My friend Sam, who had lost his girlfriend and was on the edge of losing his job, made the same discovery. He tried to confront his misfortunes — discussed them endlessly, worked them through in his men's group, cried. And when he was done, he felt wiped out, all his reserves spent, and sadder than ever — and with his problems intact. Now, he says, when he feels blue he rents "My Cousin Vinny," plays more basketball, rereads favorite novels, goes out with friends. These things don't make his problems go away either, but the next day he finds he has more strength to deal with them.

In relationships, we all assume that if we just make ourselves plain, then our partner will give us what we want. Steve thinks Marilyn isn't cooking for him because he hasn't made it clear to her how much he would appreciate that, when actually she's not cooking for him because she doesn't want to.

Not all disagreements can be talked away, not on a walk, not in the bedroom, not in the relationship itself. Nor should they be. When Bill and I married, we chose a particular set of unresolvable problems that we'll be grappling with for the next ten, twenty or fifty years. Some of them will never be resolved and never understood.

But for those that can be solved, there are other ways than talking. Once Morgan and I had argued for hours about her curfew, with the result that we were both angrier than ever. I ordered her into the car and we sneaked off for a day at the water slide park. By the end of the day, we easily negotiated a curfew we could both live with.

Women can learn from men when it comes to expressing ourselves without using words. He'll take your car in to see what's making that clicking noise, fix the toilet seat, get the blinds up on the back porch.

A good joke, time spent together, a shared meal, old-fashioned giving in and even more old-fashioned shutting up — all these work too, to ease the cacophony of human disagreements.

The Stranger I Married

THE OTHER NIGHT I was upstairs talking to Jim in his kitchen when Bill came up the back steps to say that Mike Lara was on the phone. In other words, while I was talking to my second husband, my third came up to say my first was on the phone. Your past has a way of catching up with you.

I didn't recognize the light, courteous voice on the other end of the phone, the one telling me he was married, living in Denver and still working for the railroad. Talking over old times with Mike Lara was like chatting with a stranger about a movie we'd both seen.

Although he seemed like a very nice man, and I was interested in what he was telling me about raising his wife's two children with her, my interest was only polite, as was his — he was passing through town, had seen my byline and thought he'd call.

He said he was 48, which proved that he was a stranger. My Mike is 21, a tall, lean boy in jeans and an ironed blue shirt worn open, showing his smooth chest and hiding arms he always thought were too thin. He rode a huge red Bonneville Triumph motorcycle, and he didn't buy fuel in huge quantities for the railroad, as this man was saying he did. Mike drove a lift truck on the night shift at Southern Pacific and played softball while I watched from the bleachers.

Mike, too, must have wondered who this strange woman was he was talking to. The Adair he knew did not have two teenage kids and a mortgage. She was the tannest human being he had ever seen. By September 1969, the beginning of my senior year in high school, I had spent the entire summer stretched out on the grass at the Marin Town and Country Club, and my skin, the color of a teak dining room table, dazzled Mike when we met on a blind date arranged by my sister, who was going out with his cousin Johnny.

I lived with my family in a house behind a park in San Anselmo. My brother Sean was in Vietnam, but the rest of us were still at home, living partly on the leftover tea cake, clam chowder and slightly stale French bread our mother smuggled home from her job as manager of the local Elks Club.

Mike and I got married the month I turned eighteen, in the middle of my senior year. We drove to Reno in his cherry red Chevy, with Johnny and Adrian squashed in the backseat.

A sign said, "Warning, Short Merges Ahead," but we paid no attention. A one-armed judge married us, and Johnny cried (he would be dead at 33, of diabetes). Mike held my hand so hard it hurt for hours.

We rented a hilltop apartment in Fairfax where birds circled below the living room window, and I listened to morning radio shows directed at housewives. I made him salami sandwiches and packed them into his black lunch pail along with love notes written with a purple felt pen.

I wrote my own absence excuses — "I was absent because I had a stomachache" — and took my husband to the senior prom. He let his hair grow, rode his motorcycle, went home for meals with his mother, and I started college.

Before I was nineteen I had packed my books and returned to my mother's house. I didn't know it, but I had already met my second husband, who was my English teacher at College of Marin.

Now here it was 26 years later, and two middle-aged strangers were politely speaking to each other on the phone. I said goodbye, and put down the phone.

I doubt I will bother to update my memory, feed into it this polite stranger who lives in Denver and thinks he has a pretty good shot at a job with another railroad, since he knows the SP system. I won't replace that blue shirt worn open with a suit and a tie. A memory is a kind of movie, and I was never a fan of movies that ended by saying what the characters are doing now, long after their story ends.

Let's Spend The Night Together

MODERN SCIENCE has proved conclusively that humans are not constructed to sleep next to other humans. Worms can cuddle up to other worms, and kittens to other kittens, but with humans there are all these arms and legs, not to mention breasts, etc., that one is obliged to take to bed with one, though they are of no earthly use there.

Add to this sharply individual tastes in number of pillows, hardness of mattresses and degree of openness of windows, not to mention huge variation in personal temperatures, and it's hard to fathom why sleeping together has ever become the fashion.

Just getting into bed strains ordinary civility. I'm already there, reading, when Bill comes to bed, and right away the trouble starts.

He comes to my side of the bed, not because the sight of me warm and sleepy has undone him, but because the sheet corner has come off the mattress, and he wants me to stand up, naked and freezing, while he adjusts it.

I have worked out a way to straighten out a sheet without leaving the spot I've warmed on it, a way involving a small spring in the air while simultaneously lifting the sheet over the corner, but he won't believe me.

"It'll take one second," he says, placing me in the impossible position of someone who won't get up for even a second.

When the sheet is snapped into place and I, blue with cold and contemplating divorce, am allowed to claim my now-frigid spot on the sheet, we both pick up our books.

"I am going to want to read for at least half an hour," I warn him.

I dread his getting sleepy first, even though experience shows this practically never happens. When it does, he turns out his light and turns his back to me. He is very sweet about this, never for a moment suggesting that perhaps I, too, could turn out the light at this time.

But the perfectly still outline of his body under the blanket suggests a man driven frantic by the light of a thousand suns coming

160

over his shoulder and by the thunderous crackling of turning pages.

I do my best to ignore him, continuing to read my book in my circle of lamplight, but his still form is about as much nagging as I can stand. I put out my light, then lie there against his back for twenty minutes, feeling a nearly intolerable curiosity to know what's happening next in my novel.

I contemplate stealing out to another room, but there are snow-drifts in all the other rooms, and it's so warm where I am.

When I'm the first to get sleepy, it's less of a problem. I switch off my light, and either go right unconscious or lie there sort of twitching restlessly, moving my legs and arms and readjusting my pillow, until he gets the message and turns his lamp off.

When it's dark, I settle down to the business of getting warm in the bed I share with a man who on the coldest winter days puts the electric blanket at 1, barely enough to keep off hypothermia for me. But anything higher than that would make him wake up sweating, dreaming of the fires of hell.

So, with only the blanket and comforter and whatever blankets I heap on my side, I'm forced to make the best use of the sleeping man-sized heater next to me.

Just after we both drift off, the cat, which was nowhere to be seen when Bill stood out in the yard at 11:30 and called him for ten minutes, now yowls to be let in. We both feign sleep, but Bill's swearing always gives him away.

In the first blissful years he got up to let the cat in anyway, but now, after an unsuccessful four-year campaign to offload the step-cat, he says, "He's your cat, you go."

Finally, everybody snuggles down warmly, the cat at my feet, the dog on the floor beside me on his rug. The sound of gentle breathing fills the room.

Brrrriiiing! On top of everything else that's wrong with sleeping together, it eventually ends.

Love Has Appetizers Before Main Course

THE MARRIED COUPLE had some people over for dinner the other night, a friend and her new boyfriend. The courting pair seemed very fond of each other, often breaking off in conversation to kiss, or embrace. By dessert they were holding hands under the table and looking at their watches.

The married couple clinked their forks, and drank their wine, and talked about movies, but they had the feeling they were keeping the other couple from something, if you know what I mean.

There the wife was, brilliantly analyzing "Cliffhanger" and they were looking at her with what they clearly hoped was a rapt expression, while all the time imagining each other naked in whichever of the bedrooms was nearest.

Refusing all offers of coffee and mumbling lies about work in the morning, they made their disgracefully hasty exit at 9:45.

For every married couple who has ever invited such a pair into their home, the comparison is there for anybody to make: their level of romance and yours. Their sex life and yours.

Left alone, the married couple cleans the kitchen. She rinses the dishes while he wraps up the remains of the roast chicken. They both know that the other couple are off somewhere in the city, removing each other's clothes with their teeth.

When the kitchen is clean, the married couple gets ready for bed. He tries to get the cat to come in; she brushes her teeth. "Cute butt, mister," she mutters as she passes him to take the dog out for a pee. "Keep your eyes to yourself, lady," he answers, giving up on the cat and taking the garbage out.

Not much romance going on here. She knows him pretty well now, this human being raised eating different cereal in a different town, whose enthusiasms and tastes and ordinary stubbornnesses were formed long before she came along, with her quite different tastes and stubbornnesses.

She knows his biggest dilemma is to figure out which side of the bed he likes more so he can hog it. She's resigned to his opening windows just before he goes to work and getting upset about a little thing like the dog chewing up the sunglasses he left on the bed.

He knows her, too. There she is every morning, reading funny bits of the paper aloud to him while he's trying to read the sports. When they go out for coffee she will say she doesn't want a pineapple muffin, then will stare fixedly at his until he gives her a bite. He knows she has abandoned her early pretense at being a maniac for fresh air and is "studying" the new fall TV shows. Sometimes she absentmindedly opens and drinks the wine he was saving.

He knows when they go to bed, warm back to warm back, the cat will yowl outside the window, and she'll feign sleep.

Meanwhile, the courting couple, their passion spent, lie awake, side by side, staring into the darkness.

She's trying to get over the ducks on his shower curtain, and he's wondering if sitting cross-legged on the bed while flossing her teeth is a regular nightly routine for her.

Of course, a lot of discoveries still lie ahead of them. She doesn't know yet that he feels better when all the pot handles are facing the same way, and is not exactly divorced.

He doesn't know she'll look at the rock formations that excite him and say, "They're just rocks, OK? I'm going back to the car."

The married couple, miles across the city, go to sleep almost immediately. When he turns over, so does she, automatically.

They are awakened minutes later by a strangled yowl from outside the window. The wife doesn't stir.

"Hell," says the husband.

The Grass Is Greener in The Kitchen

IT WAS SAID that whenever matrimonial disputes were brought to his notice, Samuel Johnson always sided with the husband, whom he was sure had been provoked. "Women," said Johnson, "give great offense by a contemptuous spirit of noncompliance on petty occasions."

Asked by her husband to walk in the shade, he said, a wife will experience a strange desire to walk in the sun. "He offers to read her a play, or sing her a song, and she calls the children in to disturb them, or advises him to seize that opportunity of settling the family accounts . . ."

This is not to be mistaken for a sage observation on modern marriage, of course. When was the last time your husband offered to read you a play? Mine doesn't even read plays. Nor does he sing to me. But he has been blessed, nonetheless, with a compliant wife. I was thinking about this just last Saturday morning, when Bill was mopping the kitchen floor.

We have drifted into a sort of system. I shop, do the dusting, the laundry, pick up the dry-cleaning, pay the bills, argue with the cable guy. He cooks, does the floors, takes out the garbage, argues with the other repairmen.

"Are you OK out there for a while?" Bill asked, coming around the corner with his mop and bucket. I was sitting at the desk in my office, surrounded by piles of bills. "I don't want you walking on the wet kitchen floor."

"Sure," I answered.

"Have everything you need? Coffee? Newspaper? Need an apple?"

"No, no, I'm fine." He disappeared into the kitchen with a last nervous glance back at me, and I settled down to work. After awhile, I noticed I was a little chilly and just thought I'd get my sweater that's hanging on the hook in the hall, on the other side of the kitchen. I stood on the threshold looking at the shining wet floor. If I took a huge step . . .

"What do you want? I'll get it for you," Bill said suddenly, coming around the corner. He threw me the sweater.

I retreated to my desk. I didn't want the sweater now. What I wanted was the tempting peach I had spotted sitting in a bowl on the counter. I returned to the kitchen. A ray of sunshine hit the peach. It was ripe and perfect. If I had a towel, I could skate across the floor, drying it as I went, and get that peach.

Beyond the kitchen I could see Patrick's room, and the back yard. The sun was shining out there. Suddenly I forgot about the peach. I could plant something. Flowers, or vegetables. We could spend bucolic summer afternoons in our new garden. Bill could read plays to me under the grape arbor.

It was the tiniest bit annoying, having to stay out of the kitchen when everything I needed for happiness was there, or just beyond, on the other side, shimmering in the distance. The peach I hadn't wanted for breakfast was more worth having when I had to cross a river to get it, and risk being glared at. The very kitchen itself, which I am ordinarily able to ignore for hours at a time, was more elusive, more of a challenge, more worth visiting for being forbidden. I returned to my desk, tried to concentrate. My foot tapped rhythmically. I stared at the screen.

I suddenly realized I needed some coffee. It wouldn't hurt the floor for me to just leap, gazelle-like, across it, taking care to land lightly on my heels.

I returned to the threshold. I sprinted to the counter, made a quick cup of instant coffee, ate the peach, the juice running down my chin, then settled down to read the paper, to rest up before heading out to plant a garden.

"Look what you did to the floor!" It was Bill. I looked where he was looking, and saw a trail of footprints circling the table where I sat. It looked like the sidewalk outside Grauman's Chinese Theater.

This is not being noncompliant. This is just the sort of thing that happens when one person decides to mop the floor at the exact same time another person is planning to plant a garden.

Courting The Perfect Couple

WE WERE at our table in the Chinese restaurant, waiting for another couple: He's the pastor of an Episcopal church, and she teaches English in a Catholic high school. It was our first date with them, and we were eager to make a good impression.

When Bill and I got married, we thought the horrors of dating were behind us forever. We would walk through life hand in hand, looking into each other's eyes.

Now we've discovered that we're dating as much as ever, searching as before for the perfect one, the one who will laugh at our jokes and tell us all their secrets and stick with us through thick and thin. The only difference is that we're now looking for the perfect couple.

With some couples we were mad about her but hated him, or the other way round. To solve this, we kept trying to introduce our single friends to each other, trying to make them into couples for us to date.

It worked spectacularly in one case, except they fell head over heels in love and neither of them had time for us anymore. In another it backfired: We found we had made two people we both liked into a couple that neither of us liked much. Her excess energy made him look lackluster; his dry wit made her seem fatuous. We had them over for dinner and heartily wished one of them would go home.

Or they had a baby. Couples with babies, like couples with newly remodeled kitchens that they did all the work on themselves, are best off with each other. I was part of a couple like that: Our way of entertaining adult company during those years was to urge Morgan into the middle of the room to do her dance.

While you are not actually going to sleep with the other couple, there should be some sexual attraction, some undercurrent, some flirting. If a woman looks at Bill with obvious admiration, I may make a mental note to scratch her eyes out later, but it reminds me how nice-looking he is, which I am likely to forget if I'm home squabbling with him about where to put the couch. But we also want the couple we're dating to be in love with each other. We want to warm ourselves at their fire.

They should also be prone to blurting things out. Good couples are like good movies: You enjoy them at the time, but what you really like are discussing them afterward.

Gossip about other people is one of the world's underrated pleasures. Couples make the best gossip because you see them together and can thus store up tidbits — dropped hints, funny looks, odd remarks — for the ride home.

We know one couple who just drive us nuts. They're always breaking up — he storms off to New York to produce a show, he comes back, they show up together, and they tell us nothing, *nothing*.

Sometimes we find the perfect couple, but they live too far away, or they're going to India, or they're divorcing, or they are impervious to our charms. We have had our hearts stomped on by couples who led us on, even going camping with us, and then never called. Was it something we said? Something we did?

One couple pops up here and there at parties, smiles, leads us into dazzling conversation, then disappears again, leaving us wondering if it might have worked out, if only we had got their number.

Our new couple arrives at the restaurant, and a lot of animated conversation follows. A week later, we got a note from him. It said his wife had told him he talked too much at the dinner. They had argued about this, and he had written to apologize, "if I really did talk too much." I wrote back, saying don't be silly, we were the ones who babbled like teenagers.

We're hoping they'll call us.

At Times a Stranger, Always My Beloved

I'LL GIVE YOU a thousand dollars if we can go to bed right now," I said to Bill as the last of our guests said their good-bys and disappeared out the door at 1 a.m.

He glanced over from where he was briskly carrying a blue recyling bin around the living room, gathering plastic cups and Calistoga bottles. He hesitated, his very stance pleading for permission to stay up and clean.

"How about if I just put the food away?" he said.

"All right, but just the food," I said. We have this same debate after every party: I want to dive for my warm bed, and he wants to restore the house to museum status before he so much as turns out a light.

There is nothing like getting ready for a party and then cleaning up afterward for making two people feel married, shackled for life to each other's stubbornnesses. It's still amazing to me that two adults can live in a house together without getting into fistfights.

We didn't used to be able to have people over for dinner at all. In the sort of disillusioning discoveries with which marriage is rife, I discovered Bill has some severe hangups about needing to know the exact number of people coming, and who they're bringing with them, and what time I told them to come.

His preoccupation with such trivial details forces me to become even more casual than I am by nature, so that I say things like, "Let's just invite a bunch of people over, and we'll figure out everything when they show up."

In our regular life your mate's otherness is often an irritation, as his needs collide with yours, and you spat over whether to put wine glasses in the dishwasher and whether your dad will be allowed to smoke in the house, and whether to clean up after the party or in the morning.

But at parties, you look at your beloved from across the room, and even though an hour ago he was stomping around the bedroom in his underwear, asking you where his green pants were as if you have hidden them from him on purpose, now he's wearing his black silk shirt, and laughing at a joke you can't hear and might not even get, and he is suddenly, attractively, Other.

At our St. Patrick's Day party in which everybody had to deliver a piece of Irish verse or song, Bill read a passage from his Irish history book and then delivered a short, impassioned speech on the Irish struggle. As he acted as the emcee with a grace and enthusiasm that astonished me, considering the man has not voluntarily made a phone call in the five years of our marriage, I was sitting on the floor, hiding behind an armchair in case someone should remember that I ought to do something in front of the group too.

Later I saw him laughing with some people, and it reminded me of watching Patrick get on a bus, knowing that the minute he swung out of sight he was on his own, moving in a world that didn't contain me, his own private thoughts jumping under the soft brown hair I ran a comb through before he left.

Watching Bill talk to someone else at a party reminds me of the day he said he felt out of sorts when he didn't have a serious book going. I stared at him. He had become mysterious, unknown, a man who could be made unhappy by something that would never bother me, a man with his own peculiar set of requirements for happiness.

I wondered how I could not have known such a big thing about him.

This must be why they don't seat couples together at parties: so they can flirt across the room again, stare at each other through a doorway. You see him flirting, or teasing, or telling a story, and for a minute it's as if you are both single again, and you wonder what he'd be like in bed.

Now, though, Bill was running a vacuum over the floor. I glared at him. "I was just doing this while you were brushing your teeth," he said guiltily.

I'd like to believe him, but I know him too well.

A Marriage In Intimacy Only

I WENT AWAY to Napa for the weekend with a man not my husband, while his wife was away. Bill was in New York, and Jon's wife, Tracy, was in Nigeria, and Jon and I were driving together to Napa for an author's event in support of the local library.

When I picked him up at his house in Oakland, I noticed that we didn't hug, as we usually do. As he was throwing his bag in the back of my car, his neighbor came out with her new baby. Jon introduced me and told her where we were going. As we drove off, I imagined her looking after the car, bemused by her neighbor's brazen sexual adventure.

Maybe it was that imagined glance that made us feel even more like a husband and wife setting out for the weekend. Jon drove, and I read him the directions. We settled into our rooms at the Cedar Gables Inn in Napa — he in the Master Bedroom and I in the Maid's Room.

At the crowded book party, since we knew no one else, we talked to each other in that undertone couples use. We established the signal to leave — the ear-tugging gesture Bill and I use (except that only I use it — Bill never wants to leave a party). I told Jon I was nervous about my ten-minute talk, and he told me that he shocked himself by picking up the wrong glass and getting a mouthful of wine (he doesn't drink).

We spotted someone we liked and wanted to meet, and there it was, that odd, smug, irritating, comforting "we" that you have in marriages. I had a newlywed friend who said her husband used to tell people, "We wouldn't consider living in a house built after 1900," and she would glance over at him, and think, "We?"

When I married Bill, I became a "we." We like to go to Europe, we like parties, we read in the evening, we vote the Democratic ticket, we like our new cat more than our old cat.

And so it was at this party, in my pseudo-marriage. Jon and I conferred in a whisper, then he marched over to a woman we had both liked when she read from her work and said to her, "We think you're fabulous, and we want you to come to our next event with us."

We stood back to back, talking to people, and occasionally I'd hear my name, as Jon told the story of how we'd been afraid no one in Napa had heard of us. That's what real couples do, standing near each other talking to other people, half of you listening to the story the woman in the green coat is telling, and half of you straining an ear backward jealously, listening to your mate tell the story of the run-in with the IRS when he always leaves out the best part.

Later, at the next event, we ran into a woman named Kathy we'd met at the party. Now we had friends we'd met since we got together. When we split up, we'd have to figure out who got Kathy.

The weekend made me think of how much being married, or being in any couple, is a matter of meeting the world together, and of the small details of "what are you wearing?" and "who do we like?" and "when shall we leave?"

Part of the intimacy comes from arriving together and having everybody know you'll go home and take off your clothes in front of each other and sleep in the same bed. Part of it is the fun of seeing yourselves arrive at the party, the secret, private two of you, and watching each other's transformation into your more public selves.

Bill seems so quiet and self-effacing, and I watch, startled, while he comfortably holds the interest of a circle of people while he tells a long story in an Irish accent.

It felt both odd and comfortable and in a way exciting to instantly fall into such a routine with a new man. It was like a marriage without sex, without issues, without history or baggage or habit. We both knew how to be married, how it feels, and that's how we behaved.

The Urge To Nag, Nag, Nag

I SOMETIMES FEEL a need to nag Bill when he eats tortilla chips. "Don't," I silently implore him. I bang the dishes around. I stare at him, then I look away. I struggle not to give voice to my theory that only a deeply self-destructive person would sit eating those oily pieces of chip-death in that absentminded way.

Meanwhile Bill, to all appearances engrossed in the game, is silently vowing not to mention the amount of water that escaped during my shower and filtered through the floor to the downstairs bathroom. He says nothing, but wonders to himself what's so difficult about shutting a shower curtain all the way.

Our decision not to nag each other was easy enough for me — Bill's so neat he can remind himself of something just by putting his keys down in a new place — but I'm the sort of person you can't pass on the street without wanting to tell her to tie her shoe.

Previous roommates have sunk to a low form of discourse: the rhetorical question. Did I know there was green scum on the top of the spaghetti sauce? Was it possible for me to return the milk to the fridge? Did we need seventeen kinds of cereal? Was it OK with me that Patrick was dumping the sand out of his shoes in the living room?

It isn't that I don't try. I screw the lid on the jar of pickle relish before putting it back in the fridge, wipe the toothpaste out of the sink, put my clothes away even though I might need them again any minute.

But while I'm doing all that, other things are escaping my attention, and I'm absentmindedly jotting notes on Bill's smog control papers, walking around with toilet paper on my shoe, putting the dishes away in such odd places they don't surface for months.

I am consequently used to being nagged. One former squeeze hinted I should like different music, keep more food in the fridge, and stop hogging the blankets in my sleep.

One day he came into the living room holding a wet wash cloth by one corner, and said, "Could you tell me what this was doing on the floor?" I opened my mouth to explain, and then closed it again. My floor, Jack. My wash cloth.

We had flunked each other's tests: He wanted me not to leave a wash cloth where it could annoy him. I wanted him to take no notice of such a trifling event: a rag crumpled on the linoleum.

But, of course, as always, more is going on. To keep quiet, to leave each other alone, wipe up the spilled shampoo and forget about it, is asking almost too much.

Fate has, after all, delivered to you a manifestly imperfect creature, a creature who ties the newspapers so carelessly they fly all over the yard, and it's so clear that just a word from you now and then, the tiniest hints about personal grooming and how to clean out sink drains, would transform that creature into a civilized being.

It's hard not to nag, too, because of our conviction that we are not being loved when we are being deliberately annoyed. If he loved you, would he honk at other cars when you've asked him nicely not to? Would she eat rice cakes at the counter and drop crumbs all over the floor you just mopped? Of course not.

I am still watching Bill as he watches the football game. "I hate chips," I finally blurt out.

I'm not nagging him, not really. Just making a random remark about which foods I hate.

"Fine," he says, squeezing my hand and smiling. "Don't eat them."

The Dubious Pleasures
of a Good Long Sulk

WE HAD AGREED I would follow Bill to the tire store across town, as I had no idea where it was. This plan worked fine until the first stoplight, when he sped through the yellow and I got caught on the red and watched him disappearing around a corner.

I spent the next 45 minutes driving all over town, going to two wrong addresses, trying to find the tire store.

As I drove, seething, my knuckles whiter and whiter on the steering wheel, I wondered how many days were going to pass before I'd be able to speak to Bill in a really warm tone of voice again. I was cursing the day I was born and the day I met Bill, but I was also, underneath, enjoying the feeling of being flat-out mad.

Then the bottom fell out of my fine black mood. I found the tire store and stalked into the waiting room where Bill was lounging with a magazine.

He put his arms around me. "I'm so sorry," he said. "It's all my fault. Since you're the one who recommended this tire store in the first place, I was sure you knew the way."

As he spoke, any hope of making him suffer as I had suffered flickered out. I didn't get to be mad for days. I didn't even get to be mad for as long as I'd been searching for the tire store. We just went off food shopping, as planned, while they put new front tires on my car.

This is the disadvantage of a mature relationship. You miss the satisfactions of a really Richard Nixonian sulk, of getting mad and staying mad, and not listening to any efforts to bring you out of it.

When you sulk, you're never in the wrong. You're the Queen of the May, the gloriously innocent party hugging your injustices to your breast. Access to your person is restricted. Windows are slammed down, doors boarded over. You can pretend you adore the abalone shell earrings, then seethe secretly every time you remember you got him a jacket and an expensive jogging suit.

When the person you are punishing is absent, sulking is transformed into that other delicious but necessarily more solitary activity, brooding. I've spent many a happy hour vacuuming topsoil off the venetian blinds after a fight with someone, letting the phone ring while luxuriously remembering my injuries and rehearsing my remarks.

I used to be so good at feeling wronged that I didn't always require a partner. As I pushed my cart through the aisles at the grocery store, I'd get mad at my roommate for telling me not to buy diet drinks when it was none of his business.

It made no difference to me that he was out of town when we had this falling out.

Sulking and brooding, and that other lost pleasure of immaturity, martyrdom, make the other person miserable and allow him to appreciate the unhappiness he has caused you. This satisfies your child's sense that if people upset you, they have to pay. It magically returns you to that happy childlike stage when you were the center of the universe and the tedium of considering other people's feelings was still far in the future.

Mature fights are by contrast dreary and unsatisfying. You have to make concessions, admit you may have been wrong or cop to what's really bothering you — for instance, that he held all the money in the garage sale when you wanted to hold some of it.

Or, worse, you have to just forget it, never even tell her you noticed the huge chip she gouged in the doorway when she was trying the bookshelf out in various new locations.

All mature fights do, really, is clear the air and promote lasting relationships. And you're just not always in the mood for that, are you?

A Few Moments of Clear Peace

Random Acts of Kindness

I T'S A BRILLIANTLY sunny day. Joan drives up to the Bay Bridge toll plaza in a red Honda. "I'm paying for me and for the six cars in back of me," she says, handing over seven commute tickets.

One after another, the drivers of the next six cars ease up to the booth, dollar bills waving, only to have the toll taker say, "Your fare's been paid. Have a nice day."

When I heard Joan's story, I thought it must have come as a pleasant jolt for those drivers, starting their day that way. Who knows what they might have done later themselves — perhaps waved someone into their lane at the next on ramp, or told a passing stranger how wonderful he looked in that shade of periwinkle blue.

You might do almost anything if you have been surprised yourself by a random act of kindness.

It's true Joan happened to have a surplus of commute tickets, but she was also a bit under the influence, not of drink, but of a tender phrase she had seen on an index card taped to a friend's refrigerator: "Practice random kindness and senseless acts of beauty."

It's one of the phrases that seem to be everywhere all of a sudden, floating on the current, diving down to nip the toes of the unsuspecting. Judy Foreman of San Francisco was strolling along in Santa Cruz when she saw it spray-painted on a warehouse wall. It stayed on her mind for days, and finally she had to go back and copy it down. "I just thought it was incredibly beautiful," she said, "like a message from above."

Judy started writing it at the bottom of letters. Her husband, Frank, liked it so much that he put it up in the classroom for his seventh-graders, one of whom — my daughter, Morgan — brought it home one day. I used it in a column in January, saying I liked it, but admitting I didn't know where it came from or even what it meant, really.

Two days later, I heard from Anne Herbert, who said she first scribbled those words in the Sausalito Land Company restaurant eight years ago. "I thought it was kind of neat so I was writing it in 24-point type on this place mat. I guess I knew I had something when this guy at the next table looked over and kind of wet his teeth and said, "'That's so wonderful!' "

Tall and blond, forty years old, originally from Ohio, Anne's an odd bird. She house-sits, takes little jobs, gets by. She has fantasies of being normal in which, she writes, "department stores don't depress me/I have a favorite brand of everything/I say what I think and it blends right in."

Right now she lives in Mill Valley but takes the bus every day to write down her thoughts about man's violence to man at a coffee-house in Berkeley because, she says, the level of rage there matches her own. "I can't write in the essential contentment of Marin."

She's hard to track down, but rumor is she'll be at the Berkeley Store Gallery this Saturday night, talking about her real job, which is, she says, "to worry ahead."

Her self-published book, *Compassion 101*, uncannily predicted the Gulf War, but Anne isn't impressed. She wears a button that says, "If I'm so smart, why are they dead?"

Anne has fantasies of positive vandalism — breaking into schools to paint the classrooms, leaving meals on tables in the poor part of town, "secretly planting daffodils in every gray place there is."

"The idea is," she told me, "anything you think there should be more of, do it randomly. Kindness can build on itself as much as violence can."

What the Mothers Of Russia Know

A NY MOTHER is shocked by battle. A bullet fired in a split second can shatter the throat, the heart, the freckled skin of a child she had raised up to a man, taking in an instant that hard-won mastery of the multiplication tables, of how to tell a joke, tie a tie, conjugate French verbs. The bullet will stop him cold, take away, as Clint Eastwood says in "Unforgiven," " . . all he has, and all he's ever going to have."

It won't matter then that you forgot to pack his swimsuit for summer camp, or that you didn't get after him enough about taking out the garbage.

Yet mothers send their sons off to war. Some do it because they are fierce themselves: In ancient Sparta, mothers commanded their sons to return with their shields, or on them. But for most mothers, every cell cries out against it.

The bravery of sending a son to war is ten times what it takes to go to war. Soldiers have the drumbeat coming through their boots to protect them, and their scared pride, and the nervous joking of the other soldiers, and their ideals. But the mothers stay at home with the school pictures, the discarded footballs and the marks on the kitchen wall where he grew taller each year, and they listen to the distant booming of the cannon.

Now I read that the mothers in Russia are marching into army camps and claiming their sons. One, Valentina, drove three hundred miles to her son's army base, made him change into civilian clothes and took him home to Moscow. More than five hundred mothers have done the same, say the news reports. At least fifty of them have gone all the way to Chechnya to remove their sons from the battlefield, though the Russian authorities say such deserters will face long prison terms or firing squads.

The mothers cite reasons for their actions, some blaming Boris Yeltsin, others hoping that using the army to put down an internal rebellion will be declared against the Russian constitution.

Meanwhile, though, they're just journeying to get their children, because it's dangerous out there. You wouldn't let a child play in the street: Why would you let him wear a soldier's uniform in Chechnya?

It's such a primal act, that journey, cutting through the politics and the moralizing and the hand-wringing. I can imagine how it would feel, to just go get your boy. It reminds me of what my dad said when Sean ended up in the hospital ward last year: You just go get him. If he's your son, or your brother, you just go get him. That's all.

And from all reports the boys are going willingly. There may be a time to put away childish things and be a man, but this isn't one of them, not for the scared young soldiers being sent to Chechnya to be killed by their own countrymen.

And it works. Of the soldiers taken home by their mothers, not one has died. Not one lies dead in the smashed streets of Chechnya, his arms flung out from his body, his face looking blankly at the sky.

I don't like to put emphasis on gender differences, but I think this is a real one: When women think of war, we think of bullets striking soft flesh, of all that aching, feeling, thinking beauty lying in a muddy field. With us, it comes down to one boy, and we don't see the uniform.

When Patrick was three weeks old, he went into the hospital with a high fever and was given a painful spinal tap to check for meningitis. I allowed it because it made sense to check, even though he seemed to have the same flu his sister had. When they wanted to do another one three days later, just to make sure, I said no, and kept the interns at bay until my pediatrician called and sided with me.

For Russian mothers, this tragic civil war is that second spinal tap, and they are saying no. And what if everybody behaved like this, you ask? What if every Russian mother took her son home?

Then all the sons would be home, and you could hear the birds again, over the clear blue skies of Chechnya.

Gingersnaps And a Clear Blue Sky

A FEW YEARS BACK, when I was going through a rough patch, I took a few minutes every night to write the ten times that day when I had felt happiest. It was a deliberate attempt to cheer myself up, and it worked.

I noticed that my husband had filled the car with gas, so I didn't have to. I got a lift from joking with somebody at a garage sale, making tuna fish sandwiches with Patrick, getting work done, talking to my sister on the phone.

I thought I was miserable, yet here were these small moments, like daisies in the grass, when I would have said I was purely happy.

This would not be enough, by some modern standards. In the Declaration of Independence, our founding fathers gave us the right to pursue happiness, and we've been busy ever since trying to turn it into a desperate obligation.

The women's magazines, with articles like "When You're Afraid to Be Happy," "Who's Happy and Why," and "Time to Stop Sabotaging Happiness," telegraph the message that we can all be happy if we just find the right partner, or the right black dress, or the right set of cheerful beliefs about ourselves. One article concludes, "Joy is our natural state."

If joy is our natural state, then we must be happy all the time. If we aren't, then something is wrong, and we ought to be worried.

I'm not sure I believe this. I'm not even sure I believe in happiness, at least not as a permanent condition.

In my life, it's more like a visitor, a smiling Aunt Tilly who sweeps in and out, trailing a scent of orchids, turning up when you least expect her and ordering an extravagant round of drinks, then disappearing for days on end. I would guess that what most people experience is not an endless state of bliss, but something more ordinary, what Hugh Prather called a "mixture of unsolved problems, ambiguous victories and vague defeats — with a few moments of clear peace."

I wouldn't say that I was happy yesterday, for example, since I had a houseful of teenagers and a lot of work to do.

But still the day had its moments of clear peace. I was cheered up when I went outside to get the paper and saw the sun was out. Later I had a stroll on 24th Street, eating gingersnaps and looking in the shop windows, and a stranger asked me where I get my hair cut.

After lunch, I rolled some oranges down the steps to the teenagers collected there, playing Ping-Pong, wrote something that I didn't entirely hate. The mail brought a funny letter from a friend I haven't heard from in a long time.

Later when Bill and I went for a quick walk, we came back to find that Morgan had hung a banner out the front window, saying, "Welcome home, Mom and Bill, I missed you."

A moment can be nothing more than a line in a book. In *Joe Jones*, by Anne Lamott, someone looks up the word "blue" in the dictionary and finds, "the pure color of a clear sky."

The kids and I spent ten minutes looking up all the other colors in the dictionary, but the character in the book is right: The definition of blue is the dictionary's finest moment.

Maybe that's all happiness really is, a series of fine and careless moments.

Gingersnaps and the pure color of a clear sky. Mice and hummingbirds and cats that hide in the rug and someone flirting with you over the drama titles at the movie store, and the first bite of a turkey on French with mustard and tomatoes.

Could be our job is not to pursue happiness, but simply to be around for those moments of peace, to grab them out of the air as if they were balloons drifting seaward in a bright blue sky.

New Year's Ruminations

ORGAN AND I had just watched the British documentary called "The Dying Process," about baby girls dying in overcrowded Chinese orphanages after being abandoned by their families. Chinese families are allowed only one child, and most want sons. The girls are aborted, or drowned at birth, or, for those parents who can't bring themselves to murder, are left in the road or on doorsteps, from where they are eventually brought to these orphanages.

The film was difficult to watch. It showed baby girls tied to potty chairs, five in a row, all day long. Sick babies left in rooms to die alone. The Chinese government, incensed by this film (shot in secret by film makers pretending to be just touring the orphanage), has halted all internal adoptions and is preparing its own film.

My sister-in-law had wanted to adopt a Chinese orphan rather than have a third child of her own, but discovered it would cost $20,000, including the cost of going to China to choose a child. They just didn't have the money. Had I lived in China, would I have drowned Morgan, my first born, and then had Patrick, a son, a child the family could be proud of?

Morgan has just been reading *The Woman Warrior*, by Maxine Hong Kingston, for school; part of it is about the contempt in which females are held in China, a contempt that many emigrant villagers brought with them to California. "Feeding girls is feeding cowbirds," Maxine's mother in Stockton would say, unimpressed by her daughter's straight As. When Maxine fell to the floor in a rage, her mother's friends would say, "I would hit her if she were mine. But you know how girls are. There's no profit in raising girls. Better to raise geese than girls."

The next morning after Morgan and I watched the documentary, I read a story in the newspaper about polygamy in France: Muslims who bring home extra wives from Africa, forcing their old wives to live with them all together in cramped apartment buildings. The wives hate it, but until recently the French government had put up with it. Polygamy is a tradition in parts of Africa.

We forget how it is out there. A woman from Bill's office left her job to follow her husband to his two-year job in Saudi Arabia. They got a postcard from her: Michelle has to wear an *abaya* (a long, black garment) and is not allowed to work or to drive. If she does, her husband would be punished, as she is his possession.

In this country, we've made more progress. Bill says he's never forgotten the expression on my face when his mother, who used to be a nurse, told me she remembered when all nurses had to stand up whenever a doctor entered a room.

All these stories, and the film, remind me how new, how fragile, is this trendy American idea that women are as valuable, as human, as important and necessary as men. I grew up ina female household, where most of the strong people were girls. Mother was stronger than Dad, my older sister Connie was strong where my older brother was not. I grew up without anger at men, because I never for a minute had been led to believe that women were inferior. Later, when I was grown, if a man made a derogatory remark about women, I immediately lost interest in talking to him, as I would if someone made a slur against blacks or Asians or gays. I wasn't angry. It never occurred to me that women's equality was a principle that needed defending.

And yet I have to remember that until I was eleven or so, it was my most ardent wish to be a boy. The pronoun "he" thrilled me. "She" didn't seem like much of a word. I didn't even like my siblings to refer to our mother as "she" by my brothers and sisters. It seemed too impersonal, and somehow faintly demeaning.

My daughter is growing up strong and confident. She likes her body, and would be astounded to discover that some people consider women second-class citizens. Yet she too sat and watched the faces of those abandoned babies peeping from under their covers, those babies with no one, ever, coming to pick them up.

Note to Self: Smell the Roses

M Y MOTHER used to wash our clothes in a wringer washer and then hang them on the lines. As she pinned up each garment, she said, she thought about the child it belonged to. She never wanted a dryer, even after we could afford one, because it would steal this from her, this quiet contemplation.

Thirty years later, I carry the laundry to the basement and toss in the clothes, switching them in a wet clump from washer to dryer. The clothes go by too fast for me to do anything but scoop up the wet socks that fall on the floor and toss them in with the rest. I am doing what she did — drying the family clothes — but not getting as much satisfaction from it.

I don't mean to wax sentimental about the domestic drudgery of the '50s. Nostalgia is a tender trap: For all I know, Mother was really fantasizing about shooting up a shopping mall as she hung up each of a seemingly endless line of sodden little garments.

I just wonder, sometimes, how I can learn to slow down like that. I am just as busy, or busier, than my mother was, with the job and kids and my zillions of projects.

But it's a different kind of business, a faster, jerkier kind, one task over and on to the next. It's hard to get a rhythm going, harder to draw the proper quotient of satisfaction from each task.

I know I'm supposed to stop charging around and stop and smell the roses. But I get caught up, like a swimmer in a pool full of floating junk, in what's coming at me.

I call the dentist for an appointment, go to lunch, meet deadlines, throw a load in the washer, call back a friend and then think, later, that I must have sounded rushed and unfriendly, when that's not how I felt at all. I fax the mail, scissor open instant meals, check off one item and go on to the next.

I don't spend a meditative moment really tasting the blackberry jam, or gazing at my sleeping children, or stepping out to the porch to feel the rain on my face.

Or I do it quickly, checking it off the list: Gazed at sleeping children. Lifted face to rain. Note to self: Smell roses tomorrow.

Somewhere at the center of our minds is a sunny spot in the tall grass where we can lie on our backs for hours and trace the shapes of clouds in the blue sky.

But we can't quite get there because modern life jerks along: The cat missed the litter box again, the vehicle registration is due in two days, we have to drive to the store to buy boneless chicken breasts and Calistoga, then stop by the dry cleaners to argue about the brown slacks they lost.

Much has been given us, with modern conveniences and faster ways of doing everything from mailing letters to doing the wash.

But something has been taken from us, too — a rhythm to our days once provided by the time it took to do everything. It used to take half a day just to saddle the horse and ride to town.

Our challenge is not to look backward at simpler times, but to find new rhythms, new ways of slowing down in a world that speeds up more every day.

If you have a fax you will naturally use it, rather than stroll out to the corner mailbox, feeling the sun and the wind and saying hello to the neighbors.

But what will you do with the time saved? Too often, we use it to fret about what it all means, what it all adds up to.

My Mother, My Prime Minister

L AST NOVEMBER the president of Sri Lanka chose for her prime minister the person closest to her: her mother. At the time, I wanted to call the president, Chandrika Bandaranaike Kumaratunga, and ask her whether she had thought this out. Being a daughter myself, I wanted to say, "She's your *mother*, Chan. How will she accept you being her leader when she won't let you out of the house looking that way?"

On the other hand, I'm also a mother myself, so I was charmed at this show of devotion. I think making me prime minister of something would be a nice gesture from Morgan, after my long years of refolding the clothes she flings down and accepting her preposterous excuses for missing the bus.

If I were prime minister, I would let her run her own country exactly as she pleased, as long as she was true to herself, and to what she was taught at home, and at least tried to keep the country picked up.

It would be nice to think a mother and daughter could run a country like Sri Lanka together amicably, but, alas, it seems it was not to be. The other day the mother's name was struck "by mistake" from the president's reception list for Hillary Clinton. Mother and daughter now barely speak, and rarely appear together in public. The entire government is splitting into rival camps.

At first the rift appeared to be over such issues as who deserves the credit for ousting the right-wing government of seventeen years, who forged which coalition, who supports free-market policies and who favors privatization of state-owned enterprises.

But a closer look reveals the same mother-daughter politics you find the world over. The mother says the daughter is behaving disgracefully for a widow (Kumaratunga's husband, a popular film actor, was assassinated in the 1980s), going to late-night hotel parties with an actor. And the prime minister stormed out of a cabinet meeting recently after waiting for her daughter two hours after the appointed time.

"One of the things I learned at boarding school was punctuality," sniffed the mother.

The president, for her part, has begun sending agents of the country's spy bureau to watch her mother's comings and goings to keep her from meddling in affairs that don't concern her.

Everybody knows that having your mother hanging around the country would be like having her hanging around your apartment, telling you the dining room is too small and the kitchen curtains are a mistake. You can wait forever to hear her say something nice about the way you're running the country. After all, she's the one who told you "You know, from the knees down, your legs aren't so bad."

And taking a job with your grown daughter as your boss? It upsets the laws of nature.

We women in a sense all appoint our mothers prime ministers of our lives, then wage furious power struggles with them, even after they're dead.

Even our rebellion is tied to our mothers: We have to wear silk blazers and pursue careers in dentistry just because she wore baggy old jeans and followed the Grateful Dead around the country. If she hates it when you dye your hair red, then you have to leave it red, even if you're 52 and weary of the color.

In Sri Lanka, the mere fact that the prime minister favored the Buddhist ethnic Sinhalese majority meant that the president had to back the rival Tamil Tigers.

And Mom always wins, even when we grow up to be president. Your mother is your other self, your eerie twin. Just as she used to say, "Don't even think about punching your brother," before you had time even to make a fist, so she'll know, just from the look on your face, the moment it crosses your mind to unseat her from her role as prime minister.

What I want to know is, did they actually think this would work?

Warnings That Can Never Be Heard

T HE BOMB will explode at 3:10. It's just 3:05 in Omagh, Ireland, so there's five minutes to go. Plenty of time to get away.

Brenda Pogue, seventeen, a soccer player, is in a shop with her mother. Stay in the shop, Brenda. No, her hand is on the door handle, she is going out. Her mother, absorbed with something she's thinking about buying — a package of T-shirts or some blue thread — lets her go. There is a blur at the edge of her vision, her daughter leaving. Going out into the street, attracted by the commotion. "I'll be over there, Ma. See you."

Two minutes to go. Brenda heads into the summer crowd on Market Street. The police have got word of a bomb threat and are herding the carefree summer crowd from the courthouse steps to safety — in Market Street.

Stay on the courthouse steps. This crowd is used to bomb threats that turn out to be nothing. But they go along with it, good-naturedly.

Near Brenda are young exchange students from Madrid, a woman shopping with her pregnant daughter, her little grand-daughter, a scattering of small boys — look at blond-haired eight-year-old Oman tagging along with his friend Sean. There's broad-faced 21-year-old Adrian Gallagher shopping for jeans. What do you need jeans for, Adrian? Wear your old jeans, for Pete's sake. It's reckless to go out shopping on a Saturday afternoon, don't you know that? Shop tomorrow. This Saturday's afternoon light is dangerous.

Julie Hughes, 21, a university student, has run out of her summer job at the Image Xpress to see what's going on. Go back in, Julie, go back to developing pictures. Don't listen to the music. Get your head down.

No one is paying attention to the danger. Kevin Skelton is shopping with his wife, Philomena, 39, and their three teenage daughters. Philomena. What kind of name is that? Go home, Philomena.

Your daughters will live, but you, you are going to have your clothes blown right off, right here in what is at present a shop but soon will be rubble. Right in front of Kevin. Philomena, go home.

Nearby is a festival, with floats and music. The crowd mills past a maroon Vauxhall Astra. A couple of teenagers even lean against it, maybe, as they talk. What are they talking about? Why don't they listen? Go somewhere else, kids.

What kind of car is that? An absurd purple plum of a car, packed with explosives. The men who put the explosives there have hurried away. They did not stop to finger a T-shirt, or riffle through brightly colored pairs of socks, or try on a pair of jeans. They are no dummies.

Brenda strolls near the car. She's not thinking about getting that job she wants on the mushroom farm, or about playing soccer, or about her twin brother, who sensibly stayed home on the farm. Like Julie, she just wants to see what's going on out here.

Some of the fathers have gathered in the Kosy Korner pub to wait for their wives and daughters who have, against all reason, chosen to go shopping today. One mother has gone out to buy a school uniform for her youngest child. This can wait. Buy it next Tuesday. Discover you have no cash and step to the safety of the bank in the next street. Go on, now, while there's still time. Remember that you have to call your mother or that you haven't fed your parking meter.

Oh, God, it's 3:09. There's a man getting in his car, driving away. Smart man. Don't wait for the light to turn green. Just go now. He's turning the corner. Oh, the relief. He's out of sight now, but we imagine him, driving into the rest of his life. The blast will fill his rearview mirror with rubble and smoke and orange flame.

Brenda, go back into the shop. There's just time.

Oh, Brenda.

Raising Your Happiness Set Point

I READ IN THE PAPER that how happy we are is largely determined by our genes. Just as our bodies want to be at a certain weight, despite our zealous plans to the contrary, so our spirits want to be at a certain level, whether things go badly or well.

Lighthearted people tend to zoom back to being lighthearted, even after getting fired or divorced. They will truthfully tell you they had an extremely happy childhood, though further questions reveal they were one of 18 children, were destitute, suffered from St. Vitus' dance and dropped out of school in the 10th grade. And gloomy people have no trouble boomeranging back to their gloomy set point within days of even winning the lottery.

However, one of the researchers, Dr. Lykken, pointed out that we aren't completely stuck with the temperament we were born with: You can't change your fundamental outlook, but you can nudge it into the higher registers.

"Be an experiential epicure," he says. "A steady diet of simple pleasures will keep you above your set point. Find the small things that you know give you a little high — a good meal, working in the garden, time with friends — and sprinkle your life with them."

My friend Ginny agrees. She felt bad her whole life that she wasn't a happier person, until, copying the moves of a happy friend, she just started filling her life with the things she liked: Häagen-Dazs ice cream, long cool dawn runs in the park, People magazine, bad TV, weekly lunches at dives with her female friends (one of the restaurants was so small they had to bring their own lawn chairs).

It's as simple as doing what you like to do. Jim carefully chooses melons and peaches at the Farmer's Market every Saturday morning. Morgan takes long, hot bubble baths with her Blondie CD turned way up. Bill gets up at 5:45 because he likes to start the day by quietly reading the entire paper. We take bike rides, and he keeps catching up to me to say, "I love this!"

When we were little, my mother curled up in the afternoons with the napping kids arranged around her like puppies. When Dad had to replace a section of bridge he and a friend drunkenly crashed through, he had fun while he was at it, making the new section barbershop-pole red and white.

If I were to think about what gets me above my set point, I'd have to include rambling along and stopping at garage sales on Saturday mornings, chatting with the proprietors and picking up radio headphones, baskets, black leather jackets and other things I don't need. Listening to that scamp Darien O'Toole on 98.1 interviewing some poor sod of an instant celebrity, like John Wayne Bobbitt. Watching the small, furious terrier up the street, yipping as he chases the big ball across the basketball court.

Reading Richard Wilbur's poems ripped out of my old college textbooks to Bill on the hiking trail while he holds my arm to keep me from tripping on roots. Eating grilled hot dogs with relish and regular mustard. Running into people who infuse the simplest transaction — the purchase of a Coke in a corner store — with such genuine warmth that you go on to your next encounter cheered up.

And riding Muni through the tunnel. I've liked this for months, ever since the day twelve five-year-olds got on just before we went into the tunnel. They hung on and oohed and aahed and the train tumbled on, and for all of us dozing, jaded commuters who had gone through the tunnel a thousand times without noticing, it was suddenly as thrilling as the roller coaster in Santa Cruz.

To stay above your set point, it seems to me, all you have to do is pay attention to what you like and hang out with people who are doing that too, like those kindergartners.

Doing It Just for the Consequence of It

I WAS ON my afternoon walk, musing about my last book club meeting, in which we talked about "Madame Bovary." It occurred to me that I am 46, and that when I die, all my slender knowledge of the misadventures of Madame Bovary will die with me. And it will have done me no earthly good in the meantime.

I can't get a raise in my salary because I have a passing acquaintance with the work of Gustave Flaubert. It hardly ever comes up in conversation. It certainly won't help me file my already tardy taxes or help me find my dad the housekeeper he needs.

Yet somehow it seems worth doing, just as for some reason this walk in the flickering afternoon light seems worth taking, though I gain nothing by it.

My friend Georgia explained it to me by e-mailing a passage from Henry James' "The Tragic Muse." After some discussion, a character asks why we bother increasing our capacity for appreciating the good in life.

"Where are the fine consequences?" he asks peevishly.

"In one's own spirit. One is oneself a fine consequence," the other replies serenely.

Which explains to me why I can read Flaubert and then have Madame Bovary in my head as an end in itself.

I am myself a fine consequence.

It's a suspect argument: "Why am I mainlining heroin so early in the morning? Because I'm worth it."

So this is not that argument. "I am myself a fine consequence" says filling up one's senses by going to museums, reading wonderful books — I'm now into Edith Wharton's *The House of Mirth* — or getting very hungry and then having a really good plate of hot pasta is good in itself.

"I am myself a fine consequence." It's the answer every child should give when his daddy demands to know why he is studying watercolors instead of global economics, when art seldom pays. It's the answer of everyone who prefers being educated to being trained, or at least insists that both kinds of learning take place.

It's the answer I think Bill should make if anyone ever asks him why he spends his evenings at the kitchen table studying the great sweep of history, when his field is editing cookbooks.

He doesn't even bring his vast knowledge of history into conversation much. He likes to walk around with that great surging tide of history, the stamping of horses and the roar of cannon, in his head as he bends over his deal sheets in his white shirt. He is himself a fine consequence.

It's the answer my dad might make if you ask why he reads only Joseph Conrad now, although he has no one to discuss it with except me in the letters he continues to write but no longer sends.

It's the answer of anyone who puts on a nice blouse and fresh lipstick when she will go through the day and back to bed and meet nobody at all. She might catch a glimpse of herself in the bowl of a spoon and be pleased by the reflection.

It's the answer my French friend Francoise might make if you asked her why she recoils in horror at the idea of saving time by eating anything standing up, but instead lays out a nice place setting with an ironed cloth napkin, even when she's only eating a peach.

We are, ourselves, fine consequences.

A Life That Teaches

I NEVER MET Sylvia Sanders. You've never heard of her. She wrote no books, built no bridges, did not invent a new and improved pudding mix. She was never photographed with the President. She led an ordinary life. She was married, she had kids, she had a job she went to every day.

She was a third-grade teacher here in the city, at Commodore Sloat School. Born in Arkansas, Sylvia had a molasses-thick southern drawl; she was stylish and tall and lean, although, according to other teachers, she was always eating trail mix.

She drove to school in a Ford — she wanted her car to be American — arriving at 7 a.m., after going running. Kids who were dropped off early by harried parents could always find a quiet refuge in her classroom, though there was rustling at the back from the pet rats and the snake called Slither.

Later in her illness she wore a baseball cap to class rather than a wig to hide her baldness. "Being the teacher she was," said Dana, one of the parents who told me about Sylvia, "she couldn't pass up a chance for another lesson for her students."

Under mobiles of the solar system that swung from the ceiling overhead, she played Chopin to the kids —there was a piano in the classroom, naturally — and sent them home with shining faces. Twice she led the school choir in "The Star Spangled Banner" at Giants games. Her kids literally hung on her, said Dana. "She never went out the door without at least two of them holding her hands."

As a class project, she'd trace each kid's outline on paper and cut it out. The child drew in the hair, and muscular, skeletal and circulatory systems were added as each was discussed in class. Finally they glued on various internal organs amid excited shrieks of "She's standing on my kidney!" or "I have a torn lung." Like many teachers, Sylvia spent her own money on school supplies for her classroom.

She could be tough. In a Costco parking lot she fought off a 200-

pound ex-con who wanted her car, and she made sure he did time. And she could be strict. She called parents "Mr." and "Mrs." because she wanted the kids to. She believed in the theory that children will achieve very close to the levels at which their parents and teachers expect them to achieve.

She had high standards for herself, too. Her daughter Jennifer reports that she was an ardent flosser — she was even urged by her dentist not to floss so much. She knew the name of every bird and every flower in California. ("Yeah," her cousin adds, "but she walked too fast to see them!") Vigilant about her credit rating, she'd been known to call a store and demand to know why her bill had not arrived. When she heard a siren she'd race to the end of the street, fully expecting to help out in case of some disaster.

At home, though, she made such good fried chicken that it has been memorialized in the lyrics of a hip-hop song written by a friend of her son.

After she was diagnosed with cancer, she ran ten Bay to Breakers races in a row. She read everything she could about non-Hodgkins lymphoma, and discussed her condition with anyone who would listen. Rather than wait for her hair to fall out on the pillow, she shaved her head.

"We all have our problems," she said, "but at some point you just need to deal with them and get on with your life."

Dana's seven-year-old son was going to get Sylvia for a third-grade teacher next, after watching his two older brothers come home happy at having been with Mrs. Sanders all day. He had looked forward to getting the handwritten welcome she sent each new pupil before the school year began, inviting them to write back to her and tell her about themselves.

But Sylvia died September 27, at the age of 56. I think about her, about the simple heroics of a life lived well, and I see in her example that there is no such thing as an ordinary life.

Clearing a Space For What You Want

M Y FRIEND K. and I were having lunch. She has been going out with a man who is very nice, with lots of money, vintage cars. He's involved in the community, and not particularly bad looking, with a beaked nose, glasses and a buzz cut. He'd be perfect for her if only she could force herself to be attracted to him.

This was, she said, the view of many of her friends, many of whom claimed it was perfectly possible to learn to be attracted to someone you weren't attracted to, once you got to know and admire his other qualities.

K. shivered over her seafood pizza and seemed to change the subject. "I loved my new house from the moment I saw it. I've found out since that it was put together by idiots, with poor insulation and gaps that let in the north wind, but at least I was passionate about it at the beginning."

We have all met people whom it would be convenient to be in love with — convenient because they're offering marriage, or have lots of money, or because they're such nice, funny, friendly people who share our interest in 19th century African stamps.

I remember trying once trying to fall back in love with an exboyfriend. He seemed to want me back and I missed having a boyfriend, so I thought, there he was, why not take him? One night he came to take me to the movies. I worked at my desk, enjoying the feeling of waiting for him. Then he walked into the room, and instantly I knew this wouldn't work. The feeling was gone, and I couldn't do without it.

Passion is walking into a department store and seeing a red wool sweater that you feel so strongly about that you plunk down full price right on the spot. Anything less is a sweater you'll buy if the price is right, or if you happen to feel chilled that day, or because it would go with something else.

It makes you feel alive, wanting a sweater that much, or feeling that way about a man. The only way to get it is to wait for it. As my dad said to me once, "Remember to practice a little moderation now and then, to increase the pleasure of the blowouts."

If you buy the so-so sweater, you might be wearing it when you pass the perfect one in the store window. You risk passing it by without a glance, or seeing it but remembering you just bought a sweater.

It's hard, goodness knows, to endure the chill until the right sweater comes along. I have another friend, J. She and her boyfriend have decided their relationship has no future — he wants kids, she doesn't — but they've agreed to go on dating until one of them finds somebody else. They are determined not to be cold, not even for a little while.

I was lucky. I cleared some space in my life, quite deliberately, and then one day I walked into the elevator at work and met the man I would marry a year later.

"But you still would have gone into the elevator even if you hadn't stopped seeing the other guy," J. insisted when I told her the story.

"But I would have gone into the elevator differently," I said.

I was convinced that if my senses had not been sharpened by solitude, I might never have noticed the handsome guy in a suit standing there holding the Sunday paper. I might never have said hi, and asked if he worked in the building.

Last time I saw her, K. was still resisting her friends' insistence that she go out with the nice guy with the buzz cut. She preferred to stay home, in the jerry-built house she was passionate about, and wait.

A Last, Wild Look Around Your House

SOMEONE POUNDS on the door. You stumble out of bed, grabbing a robe, as the sound of knocking echoes through the still house.

You open the door to men dressed in black, wearing crosses, with their faces covered in black paint. One of the men jerks his head toward the open field, toward Albania: "Go now, with your family, or be killed."

What do you take with you when a man with a gun gives you an hour?

As your kids, pale with shock, hurry to put jackets on over their pajamas, you take a last wild look around your house.

Strange thoughts must come into your head: that load of wash on the line. The milk souring in the fridge. The book you borrowed from your sister and haven't returned yet.

You see family photos on the piano, letters piled on a desk, the birdhouse your son is making out of Popsicle sticks.

Many things you know you won't need. The electric bill, the Yugoslavian stamps, the notices on the fridge about next week's parent- teacher conference. The green leather address book.

The kids are in the kitchen, each clutching something: a pet hamster in a cage, a pair of battered skates, a collection of dolls in a pillowcase. "No," you say. "No, we can't take any of those things."

You race through the house once more, grabbing anything that meets your eye: toothpaste, paper towels, an afghan off the living room couch. Your husband, white-faced and shaking, has to stop you from making the bed.

It's time. They're pounding on the door again. Your husband has persuaded you not to make the bed, but he's the one who, out of habit, locks the house and puts the key in his pocket.

He's the one who stops in the road to look back at the house one more time.

You join a long line of cars and farm vehicles heading for the border. Every tractor and harvester is piled high with huddled forms, many incongruously dressed in bright colors, yellows and reds, and many of them small children.

It's a strange spring harvest in Yugoslavia.

You ride for hour after hour, numbly watching the trees go by. Finally, you follow a man trundling his bespectacled mother across the Albanian border in a wheelbarrow.

In time you learn you are one of the lucky ones, like the math teacher who escaped into the woods and was forced-marched to a bus that would take him to the border.

Like the man who was about to be executed — "Choose which one you want to kill you" — but was released after he blurted desperately: "My brother saw you when you picked me out, and he knows you."

You are not the man whose four small kids, three daughters and a son, were killed when a shell hit the tractor they were fleeing on.

"My life has no meaning now," the father would tell reporters, standing huddled in a red jacket in a light rain, too shocked even for tears.

You are luckier than the family who may have had time to hear glass breaking as the grenade sailed in through the window, but no more time than that. They were killed to frighten their neighbors into leaving.

You are not the family who gave the Serbs who came to the house German marks, and the necklaces from around their necks, pressing into their hands even the earrings from the mother's ears, and whose trembling seventeen-year-old son was still taken out behind the house by the armed men.

Pop the Bottle

FRIENDS OF OURS, a couple, were given a bottle of expensive champagne as a wedding present and are planning to open it when they have something to celebrate. It's still on the shelf. They dust it off once a week, along with the china and the bric-a-brac that lines the rest of the shelf. It's stayed there through the births of their children, their anniversaries, the closing of escrow on their house, and the day her biopsy came back benign.

I know why it stays there. I have on my desk a Philip Larkin poem a friend sent me. "Always too eager for the future, we/pick up bad habits of expectancy./ Something is always approaching; every day/ Til then we say,/ Watching from a bluff the tiny, clear,/ Sparkling armada of promises draw near/ . . . We think each one will heave to and unload/ all good into our lives, all we are owed/ For waiting so devoutly and so long."

Waiting for something to celebrate becomes a habit. Thinking that all good is in the past (the good old days) or in the future (when my ship comes in) is a habit. It's an easy enough one to get into — as a child, you wait to grow up. I remember wandering aimlessly around our neighborhood, reading books in the grass, thinking, I don't have to do anything right now, because I'm not a grown-up yet. My life hasn't begun yet.

Waiting becomes a habit. You wait to get taller. Girls wait to get breasts. You wait for your face to clear up, to get your driver's license, to get your own apartment.

When you do grow up and have babies of your own, you wait for them to go to school, so you can get to your real life, which is painting, or running a corporation or restoring Chevys.

And when you're at your real work, you're thinking where it might lead, how if someone buys this company it might get you out of the quagmire that is your life, and you can get a new stove, and $200 shoes and retire to a sun-soaked hamlet in Sonoma, and then you would be happy.

And if you sell your company for 200,000 smackeroos and buy a place with its own apple orchard, then you think, If I can just get the roof of the barn fixed, and get these apple trees pruned and the pond cleaned, then I would be happy.

I know because I am in limbo, somewhere between the good job and the better job, between the first roof owned and the sunsoaked hamlet in Sonoma. Things are going along about as well as could possibly be expected. We're in good health, we have enough money, work we enjoy, friends, trips aboard.

It's not enough, of course. If I could write a book that hit really big, maybe then it would be enough. I think that even though it hasn't been enough for the people I know of who have done that — friends who now stare dismally out the window, wondering if they'll ever be able to write anything as good again, or fretting that the publisher is neglecting them.

Discontent is man's (and woman's) natural condition. We'll always be waiting for that ship that never docks. Essayist Hugh Prather said all any of us can look forward to is a succession of unsolved problems, ambiguous victories and vague defeats.

He did add, though, that we could, in the midst of all that, look forward to some moments of clear peace. Moments like yesterday, when just as I was gloomily recounting some tale or other to Bill on our walk, a man with a green mohawk and wearing a black leather skirt walked by us. "You have to love this town," Bill said, and we both felt better. I left my car out on street sweeping day and didn't get a ticket. I may never see the Grand Canyon in the purple dusk, but I could try not to miss the heartstopping view of my kids quietly doing their homework — a sight worth any number of sunlit gullies.

You can make up your own list. So can our friends with the champagne. Come to that, maybe just having been given an expensive bottle of champagne is sufficient reason for rejoicing.

Or, if not, then a pair of good (and thirsty) friends dropping by.

Pop that bottle.

It's
All
Relative

Confessions of An Only Adult

SOMETIMES I'm asked how it has affected me to come from a large family. This question isn't always posed by a boyfriend reeling from a nightmare family dinner, but sometimes comes from a friend who grew up without brothers and sisters and wonders what he missed.

I don't always know what to answer to this. If I didn't have six brothers and sisters, I'm convinced I'd be pretty much the same person I am.

For example, I'm sure lots of people jump on their own couch yelling "Dibs!" even if they're alone in their apartment. And lots, hearing a crash out in the street, will automatically blurt out, "It wasn't me!" It's pretty normal, I think, to hide your deli sandwich behind the milk in the fridge so that nobody will steal it, even though your closest siblings live fifteen miles away.

Anyway, I know what I missed not being an only child, because here I am an only adult. I know now what it's like to be alone in a house, and I'm very comfortable with that, as long as it's as it is right now, with three girls practicing the Running Man dance in the kitchen, and two little boys clubbing goldfish in the living room to feed them to the new turtle, and the TV and radio blaring and the phone ringing. Otherwise it might seem, you know, a little quiet.

What I don't know is what it would have been like to grow up without all the special moments I remember, like the one when Mickey burst into the house after we'd all been reading about the robbery at a local store and yelled, "Guess what! Mr. Lacy's store was robbed!" To this day, no one in my family can say "Guess what?" without someone else answering, wearily, "Mr. Lacy's store was robbed."

If I had been an only child, I would've missed the sight of Connie walking apart from the rest of us on the way to school, absolutely convinced that everyone would take her for a charming child walking prettily to school by herself, and not one of those rowdy Dalys that she so exactly resembled.

I wouldn't have seen Sean pluck a dead rat out of the electric heater after Dad, Dangerous Dan McGrew, had fainted dead away. Or quick-thinking Connie slap out the lighter-fluid fire on Shannon's leg.

There was the windy afternoon when Adrian rose triumphant on water skis after Dad was about to be disgusted with us all, and the morning when I called up three of Shannon's little girlfriends on the same morning, pretending to be him (I was thirteen, he was eleven, and our voices were identical), and asked them all to go steady. (He had told everybody I was kissing a boy out by the driveway).

Then one day everybody was grown, with his own refrigerator, bathroom and closet, and pretty soon the moments when you actually like being from a large family come closer and closer together, and then there's this payoff.

Instead of six rivals for your mother's attention, you now have six friends you can't lose, six people who knew you at thireen and pretend to take you seriously anyway. They talk to you and tell you what their lives are like.

If you're one of the younger ones, as I am, birth order is finally working in your favor.

By your thirties, you are very glad to have all of them. But you are grown-up now, mature.

Even as you feel a little thrill of joy when you think you're getting sick, because deep down you still think it means a day on the sagging green couch in the kitchen, having mother all to yourself, still you wonder what all the fuss is about.

As if it makes any difference what kind of family you come from.

Problems of Aging: My Tattletale Twin

N O WOMAN should ever be quite accurate about her age," Oscar Wilde said. "It looks so calculating." I couldn't agree more.

Every woman has the right to choose the age she feels comfortable with, rather than tediously counting the number of times the Earth has circled the sun since her birth.

Every woman has the right, that is, except me. I have a twin sister, an extremely pigheaded and uncooperative one, and if we agree on nothing else, we must agree on how old we are.

But we can't.

Tomorrow is my birthday, my 37th. Not to boast, but I think I have accepted the passage of the years with a certain grace, a certain readiness to embrace the blessings of maturity.

I wish I could say the same for Adrian. She is turning 38 tomorrow, and not a bit gracefully. She goes on pathetically shopping for size four jeans in the juniors department, and, sadder still, fitting into them. She pays no attention to the nice powder-blue ladies' polyester suits I try to interest her in.

Most annoying is her pedantic insistence on adding another year to her age, just because a year has passed. If she keeps doing this at the present rate, we'll be forty in two years.

I told her I had decided to stick with 37 for a while, as I was just getting used to it. I said it would look a lot better all around if she did, too.

She said no. She wouldn't budge even when I pointed out that having a twin a year younger was going to be an inconvenience for her. It suggests an inattention to detail.

It also suggests a nightmare labor, which wasn't the case at all.

We were born ten minutes apart, Adrian first. She always said she was the real baby, and I was a kind of backup.

She may have been right, because only one was expected. The

intern at the hospital was heading for bed after delivering Adrian when a sound made him turn in the doorway.

"What're you doing?" he asked. "You just had your kid."

It was 1952, year of siren sheaths, ponytails, hot rods, flying saucer sightings, and "I Like Ike!"

Mother brought us home to Stinson Beach ten days later in a cardboard box. We met our three siblings, Sean, four, Connie, three, and Mickey, two. Mickey piled fourteen blankets on us because "baby cold."

The *Stinson Beach News* wrote Mother up for having five children under the age of five, her mother asked her if she had ever heard of birth control, and the landlord gave us thirty days to get out.

These early trials drew us together. You can't share a cardboard box with someone without feeling something pretty special for them. Go ahead — try it.

We had older sisters — who don't enjoy that term as much as they once did — and eventually a younger one, but being twins was a different feeling.

When I was little, I was convinced that I would expire exactly ten minutes after Adrian. I wondered how it would feel, being alone for those ten minutes, my twin gone. As writer Gregg Levoy commented, others are born separate and must learn intimacy, but twins are born intimate, and must learn separateness.

I don't want to learn too much separateness. On the other hand, I'd like to sneak up on forty a little more gradually.

So there it is. I'm going to miss having a twin, now that Adrian is just another big sister. It was nice, having a companion through life. The best part about it was that no matter how old I got, there she was, my twin, my mirror, getting just as old — and even ten minutes older.

Home Sick And Homesick

THE SAD TRUTH is that there is no point to getting sick when you're a grown-up. You know why? It's because being sick is about you and your mother.

It's not like when you were little. Getting sick then meant a trip to The Couch, the sagging green one. There, propped by pillows and blankets, comforted by your mother's cool hand on your sweaty little brow, you entered an infinitely gentler world, the mysterious one your mother inhabited when everybody was off at school.

In this world, the pace of life slowed down to the buzzing of an insect out in the yard and the sound of your mother clinking glasses as she dried them and put them away. It was a world without brothers and sisters. In this world, Neapolitan ice cream—ice cream someone has made a special trip to the store to buy for you—melts on your tongue, tasting slightly of the metal spoon because you are eating so slowly.

To get to this favored spot, you sometimes had to let your head loll rather obviously on your arms at the kitchen table. Other times, though, your mother would notice you dragging the broom across the floor and ask you tenderly if you felt all right. Once, when the seven of us kids were all hanging around the house, mother said, "Shannon is really sick. Look at his eyes." We all looked at my brother's stupid eyes. They looked fine to us—maybe a little glazed, but wasn't that normal, at least for Shannon?

Ten minutes later, he was installed, grinning, on The Couch in his GI Joe pajamas while mother bent over him adjusting his pillow and the rest of us stood in a hot, jealous knot, watching. Shannon was trying to talk around the thermometer, insisting that he didn't want to miss the math test—all the time cutting his eyes at the rest of us.

Nothing like this happens when you grow up. If you suddenly find yourself wincing at the glare from the computer screen or the roar of the pencil sharpener, you still feel that thrill—"Yippee! I'm sick!"—running like a song underneath the discomfort. But then nothing good happens. Unless your mother happens to be at the neighboring cubicle, there is no one to say, "Gee, honey, you don't look well. You better lie down."

Without that solicitous hand on your forehead, there is no one to confirm that you are really sick. Already miserable, you now have to feel like a goldbricker, telling your boss you're not feeling well when you look the same as always, and it's a nice sunny day outside, possibly on a Friday, maybe even the day before a three-day weekend, and how is he to know that you're not making it up? So you skulk out, with everybody wondering where you are really going. You stop at the corner store to stock up on aspirin and soda, and then stagger sulkily around your apartment for the rest of the day, washing up the dishes or staring blearily at the bookshelves. You're dizzy and the colors in the room hurt your eyes, but you still wonder whether you should mop the floor or something, as long as there is no one to see how sick you are anyway.

Mothers cut right through that. "What are you doing up?" they say, drying their hands on their aprons, hustling you back into your warm covers. "Now you stay here. I'll bring you some ice cream." You want your mother, and no one else will do. Boyfriends say, "Oh, sweetie, that's too bad," and offer to pick up something from the drugstore, but they always forget.

Children are even worse. All children live in fear that someone else will think of getting sick before they do. As I lay in a pool of wretchedness on the couch, explaining to my daughter Morgan, ten, that I had to come home sick, she pointed out that her own stomach had not stopped hurting for a whole week, and nobody let *her* come home. "I'm so sick I'm sweating air," she said. Then she asked if I would make her a sandwich.

It is beginning to dawn on me that now when I get sick, I am just sick. Not special, just sick. Once childhood is past, there is no sagging green couch, no pot-bellied stove, no brothers and sisters to wheedle a bite of your Neapolitan, no mom to insist that you stay home with her. There is no point in getting sick at all, anymore, unless it really is a sunny Friday and you want to beat the crowds up to the lake.

Memory Is as Elusive as an Old Turkey

I'VE BEEN READING a lot lately — maybe you have, too — about recovered memories. People are accusing their relatives of hideous crimes, all on the basis of this fragile instrument we call memory.

I was thinking about this because I happened to be talking to some of my family about the turkey we had as a pet when I was little. We lived out in Lagunitas in West Marin then, in a ramshackle house on its own acre of land.

Dad had bought a turkey to slaughter for dinner because they were cheaper than frozen ones. I remember peeping into the washroom and seeing the bird as it lay on Dad's grease-stained pants in the washroom, looking at him out of one bright eye. He couldn't bring himself to kill it, and finally it escaped out a window and hid in the hydrangeas.

"That never happened," my brother Shannon said over the phone from the lumber company he manages in San Rafael. "Dad strung that turkey upside down from the ceiling and pulled its head off with a come-along."

"Are you sure?" I said. I was remembering how that turkey used to come right into the kitchen for crusts of toast in the mornings.

"I was standing right there," Shannon insisted. "Dad had a steel gear strung from a wire, and he'd pull it back over and over, trying to hit the turkey. He missed a couple of times and hit his own knee."

I called Dad in Fairfax. He said, "The man at the turkey farm told me it's a bugger to clean those things. He said to get a big darning needle and take ahold of the turkey's head and drive this object into his eye and he'll instantaneously release his feathers. I tried to do that with a carpenter's awl, but I could not do it. So I hustled it outside and whacked its head off with an ax in the time-honored way."

I called my sister Mickey in Idaho. She's two years older than I am, and would surely remember that we kept that turkey as a pet. Grandma embroidered a blue collar for him.

Mickey said Dad whacked the turkey in the freezer room. I didn't remember any freezer room. "Was that where the washing machine was?" I said.

"What washing machine?" Mick said.

"You know, in the room right behind the potbellied stove."

"We didn't have a potbellied stove," she said. "Anyway, the freezer was in that screened-in area behind Dad and Mom's room. Remember the day they went to the city and left us with the Wilson boy? They brought us all back presents, and I got a ring from Chinatown that I hid in the freezer so Connie wouldn't get it. I never saw it again."

I couldn't reach my older brother Sean in Washington, and Robin, the youngest, wasn't even born yet, so I called my sister Connie at her consignment store in Salt Lake City. She's three years older than I am. She'd know about the turkey who used to follow us out to the mailbox and cock his head wistfully at us as we headed down the road to school.

"What turkey?" Connie said when she picked up the phone. "We never had a turkey." She also said she wasn't the one who swiped Mickey's ring out of the freezer.

"Of course we had a turkey," my twin sister, Adrian, said when I reached her at the civil court in Ukiah where she works. "Dad killed it in the side porch room where the freezer was. It was making a lot of racket and Mom told him to go wring its neck. He didn't want to, but he did it."

I reached Mother in San Rafael as she was packing for a trip to New York. "There was never any live turkey in our house, ever," she said.

I really don't know what any of them is talking about. We had that turkey for years. It finally died of old age and we buried it down by the goat pen.

Face to Face In the Bathroom

ORGAN IS standing in the shower fully clothed, claiming the shower. Patrick, who had no interest in the bathroom until the second his sister went in there, swipes her outfit and hides it somewhere in the house.

I wander into the bathroom to do something about all the yelling, and instead feel a sudden yearning to linger at the mirror and fiddle with my hair.

It seems to be a fact of life: A bathroom is not worth a second glance unless someone else wants it, badly. It's only then that you realize that your happiness depends on your getting into the bathroom right now and locking everybody else out.

I discovered this early, back in our family home in Lagunitas. We had one tiny bathroom at the end of the house, and seven fanatically modest Irish children, each one of whom would go to pieces if someone so much as saw their ankles.

We always locked the door. A door that was merely closed was a sign that said, "Come on in and catch me doing something intensely private." Not that it helped that much. Right after you managed to sprint into the bathroom and slammed home the bolt, the furious pounding started.

"Who's in there? What are you doing in there? I need the bathroom right now!"

What you were doing in there, a lot of the time, was finding out that the toothpaste tube was empty and the only roll of toilet paper lay like a half-submerged island in a puddle by the tub. Like many relief agencies, mother believed that her job ended with getting supplies to the troubled area. It was up to us to get the toilet paper from the kitchen to the bathroom. We couldn't, though, because when we were in the kitchen we didn't need toilet paper and when we were in the bathroom we were in no condition to stroll to the kitchen.

You could, in theory, ask the person waiting outside to get you some toilet paper. This seldom worked, though. The impatient sister outside the door would always remember that no one ever got *her* anything when *she* needed it. A brother would be reminded of injustices and slights going back to when he was six and no one would help him drag his wagon up the steps.

Even when you were done scraping off the top of the soaked toilet roll and standing on the toothpaste tube, you were reluctant to leave the bathroom. In a crowded house, it was the only place you could be truly alone, truly face to face with yourself.

The bathroom was, for us, associated with the intense rumination that comes with growing up. You learned to put on a bra there, said speeches to the mirror, pulled your skin tight against the bone to see what you'd look like if you lost ten pounds, prayed that the gods would smite down Debbie Richmond.

You experimented with Nair and Noxzema, tried to figure out if your period was overdue, tried on clothes. You came to terms with yourself in the bathroom, learned to do what you could with what you had and with the one wet towel the previous occupant left you.

Then you grew up, and it became just another room, the one with the sink and the shower and all that. You could get into it pretty much whenever you liked. It was no longer a refuge, a haven, a fine and private place.

But it remained a place for coming to terms with yourself, for holding a hair up and deciding that the lighting was making it look gray, a place for learning to shrug off the wrinkles and sags, which could also be a trick of the light. It remains the place where you come to fiddle with your hair while listening to the radio and to the comforting sounds of your own children pounding heatedly on the door, asking what on earth you're doing in there.

Siblinghood Is Powerful

O NE OF THE world's most succinct pieces of advice comes from a book on how to avoid sibling rivalry. "Have only one child," it says.

Last night Patrick, eleven, told Morgan, thirteen, that her outfit — Santa Claus boxer shorts over gray sweat pants — was "fingernails on a blackboard."

She stole his red blanket, then accused him of not caring about anything or anybody when he demanded it back. Ten minutes later he bought an ice cream at the store, pretended there were more in the fridge, and grabbed her place on the couch when she got up.

Each of them resents every mouthful of food the other eats, every stitch of clothing he owns, the very air the other breathes.

I used to tell them that it was impossible to be absolutely equal all the time, but that when they were 21 and each added up everything I had ever given them or done for them, every quarter for the bus, every pair of roller skates, they would find it was equal.

They actually bought that.

I thought I was doing Morgan a favor when I gave her another child to grow up with. I even made it a point to have them close together.

I should have remembered from my own childhood that a sibling is another rank weed to fight with for sun and water.

I had six brothers and sisters, and we had no more regard for one another than puppies in a litter. Everything they got was something I didn't get. Every smile at one child was an arrow in a sibling's heart. After Sean was born, my parents had four girls in a row in an attempt to provide him with a brother, and when Shannon finally came along Sean did his best to enlarge the room they shared by using Shannon's head as a battering ram.

Connie, born second, was presented ten months later with a nice sister to play with. She drew a yellow line across the floor of the room she shared with Mickey and dared her to cross it. Just the sight of Mickey's blond curls made Connie pull more stuffing out of the mattress they shared.

I was never what you would call friends with any of them. Connie was cranky, rolling her hair in Minute Maid cans behind a locked door. Sean and Mickey were too old to talk to me, Shannon and Robin were too young for me to talk to them.

Even Adrian, my twin, was a mystery to me, locked away in her own world, as I was locked away in mine. I had no idea what she was like, what she was afraid of, or what she thought of me. I knew that she liked Lorna Doones and could run faster than anyone else in the third grade, and that later mother was always trying to get her to pose for pictures in her bathing suit, even when I was already posed winningly on my towel, trying to get her attention.

Then we all grew up. Connie and Mickey still don't talk to each other. The yellow line is now the state border between Idaho and Utah. I don't see much of my brothers, though I wish I did. But I have four sisters.

They'll still be here when my parents are gone and my children have families of their own. We will still be on the phone to one another every day, checking in with one another as we move through life.

He doesn't know it now, but Patrick is going to like having a sister. And Morgan is going to like having a brother.

They'll come together to visit me when I'm a wheezing old thing in the rest home, and I'll give them their lists of every single thing they ever got from me. They'll see that it was equal, for at the top of his list it'll say, "A Sister," and at the top of hers, "A Brother."

An Unremarkable Life

A WOMAN CALLED ME yesterday to ask me to write about my mother. "How come you never talk about your Mom?" she demanded to know. I tried to explain to her that it's just that my mother has never done anything all that remarkable.

I wouldn't know what to write about, wouldn't know where to begin, really, unless it was back in Stinson Beach in 1951, when Mom and Dad lived in a $50-a-month cottage. They already had three kids, Sean, Connie and Mickey, and she was pregnant again.

I have carbons of letters she wrote to friends, like the one that begins, "Gaining weight like mad, sleep all the time. Not flat-chested anymore. He should be born around the 14th of January."

The next letter begins, "Twins are all paid for, now have to get a safe secondhand car." She tells about having been written up in the *Stinson Beach News* for having five children under the age of five, then goes on cheerfully to describe how she was washing dishes in the bathtub because the sink was broken and Dad hadn't got around to fixing it: "The youngsters think it's enormously funny."

Dad had been out of work for weeks — the carpenters were striking for fifteen cents more an hour — but Mother wrote about how beautiful the weather was.

"Don't have a buggy, so have the twins in a banana box with another box for sunshades, then put the box in the kids' wagon and off we go to the beach. Works fine."

The next letter reports they've been asked to move: "Too many kids." It didn't help that a diaper had gone down the toilet, and the landlord had had to expose pipe after pipe in the back yard before he found it.

When Shannon was born two years later, mother had tuberculosis. The baby was taken away, the kids parceled out to foster homes, and Dad took Sean, six, who was TB-positive but not infectious.

Mother still recalls with fondness her lovely rest in the sanitorium, reading books all day long, eating meals someone else had cooked. Years later, when people asked her why she had all those kids, she would say, "I was making friends."

When everybody was well again, we moved to Lagunitas, buying an old shingle house on a half acre with a creek running through it.

Sometimes I would sit in my desk at Lagunitas School, staring out the window at the poppies on the hillside, and pretend that someone had come in and told me that my mother was dead.

I did it because it felt so good to open my eyes and tell myself that she was fine, that when I got off the bus and walked into the yard, she would be there, hanging out the wash, reading her book on the porch swing, listening to Doris Day singing, "Whatever will be, will be" on our phonograph. It seemed to be our theme song.

Years later, when Dad quit his shilly-shallying with the question and finally took off, mother did what anybody would do — pawned his tools and stuck us all in a matinee for safekeeping while she went out to find us all a new place to live.

During all this she was pregnant with Robin, the seventh friend. She found a job at the Elks Club, and was eventually made manager, though it was a men's club.

We never went hungry, never spent a night in juvenile hall. Mother finished raising us pretty much as she had begun — without Dad's help. If she ever felt that raising seven kids was not always, every minute, what she wanted to be doing with her life, she didn't let on.

She had simply done what women do.

Turkey Is Nothing Without Seasoning

THIS IS THE time of year when the red-faced, sweating cook brushes the bangs out of his eyes with the back of a flour-covered hand and desperately consults turkey recipes, trying to make the dry old bird as palatable as possible. Two small turkeys or one big one? Fresh? Frozen? Free-range? Meat thermometer or juices running clear?

No one struggles with such questions in March, or in August, even though you can have turkey any time of year. I see its fat bluish-white legs there in the cold case at Safeway, cheaper and more nutritious than chicken. As far as I can tell, nobody gives it a second look.

Only at Thanksgiving and Christmas do we have the ingredients for a turkey dinner: the right proportion of family arguments, jokes, laughter, affection, stifled resentments, unsolicited advice, the frayed nerves of a long car drive, the pleasure of seeing people we have missed.

Turkey is the perfect staple for the holidays. Essentially tasteless in itself, it picks up all the seething flavors in the room, from Uncle Ned's fit of the giggles to Great-Grandma's secret plan to disinherit everyone to your brother's playing "House of the Rising Sun" on his battered guitar.

What the turkey tastes like depends on where you are and whom you're with. One year I got mixed up about what Thanksgiving was. I thought it was a big meal in Marin with my family, and I wasn't in the mood for that. I told them my car had a flat tire; I also told the people I lived with I didn't want to go out with them to dinner.

I stayed home alone, feeling worse by the minute. My roommates brought me back a plateful of turkey and trimming. It was succulent and tender and delicately flavored, and still it was so tasteless I couldn't choke it down.

Nothing was missing, yet everything was.

The essential flavoring seems to be family, whether blood ties or with people you care about so much that you squabble like real relatives. This year my family's going to my sister Adrian's in Ukiah, a hundred miles to the north.

Everybody will arrive in a different mood, and the turkey slumbering in the oven will pick up a little of each, the flavor becoming more complex with each ringing of the doorbell.

As we talk about gang-dyeing Adrian's hair, figure out where to have Christmas, gossip about whoever's not there, and say please and thank you and would you like more wine, every emotion in the room will float through the warm air of the overcrowded kitchen to be absorbed by the secret turkey in the oven.

It's not just the flavors. Even the ingredients change from year to year. In my family, this year's ingredients include Neil, the new man in Adrian's life. We know he'll fit in because he got thrown in the creek at Mom's birthday party in August and was a sport about it.

This turkey will be seasoned with thoughts of my brother Sean, who is ill, and the two sisters who live up north.

Then we'll all sit down and devour in minutes what it took days to prepare, the steaming hot turkey, the fragrant stuffing, pumpkin and mince pies, washed down with beer and wine and sparkling cider and coffee.

The turkey will taste of everything, of Mother's mood and Morgan's plea for a driving lesson, Shannon's piano-playing, Robin's jokes, the absence of the older kids. It'll taste of whoever's turn it is to be mad, of the unspoken love and lingering rivalry and the thousand other connections that bring us together again every year.

The next day the turkey leftovers will once again be just food. You'll mix it with mayonnaise, add lettuce and tomato and minced scallions, layer it on warm, freshly baked bread, and still it'll never taste again the way it will today, with everybody at the table.

A Happy Land of Pot And Poly-Fidelity

M Y WRETCHED sister Adrian, who already lives a hundred miles away in Ukiah, is moving twenty miles farther north to Willits, a little (population 5,000) town on top of a ridge, reportedly the highest point on Highway 101 between Mexico and Canada, to live with her new boyfriend.

Bill and I drove up from the city on New Year's Eve to go to the hot event that night in Willits, the Madhatter's Ball at the community center.

I thought Ukiah was remote, but at least it has exits off the freeway: In Willits the highway threads right through town, past the fast-food places. People speak of "parcels" instead of acres or lots, and directions to most houses start with "turn off the paved road" and involve combination locks.

A lot of hippies have come up here. I was told that there are proportionately more Ph.D.s in Willits than anywhere else in California, but I doubt that's a fact in Willits' favor.

We all trooped across the street to the dance, wearing our funny hats. We ran into a woman, blond, about 27, who introduced her two husbands, two slender, gentle men who looked to be in their late 40s.

She said the three of them live on a "parcel" about 30 miles out of town. Their arrangement (one we were told is fairly common in Willits) is called a "poly-fidelity group." Even their food is communal: They and their neighbors order it in on pallets from an outfit in Grass Valley that dumps it behind the post office.

The seven-piece Zairian band Samba Ngo was playing a kind of music called "soukous" that translates into "having a good time." An alarm clock sat on every table, set to go off at midnight. Even the local internist was decked out in confetti and dancing wildly among the tables.

When Adrian and I cut across the dance floor to get to our table, she told me to slow down my walk.

"Everybody will know you're not from Willits," she said, as if that were a bad thing.

222

But she meant it. Bill and I, being known to be up from the city, were regarded with a kind of compassion by those we were introduced to, especially when we said we lived right in the middle of San Francisco.

"It's pretty crazy down there, isn't it?" said one man.

Yes, it's a den of iniquity, we thought, as we watched the woman with two husbands (who had said they were getting up at 9 a.m. for a four-hour yoga intensive) knocking back Jack Daniel's mixed cocktails, a popular drink despite the wide availability of high-octane local grass. (People with no visible means of support here — that is, pot growers — are known as "carpenters.")

We left early on New Year's Day because we had two parties to go to back in the city. Adrian was lounging on the couch when we left, looking forward to a day of doing nothing. "We might go for a walk later," she said, and her boyfriend confirmed it: They were definitely going to go for a walk later.

It's nice that Adrian keeps meeting men who live in towns I've never even been to. Travel is so broadening.

Without her I'd never get to a place like Willits, where so many people have found exactly what they were looking for, bucolic peacefulness in a place where you can shoot off your gun without hitting your neighbor.

In Willits the Safeway doubles as the country club, you have a choice of salt or brewer's yeast on your popcorn at the Noyo movie theater, and the prosperous gardening store deals almost exclusively in drip systems.

It's enough to make you think, really, about your own choices.

The hills were a beautiful soft brown as we drove south on 101, toward the bright lights, putting the car on cruise control and listening to "Tales of the City" on a book tape, and fantasizing about moving to Manhattan.

Thicker Than Water, Thinner Than Air

I T WAS Connie's idea that the seven of us kids all meet somewhere this year for the weekend and talk about the past, meaning our childhood out on Lagunitas Road in West Marin in the '50s and '60s.

I told her idea to my sister Adrian, who thought it sounded like fun, and we suggested to Con that we meet in Ashland, Ore., which is fairly close to everybody (Mickey in Idaho, Sean in Washington, Connie in Utah and us four "little" kids in California), and which has Shakespeare plays we could go to when the talks, inevitably, ended in a fight.

"That won't work," Connie said in her finest this-is-the-way-it-is tone when I called her back. "We need to be isolated, take a house on a beach somewhere, so we can really work on the issues. And people would have to promise not to drink."

Except that she didn't say "drink," she said people would have to promise not to "take refuge in their addictions." I suggested to Connie that she couldn't control the get-together like that; it wouldn't work. When it comes to getting them to do anything they don't want to do, my siblings are about as cooperative as cats. I could just see my brothers crossing two states to listen to Connie drag them through "the issues."

"I'm not trying to control anything," Connie retorted. "These are just my terms."

So there went the retreat. But it isn't just Connie who made it a doomed enterprise: We are all consumed by our private stubbornnesses, our resentments carried over from one year's accounts to the next. I haven't totally forgiven Shannon for pointing out at a family breakfast when I was a teenager that if Johnny hadn't sneaked upstairs the night before, why was my nightgown on inside out?

Talking to Connie, hearing her slip away again, I was reminded of what I've noticed before about families: Not everything can be fixed by talking. Not every lapsed family connection is a misunderstanding. Sometimes differences are intractable. Sometimes a person is born into the wrong family, an apple born into a family of oranges.

Yet the connection remains, beneath the failure of words to resolve anything. This retreat won't happen, yet I see the seven of us, more and more, drawing together. When Sean was sick, Shannon, Robin and Adrian flew up to see him. Shannon and Robin just bought a horse together, riding it on alternate days.

In an even more bizarre development, Mickey is writing to Connie, her arch-enemy from the crib, the one who drew a yellow line down the middle of the room they shared and dared her ever to cross it. Connie is writing back. The two of them have, taking wildly different roads, come to the same place: Both take in and resell secondhand clothes, although Connie takes in only the best, like the Patagonia brand, and Mickey's less particular, because she's a skilled seamstress and can fix anything.

When we were kids, we were once down on the road, helping some neighbor kids pummel Shannon for some offense, when Mother came barreling down from the house above, furious, to pick Shannon up by the scruff of his neck and then wheel on us accusingly. "He's your brother," she said. "He's your brother."

I don't think any of us ever forgot that.

I haven't forgotten, either, a rainy afternoon when we were kids. We seemed to be worried that afternoon, I no longer remember about what, and were tying the four corners of our blankets together to the underside of Mickey's top bunk and then trying to crawl into them.

Everybody else's cocoons held — Connie tied hers so firmly that we later had to cut the blanket away — but mine was a disaster; it kept coming undone, and I sat on the bunk and cried in frustration.

Somebody helped me then, Adrian maybe, or perhaps Connie, rushing to my aid with such enthusiasm that she accidentally on purpose knocked Mickey over the side, and I crawled in, warm and safe, in our cocoon town.

The Familial Mystique

W E ALL HAVE this tender idea of them: Other People's Families. They all vacation together at the same condo at Lake Tahoe in July every year. They don't quarrel, or if they do their quarrels are lighthearted affairs, over who was supposed to be stirring the soup. The kids tease each other good-naturedly but are there for each other in the clinches. Nobody's ever screaming to get into the bathroom.

When I was growing up, I was in awe of OPFs — especially the Wilsons down the road, who, my mother liked to point out, kept their rooms neat and clean and never talked back to their mother.

Back then I thought I was in love with blue-eyed Rodney, the smartest boy in the third grade, but now I think I actually had a crush on his mother. She was like a TV mom, always seeming to hover in the background, wearing neatly ironed pedal pushers, waiting to learn what Rodney might like to do or have next.

My own refrigerator, back at the house I shared with two parents, two dogs and six brothers and sisters, was an open window, as far as my chances of ever again seeing what I put in it were concerned.

Any food that came into the house was devoured on the spot by the big kids, and we little kids snapped and growled at the edges of the feast, trying for at least a folded-over sandwich made of the left-over egg salad. Sometimes the seven of us had giggling fits at the table and were all sent to bed right in the middle of dinner.

Other families didn't do that, I knew. Being a member of my family was like my own insides: full of strange weirdnesses and embarrassments, a pervading sense of not being like other people. So I was pleased, upon growing up, to discover how screwed up not only some of other people's families are but how screwed up they all are.

I liked hearing about the spectacular tantrums over the morning toast, the icy resentments over a car borrowed and returned with the gas tank empty ten years ago, the letter from Dad carried unopened in a pocket for eight months by the guilty son, the promises made impulsively and broken deliberately — in short, the roiling stew of regret, misunderstanding, jealousy, fury and love that is the result every time you pack two or more people into one house, stir and then add twenty years.

Bill, for example, comes from a nice family of four kids, and his parents are still together, living up in Oakmont. He and his siblings grew up in a white house in a neat suburb in Massachusetts and seem to have walked out of a Hallmark card. They all hug each other and everything. News flash: They're as nice a family as you will ever meet, but they fight.

They don't tell us this about other people's families. One of the habits of my own, when we get together, is to make casual references to how awful we are. "Oh, I hate this family," one of us will say.

And, of course, we'll be right. On any given day someone will not be speaking to someone else, someone will be feeling guilty and a third person will be secretly promising himself that he will erase our freeway exits from his mind.

But on the same day, someone will be relieved and happy just because her sister found exactly the right dress for her wedding. The brother who resolved to leave the family will, of course, take off work for a family get-together. A sister whose purse clanks with stolen ashtrays will send another sister $1,000 just to cheer her up.

And yet it never seems to occur to us that our degree of obsession with one another and one another's affairs — the very idea that one sister is furious because another hasn't called — means that we have a close, typical, normal, all-American family.

In Search of a Father

An Uneasy Member Of The Wedding

I HAVEN'T TOLD my dad yet about my getting married again. He tends to take a sardonic view of these events. "We should have a justice of the peace in the family," he says. "We can use the money, too."

Dad is in any event a dangerous element to introduce to an affair one hopes will go perfectly. Asking him to a carefully planned formal event might be uncomfortably like introducing a gun in the first act of a play: You fully expect the gun to go off before the curtain comes down.

When I got married last time, back in 1976, I needed someone to give me away. Somebody like, well, my father.

I knew right where to find him. He was living in a car in Forest Knolls.

My mother was understanding. She said, "Invite your father, and you can count me out."

I pleaded, and after holding out for days she relented, saying she would come "as long as it's understood that he is definitely not to join the reception line."

A few days later I drove out to the valley to the ranch where Dad parked his car. I bounced twice around the ranch's rutted circular driveway, past barns, corrals and horses flicking their tails in the heat, before I noticed, deep in a corner, an old green station wagon with a lazy curl of smoke rising from a hole cut through its roof.

"Well, Dare," Dad said, coming out to meet me when he heard the car. He wore the usual worn brown pants and nondescript Bargain Box shirt. "What's shaking?" He had been staring down the barrel of a lonely Sunday afternoon, and here I was.

"I'm getting married," I told him, as I accepted a steaming cup of instant coffee and balanced it awkwardly on my knee. "I want you to give me away." Behind us, a potbellied stove occupied the space where the back seat had been. Further back was a jumble of paper-backs, blankets, two guitars and a typewriter.

We hadn't talked all that much in the years since he'd left the family. I wasn't sure what I wanted from him then, except that I was getting married, and wanted to include him.

It wasn't his first wedding. As we kids — seven of us — started to grow up and get married, he liked to come back from wherever he was to accept everybody's congratulations for the fine family he'd raised.

Dad showed up on time, dressed, for the first time I could remember, in a jacket and tie. Bedlam reigned at the site. The cake, made by a friend, had melted in the hot June sun, the caterer had a flat tire on the Richmond Bridge, and the bride had managed to spill champagne and orange juice all down the front of her dress, so that she had to clutch her corsage for hours longer than was usual.

Dad sat in a corner, chain-smoking as if he were going to the gas chamber. Jim explained to him that the rules forbade smoking, then added, to Dad's astonishment, "As long as you aren't doing anything, I wonder if you'd mind helping to arrange the flowers."

Dad did not help with the flowers, but he did, right after the ceremony, take his place in the reception line on my right and began shaking hands with the guests who came through. My mother stood shaking hands on the other side of my husband, a much better sport about it all than she had to be.

The gun never did go off. Hours into the wedding, Dad came up to me, his glass empty and his tie askew, to say, "Dare, I was planning to make a shambles of your wedding, but I'm having too much fun."

Negotiations Leading To a Lasting Peace

My DAD has popped up again. He's gone back to the Mohave Desert, this time in a little white van he swapped his truck for. He's figured out how to rig up a stove in it, one that runs on the mesquite fuel he collects in the wire basket of his bicycle.

It amuses him, this image of a geezer gathering firewood. He's been doing his best impersonation of an Irish drunk for most of his life, playing his role with zeal, and now at 69 he's impersonating an old man.

Instead of dismay at his deterioration, he feels a new tenderness toward the apparition he sees in the mirror, this derelict with blue-veined legs, weak shoulders and dimming eyesight.

"The more ghastly I become," he writes me, "the more I overflow, wanting to throw my arms around that haggard creep in the mirror."

He thinks I should throw my arms around that haggard creep, too. "I ran back and embraced my father before it was too late," he says pointedly, speaking of the man who sent Dad to stay with relatives and who sat in the kitchen day after day, drinking Brown Derby beer and reading Wild West magazines. It wasn't until he went to the desert that Dad forgave his father, not so much for the abandonment as for the choice of reading matter.

I can't do the same, not yet. I'm not old enough to forgive my father, for all he did and all he left undone. I'm still in the middle of it all, the life and confusion and noise. I still judge him, with a child's harsh standards.

I never thought he'd get old at all, this guy who spent his life dumping cars in the ditch, going on epic drunks, burning down the family homestead and hightailing it to Mexico. He was the kind who dies early, smelling of beer, in the emergency room of a large city hospital, far from the homes of his angry, jilted children.

But he stopped drinking, and he's doing it by himself out there, forgiving himself for what can't be changed, those long-ago images: children left in a car while he went off to play the slot machines, packing boxes, the woman he left to raise seven children alone.

Like all of us, he has before him only this moment, and then the next. He's filling those moments exactly the way he wants to, reading books and writing a journal by the light of the desert sun. He scribbles insults and then sends them to me, trying to goad me into rising above the bitter warfare of father and child.

I read those insults, back in my city apartment, and get mad all over again, scratching, "Do I have to stand for this?" in the margin.

But he goes on trying to reach me, even at the cost of driving off his only reader. We're both as stubborn as they come, but we're stuck with each other. That's our starting point. The rest is whatever grudging understanding we manage to work out, with both of us trying.

Once, as we drove away from my father's truck, me choking over something he'd said, my sister exclaimed, "Why do you keep trying? What has he ever done for you to care about him?"

I shrugged, thinking, "He's my father. They only come one to a customer. How can you not try?"

A man I know carried a letter from his father around for eight months, afraid to open it. He never put it in a drawer — he had to have it near him, for that moment when he was so up that not even his father could bring him down. I don't know if he ever opened it, but I know he never threw it away.

He was trying.

Personal Tests, Meant to Be Failed

ON THE 21st of March, I got a letter from my long-silent father in the Mojave Desert. He had, months ago, stopped sending me his writings: he prefers an imaginary reader, one expansive and wide-ranging, to one who "skims for personal themes" and then tosses the paper aside.

In the letter, Dad says he needs a carriage spring for his portable Royal Mercury typewriter. Could I send it to him before he leaves at the end of the month?

Dad has sent me on holy quests before. He's needed a chimney lamp of a type they don't make anymore, a sample of Robert Penn Warren's handwriting, a piece for the lathe he was hand-machining.

Once he wanted me to find and send him an old manual typewriter. I sent the money for one instead — he was then in Reno, the pawnshop capital of the world — and he sent the money order back by return mail. I had missed the point.

Dad's not happy with me. "You handle me like a stage prop," he says. "But if you take only what interests you, you may exclude the key that might have made me less villainous."

Reading that, I nod. I unroll those taped-together yellow pages and read fast, breathlessly, as if there is something in particular I want to know.

And, true enough, I take only what interests me — I strip-mine his pages for lumps of coal I can use to build my own fires. That's how reading works.

For all I know, Dad may be right when he maintains I want him to be, as he puts it, "one of those jolly daddies who forsake the bottle and take to the pen, wearing the trappings of slightly faded scholarliness." Maybe I would prefer a jolly daddy to the irascible old reprobate who fulminates in the desert, cocking a scornful eye at my growing pile of worldly goods and saying, "Follow me, if you dare."

The fact remains: I read, faithfully, every line he sends me. Even the scrawled yellow pages that arrive when the desert grit gets into the typewriter and breaks the carriage spring. Every line.

He wants more. "Get over your childhood tremors. It's about time you held up your share of the load, helped me to understand what I'm about. I run on moonbeams, which won't do. I can't operate on my own — even the Lone Ranger cried himself to sleep every night."

I could redeem myself with the desert-going Lone Ranger, I suppose. As in the fairy tales of old, I could have accepted this mission, saddled my horse like faithful Tonto, and plunged into the byways and back shops of the city until the hour when I emerged, dusty but triumphant, with precisely the right carriage spring.

But he didn't give me enough time. Even if I had managed to track the part down, and tried to Fed Ex it, I doubt if Federal Express would be willing to roam the desert in search of a little white van with my scowling father at the wheel.

Not that I broke my neck to try to get it to him, or anything. A short sprint through the Yellow Pages, a few calls to typewriter repair shops that had no interest in selling tiny parts, and I gave up.

"Humor thy father," you say, but it isn't just my father. Everybody seems to have his own little test. If you love me, cook for me. Quit your job. Don't wear that tie. Find me a carriage spring. Forgive me my trespasses.

Tests are made to be failed. That's their nature. All you can do is elect not to take them in the first place.

We are coming to the end of something, he and I.

Dad's Come Home To Roost

U H-OH. Dad's back. A friend of his gave me Dad's new address, an apartment in Fairfax. An apartment. We kids, long used to trading rumors about where Dad is parked, will have to get used to new phrases:

"Are you going over to Dad's? What's Dad's address?"

It's the end of an era.

I shouldn't assume that you know the whole story. Dreams of the open road have always plagued my father, but for most of his life, the closest he came to realizing them was the series of cars and trailers he lived in after he left the family, when he was still working as a carpenter.

Then six years ago, just as he was running out of work, Dad discovered he was eligible for Social Security. A man who until that minute had worked for every dime, he sat turning that first check over and over in his hands.

Then he gave away everything he owned and headed down the blue lines on the California map. On the back of his wheezing old green panel 1953 bakery truck, he hung a bright little black and gold sign: NO SOLICITING. That truck was his way of telling everybody to go to hell.

He parked on desert reaches or forest glades, with only a lazy swirl of smoke marking where he was. He was free, and doing what more than one man or woman has lain awake dreaming of doing. The drinking that had blasted his middle years ended by a sour stomach. He returned to his earliest addiction, the word. All day he sat either reading or tapping away at a thrift store typewriter, shoulders hunched against the desert chill, in front of what he called his picture window. When he needed a human voice, he dialed in the sputtering of far-off radio farm programs.

"Town Day!" he'd write in his journal once a week, and he and his little black and white dog, Fred, would make the trek to the nearest hamlet, where they'd load up on bananas, dog food, milk and secondhand books.

Dad always had dogs, even when I was little. "Living for extended periods of time with nothing wagging its tail at the sound of your voice is dangerous," he says. The rest of his social life was provided by the cops who dropped by the driver's window to discuss the vagrancy laws with him, and, in a roundabout way, by me.

I never knew my father before he went to the desert. His appearance in my life since my teens had been brief and explosive, like a bird that flies into a classroom and beats its wings frantically against the wall before finding an open window.

But this was a comfortable distance for us, Irish daughter and Irish father. I raged at him, judged him, trolled his pages for mention of my own name, stole his best lines for my own newspaper column. He flung back insults from every hamlet in the state.

It was kind of fun.

We'll have to work out something new now, he and I. His odyssey ended by degrees: a warrant or two floating around a couple of years ago (if anybody asks, he's in Montana) made him decide not to renew his driver's license, and he settled in Mendocino, in a trailer on someone's land. He doesn't like accepting favors but had no choice: He had discovered on his travels that the frontier is really gone, that someone owns every square foot of the continent now, and if you don't have your own place you're trespassing.

I haven't seen him or his place yet. I have an idea he's not thrilled with his new circumstances. Maybe it's time to remind Dad of something else he discovered in the desert: that whatever you're looking for, you'd better have at least the beginnings of it with you before you set out.

I never thought he needed that old truck to raise hell.

The Library's Full of Strange Encounters

NOW THAT the new library is up and running, everybody hereabouts has a San Francisco Main Library story, and I'm no exception.

In 1973 I was 21, living in a $100-a-month studio apartment on Polk Street, majoring in English at San Francisco State. I ate at the U.S. restaurant in North Beach with my gay friend Loyal, drank Marsala at the Caffe Sport, flirted with my English teachers, drank black coffee and Dubonnet. Thin, elegant Loyal had the apartment on one side of me; across the hall lived Pierre, a hugely fat, sweet, retired man who had worked at Hills Brothers coffee all his life. I would often end the day sitting at Pierre's table.

I was so 21. I wore green velvet caps and green cords, made lists of the men I had slept with (I called such episodes "affairs"), read books like *Jacob's Room,* by Virginia Woolf, smoked English cigarettes, got food stamps, had my teeth fixed at the University of Pacific's free clinic. And I went often to the main library, a straight six-block shot down Polk street. I was, of course, lonesome, though I never would have admitted it. I am sure I was feeling lonely that day, walking in the rain down to the library to find another difficult English major-y book to read. And there he was, studying the rows of fiction on the second floor: the father I had not seen in years, hearing only rumors of where he was, what he was doing.

"Dad," I said, and he turned.

"Well, I'll be damned." He was a grizzled 52, wrapped in a gray jacket and old brown corduroy pants, and the smell of tobacco clung comfortingly to him, as always. He had a stack of books to check out, just as I did. We compared notes, and to our shock discovered he lived around the corner from me, in a residence hotel on Bush Street.

The next day, I visited him in his room, filled with junk and library books stacked under a reading lamp, and asked him if he wanted to walk across the Golden Gate Bridge — in those days I was full of wanting to do things I had never done — and we walked all the way to Mill Valley, where I left him at the 2 A.M. Club, a dive on the main street into town. When I look back, I realize that meeting in the library was our road back to each other. And it wasn't incidental: We were reunited by our shared excitement over books, just as we've stayed connected through our shared hypergraphia — the rage to scribble.

From then on, even after he and I both moved separately back to Marin, I would go out to see him, in whatever car and on whatever hillside he was living, slide into the front seat and accept the cup of coffee he brewed on the stove where the back seat had been. He always wanted to talk about books, and he always had a library card.

Later, when he took his old bakery truck down to the Mojave, what troubled Dad most was how to get one of those cards without having an address. He had to resort to the books available at thrift stores, and what he carried with him. Today he still haunts libraries, taking the bus now to the Marin County Main Library in that grand pink-and-blue building out by 101, and hunting through the stacks, as of old.

He won't run into me there, as I mostly go to bookstores now, but I'm still a card carrying member of the San Francisco public library. I rent how-to-ski videos from them, take out Cecile Holland's historical novels and find books for the kids' school projects. It's always with a sort of surprise that I remember, when I get there, that you can take out all these books for free, and renew them endlessly. I'm almost as bad as my friend Ginny, who thinks libraries are so great she always feels like crying in them.

I bring Patrick home ten books for a 100-word assignment on the War of the Roses, and am amazed when he doesn't dive into them with a glad shout. But he has a green San Francisco library card of his own in his wallet, and he reads. If he sticks around here he will have library stories of his own.

Struggling Toward A Father

I KNOW what my dad wouldn't mind having for Father's Day this Sunday: the Ellman biography of James Joyce, a list of the spellings of such interjections as "ugh," and a book about Neanderthals he read and wants to own.

He was delighted at how they hung their dead in bowers in the trees, garlanded with flowers. "And we call them primitive!" Dad's 71 now. His scowling Medi-Cal doctor tells him he has high blood pressure, and doles out pills but little else — yet warns him of the dangers of resentment. Dad says he imagines himself any day now, when the stroke comes, adjusting the hang of one arm with the other.

He's not supposed to exert himself but does anyway. "Noticed a high, narrow bookcase behind the supermarket, and went down to steal it about 4:30 this morning," he wrote recently, "mildly curious whether the moderate exercise and moderate panic of theft would finish me off."

When I was little, he stood in the yard holding an anvil over his head, grinning at the camera. He was the sound of distant hammering, the drifting smell of tobacco and sawdust, the roar of a truck starting up. He existed on the edge of my world, as I did on his. "You were always twisted around something in the foreground, part of your mother's entourage."

That gulf increased as the years went by. He left home for good when I was half-grown. For a long time after that, he lived in a station wagon parked on a hill in west Marin. He never came near us unless he was drunk — and then he'd call and want to talk for hours. Sometimes I would go out to see him, this bantering stranger, but we got nowhere with these visits, me grown now with my city life and shiny new jobs, him lifting an eyebrow, asking too few questions.

When I was in my mid-30s, he gave me a notebook of his to read. "When you've wormed your way through all this, you'll know more about the person your father was than most kids," he said, and then left for the desert for five years. From the Mojave he wrote me long letters on yellow sheets.

It was just a stroke of luck that we both loved words and could use them to try to fumble out some sort of relationship. "I'm going to put everything complimentary to you in longhand," he announced when he suspected I skimmed the difficult handwritten parts.

We have had to work harder overcoming our similarities than our differences, both being stubborn and word-struck and a little bit spoiled. We were never friends, and we never will be. We are a father and a daughter, struggling toward each other.

I learned he was burdened by regrets. "Maybe at some point you won't be so bitter about a few bottles of milk, a loaf of bread or two or even a little dental work," he'd say, of things I had never mentioned. His regrets go farther back than my childhood. His mother died when he was five, and he never got to know his father, a discouraged man who sat reading westerns in the kitchen. Long, silent years followed until the day Dad read in the paper that his father had died. I never met my grandfather.

Now Dad has set about improving his relationship with his father, the man he realizes gave him his lifelong love of reading. "I ran back and embraced my father," he says pointedly.

I've been luckier, thanks to that notebook and what followed. I've had the chance to get to know my father as I've learned to know myself — aware of my weaknesses, and choosing not to dwell on them. Knowing I'm doing the best I can, and am in any case the best deal I'm likely to get.

We could do better at this. I could tell him things, he could tell me things. We could fall into each other's arms. But that wouldn't be Irish, and I'm not sure we need to get that carried away.

So we do what we can do. I can take him books to fill that purloined bookcase. Now that I know him a little, he's at least easier to buy presents for. It'll never be easy, though. He said, "I'd much rather be cursed than be given a necktie, the hidden significance of which is to hang yourself."

Being in Charge Of Dad

MY DAD SAID his doctor, during a routine exam, had asked him whom he wanted the remains sent to. "He wormed your address out of me," Dad said.

If you saw us when I was little, you would have voted me least likely to end up as the name on Dad's medical forms. He was unusually strong for his size, a muscular young carpenter who lifted anvils in the back yard. He used to say he could lift a tree and the baboon hiding behind it. I was a little girl in a house crowded with little girls.

Now I have, somewhere along the way, become my father's keeper. I didn't realize this until the other night, when Dad had a bad flu, and I asked one of my sisters who lived nearer to him to go over there. She refused. "You're in charge of Dad," she said.

I'm in charge of Dad? Since when?

When we went out for a drive the other day, to look at the house I grew up in, I knew he'd been sick for a day or two, but I didn't stop by the grocery store to get him food. I didn't ask if he takes vitamins, though at home I hand vitamins to the kids as they watch TV and watch them take them (a practice I intend to keep up until they put a full day's vitamins into bagel dogs).

If I had given the matter any thought at all, I would have said he can buy his own food, realize for himself that vitamins are a good idea. He's a grown man, for chrissake.

Of all the ways my dad and I have tried to be, this feels the weirdest. Despite being a mom, I'm not much of a fusser over people. And Dad is not the helpless type. I've always been in "Hiya, Pop, how the hell are you" mode. I don't take care of him, he doesn't take care of me.

Of course I look around, see a lot of my friends taking care of their parents, spending every weekend in Spokane, doing Mom's weeding and making her appointments and trying to get 92-year-old Dad to give up his driving license before he kills somebody. Steve dreads the day his aged, querulous parents will leave the chicken farm in the desert and land on his doorway. Janice suffers agonies of guilt over the fact that she doesn't want her mother in the Midwest to come live with her.

But I have assumed, all these years, that Dad is in charge of himself. He does a pretty lousy job of it, but then so do we all.

I did the other day find him a new doctor, since his old one had gone to live in Sweden. "Will you be coming in with him?" the nurse asked. I said no, but for an instant I saw myself doing that, driving my pop to the doctor, making sure he had his card with him, and maybe, just to complete the picture, buttoning up any buttons he missed.

That picture didn't seem to fit either of us very well, especially him. He casts a jaundiced eye on most offers of help. All he asks for are typewriter ribbons: "Are you telling me you can't redirect any passing copy boy to the supply room, pick up a few dusty ribbons for your poor old half-blind father, locked in the hinterland, from which the last typewriter store folded up long ago? You say you thrill to the prospect of a genetic scribbling consortium, but still the ribbons remain locked away in the vaults."

When I did get around to the ribbons, it went wrong, somehow. He didn't like the way I asked for his typewriter model, or I got off the phone too fast, or I interrupted what he was doing. Our simplest transactions are made complicated by our vastly different lives, and ages, and ideas about the relative importance of typewriter ribbons. Still, we're both diverted by his dispatches from his new frontier: He is new at being old, and finds comic possibilities in it.

We're trying to make the best of this odd new role, my name on his medical form. As he warns me himself, "Don't take your responsibilities as my keeper too seriously — don't let yourself be swayed by what, after all, is no more than the usual wheezing and burnt-out lightbulbs one finds in old people."

But since he's a geezer of 75 with a ruined landscape behind him, and I'm a relatively hale 43, we will get used to it, both of us.

'I Guess I've Crossed Some Sort of Line'

"I WAS WAITING for you," Dad said when Adrian and I came to get him at his apartment a few days ago. He was sitting on the bed, wearing jeans, with his blue shirt on backward. Flakes of tobacco nearly blanketed the floor: He can no longer roll himself a cigarette, but goes on trying.

The pills he had been given the day before for a suspected kidney infection lay in a sodden mess on the kitchen table. He'd told Adrian he hadn't taken the pills because the instructions were too complicated. She picked up the empty container and read, "Take twice a day with water."

Dad is only 74, but high blood pressure and alcoholism are doing for him early. In the past few months he's been unable to read, unable to write, unable to eat, forgetful about even drinking water. This morning he had started to drink, and so we were here. He looked at us with that old glint in his eye, the warm sun coming in the window, a warm Coors in his hand. If it was the last party, it was in his style.

"I guess I've crossed some sort of line," he told us ruefully as we bustled about, gathering his things.

Then he glanced around his place, at the typewriter he can no longer use, the books he can't read. "So this is it?" he said. "You're coming to take Dad away?"

We were, too.

"It's your decision, Dad," Adrian said. We knew from experience that Dad has little talent for being railroaded.

I was sitting beside him, trying not to cry. "One day my kids will come for me too, Dad," I reminded him. "I don't have kids," Adrian said. "Yes, my kids will have to come for Adrian, too," I said, and we laughed.

"Just give me another fifteen minutes," Dad said, and we all sat down. He drank from his Coors. I wish now I had thought to have a beer with him, while I still had the chance.

We were trying to roll him a cigarette, but neither of us knew how. After he picked up a pen and tried to smoke that, combining his two vices, I walked down to the store to buy Marlboros.

I was noticing everything, as if in this hour everything was heightened, everything mattered. On the way to the store, I passed a man playing ball with his two sons. When I came back, the little one, about four, was lying on the pavement crying, having run into a pole. "Be strong for Daddy," the man kept saying to the little boy as he stooped over him.

When I got back, Adrian packed a plastic garbage bag with extra jeans and shirts for Dad, his jacket, glasses and pills. I got him into another shirt, found his socks and shoes, and put his keys and wallet in my purse.

"When you're ready, Dad," Adrian said. She was crying.

"Hell, I guess I'm ready," Dad said. I locked his door behind us, and he sauntered to the car, with one of us on either side, lest he fall. He wasn't drunk. This was different.

At the Veterans Hospital in the city, we waited outside, listening, while the psychiatrist asked him questions in a loud voice. "What year is it?" He didn't know. "What month is it?" March? "What's three from a hundred?" He didn't know. "What are your daughters' names?" Adrian and Adair. "What did he think he was here for?" He wasn't sure.

I'm proud to report that Dad went on the lam from the VA hospital the next morning, though he didn't get farther than the front door of the building. I think he was heading for the desert, to see the last of the wildflowers.

"Guess I'm in worse shape than I thought," he told me.

And he is, too, but in another way he's in pretty good shape, going bravely, and with all his old humor, into the unknown. And Adrian and me with him.

Be strong for Daddy.

A Month Lost In a Nursing Home

WHEN MY DAD landed in a nursing home in May, unable to say what year it was or to smoke the right end of his cigarette, and finally strapped to a wheelchair, my sister and I could see that the doctor who had diagnosed him at the veterans' hospital was probably right about his having "senile dementia, uncomplicated type," as his chart said. I was uncertain, though. I'd read up on dementia, and discovered that it happens slowly, over years. But Dad had gone in three days from being able to walk to being unable to eat without help.

He didn't seem unhappy, though. He smiled when he saw us come in, and once even told us he felt a strange exuberance. There was nothing to be exuberant about: My sister and I were watching the shack of our dad's body slowly collapsing, a board flying free there, a porch sagging here.

Still, we felt doubt. Adrian's friend Kirk had looked up the tranquilizer called Tranxene that Dad had been taking for months to ward off anxiety. "He should get the hell off those pills — your dad looks drugged to me, not senile," Kirk said.

The VA doctor nodded. "Let's send him to a nursing home for a month, get all the drugs out of his system, see how it goes then," he said.

Few would have doubted that diagnosis. When Dad first got to the home, confused and weak and hooked to a catheter, he looked like everybody else there, almost all of whom were strapped to their own wheelchairs, staring vacantly into space. One woman was always collapsed into her lunch, her pink scalp shining at us. Every day Dad was smaller, more boy-sized. The nursing home doctor said he had the "dwindles," a word Dad would be charmed by. Dwindling, like an unwatered geranium.

I was so upset I was planning to smother him, the way the Chief did Mac in *One Flew Over the Cuckoo's Nest*. But the nursing home pillows were too thin. That was on my list: sunglasses, TV, sweatpants, better pillow. My follow-up plan, still a good one, I think, was to push him in his wheelchair up to the 2 A.M. Club up the street, slap a fifty on the bar and let him go out in style, on a wave of Schlitz.

Then my sister asked the nursing home what medicines Dad was on. To our astonishment, we found he had been put on Zoloft, a strong anti-depressant. I called the VA. "This is routine for people suspected of having dementia," a doctor at the VA told me. "If they seem depressed, we treat them for depression."

"Without saying a word to the family, even when the family has been telling you his trouble might be drugs in the first place?" I asked.

We stopped the Zoloft, and one week later I arrived to find not an affable but loony-tunes wraith strapped to a wheelchair, but my dad. "What the hell am I doing here?" he wanted to know. He asked whose clothes he was wearing. And he wanted to go home.

It was two days before we could get him released. So he went AWOL, climbing over the fence, crossing four lanes of traffic, a life-long escape artist on the lam again. They caught up to him at the service station, brought him back, put a beeper on him, informed me this was evidence of continuing dementia and asked me if they could administer Haldol, a strong tranquilizer. "You don't know my dad," I said. "This is his normal self. Besides, what would you do if you woke up in a nursing home?"

The good news is that it's over. Dad's back in his apartment, scared, shaky, angry, thin as a rock star — but back. He lost twenty pounds, his wardrobe (which I'm afraid I threw out) and a month from his life in his odyssey through the medical system.

We're left with the memory of a confused month, when we were never sure what was going on, and nobody seemed able to tell us. And with the hope that the woman with the pink scalp has someone to look at her chart, too, and ask, "What the hell are you people giving her?"

A Lonesome Train In Room 105

MY GRANDFATHER has been missing for a long time. No one's been able to tell me when he was born, or when he died.

It could be because that's the Irish side of Dad's family. On the other side, my father's mother, there were Mormons way back, so we know every name, every birth and death, every idle cough back to the arrival in San Francisco of the ship *Brooklyn* in 1846, bringing my skirt-chasing great-great-grandfather, Orrin Smith. In fact, last week my cousins in Livermore called in great excitement to tell me that they think Orrin Smith slept in the Blue Wing Inn, opposite the Sonoma Mission, in 1848.

On the Irish side, they were more lackadaisical about keeping track. At some point, my father's father died, and no one even thought to jot down the date.

So I went down to Room 105, the Vital Statistics Room of the Department of Health down at the Civic Center. This is where we start when we're born in San Francisco, and where we come back to in the end.

If you have an appointment, they let you perch on a stool and look through the huge books piled on the sagging shelves. Last year 7,446 San Franciscans made their final departure from this eerie train station, and 8,386 arrived.

I sat on a stool, dragged down a huge ledger. This is the pre-computer age — these are deaths entered in ledgers longhand, in flowing script. There was at least that ceremony to it: Someone had to write out your name, and the day you died.

All I knew was that my grandfather's name was Francis Thomas Daly and that when he died he was married to a Haight Street waitress named Rose. And I have some fading black-and-white pictures from my aunt's album. In one, he stands at the side of a house, his hands at his sides, staring docilely into the camera, a slender, earnest-looking man with a high forehead, dressed in black pants and an open-necked white shirt.

His pretty, flirtatious first wife, Vera, died of rheumatic fever at age 27, and his two young kids were raised by relatives, shifting from home to home.

As I turned the pages, a soft murmur came from outside the windows as people lined up, waiting their turn to get birth and death certificates. I read slowly through the ledgers, finding Daly after Daly after Daly.

Sean, Seamus, Patrick, William. I finished that ledger, pulled out another. The names started to blur.

Until, suddenly, there he was. Frank Thomas Daly, married, a teamster, born Nov. 30, 1900, in San Francisco. Wife, Rose. He died on March 29, 1954. "Length of stay in this city or town: Life." His father is listed as "unknown Daly," his mother as simply "unknown."

I scribbled down the number next to his name, and a few minutes later, outside another room down the corridor, a woman handed me a copy of his death certificate.

I stood in the shadowy corridor, scanning it. Frank Daly died of lung disease in Room 107 of a hotel at 252 Sixth St. His permanent address is listed as 214 Scott St. Oddly, that house, a dingy white Victorian, is two blocks from where I live. If my grandfather had stepped out the door, he could have seen my house.

Nothing on the certificate hinted at why he died in a hotel room on Sixth Street when he lived on Scott. I guess we'll never know. He was 53 years old.

The certificate listed him as being buried at Cypress Lawn. I called the cemetery, and they said, cheerfully, Yes, he's here, Grave 469, Elm Square.

He was here all the time, of course, in Room 105. They're all here. The train whistle blows, and the engine screams into the station — or it pulls out, puffing, majestic, until it's just a smudge of smoke in the distance, like a scrawl on a ledger.

A Life That's An Open Book

DAD'S BEEN thrown out of the Fairfax library. He went over there to get a book on Benedict Arnold, and the librarian wanted to check his address. She asked him what it was, and he didn't know, so her question infuriated him. He told her that she had no right to ask him questions, that she should just let him check out his book.

Sometimes I think the story of Dad's life is a library story. He remembers marching down McAllister Street when he was a boy to the main library to check out four books. He claimed it was the best nightlife San Francisco had to offer.

Dad learned early about running away, but one of the places he liked best to run to was books. He dropped out of George Washington High School and joined the Army, which court-martialed him and locked him up.

He spent two years reading through the prison library, holding the books at arm's length through the bars to catch the light coming in from the end of the tier, while the din of World War II faded in his ears. He remembers nearly wearing out a dictionary in that prison, memorizing words and definitions.

When they let him out, he met my mother on Ocean Beach when she was lying on the sand reading a library book. The cover didn't look garish to him, and he strolled over for a closer look.

Six kids later, he and Mother would pile us all into the Rambler and go to the library in Forest Knolls. When we left, there were gaping holes in the shelves.

"Sons of bitches sneaking into libraries and getting their own ideas about how the country's being governed is why this country works," Dad told me once, when his branch was cutting back its hours. "You used to be able to compare what your president tells you with what you found in books. Now where do you trot off to of an evening?"

Both of my parents got drunk on print, spending the grocery money on books, keeping library books long after their due date, hiding paperbacks in lunch pails, laundry baskets.

Mother said she loved going swimming, and took us nearly every afternoon, but guess what she brought along to do while we were all in the water? Library books gave Dad ideas above his station, so that he was forever walking off jobs because the ignorance of the boss got on his nerves.

Finally he walked away from us, too. I grew up without him, and gradually forgot about him, until I ran into him by chance at the San Francisco Main Library when I was 21. Since then we've stayed in touch.

He wrote letters home to me, so I knew the first thing he'd do when he got to a new place was get a library card — though this isn't an easy thing to do when your address is a truck.

Dad got old out in the desert, came back when he was 70, sold his truck and found a place to live in Fairfax. He had only $500 a month in Social Security, but there was the library just down the street.

He's 76 now, and I'm beginning to suspect that he can't read much. Nor can he really remember numbers, and he tends to get belligerent when you ask him a nosy question, like what his address is.

He says the librarian threw him out, which she didn't. She just didn't give him any books. Which is just as good as throwing him out, to him.

Another Step On a Long Road

DAD ON THE PHONE to me, laboring to speak. "What's the matter, Dad?" Silence. I hear only the sound of breathing. A neighbor found him sitting on a chair in the laundry room, bewildered. His mind, the last refuge of a scoundrel, has let him down at last as dementia destroys brain cells. His liver is a squeezed-out sponge.

He was wearing only boxer shorts and an old jacket the last time I was at his place. "I like your outfit," I said.

"I like yours, too," he answered in the same tone, glancing at the slacks and blouse I had worn to teach a workshop in Marin earlier that day.

I had him step into one of the pairs of warm-up pants I'd bought for him. It's been months since Dad dressed himself. He claims it's because it's nice and warm in his apartment.

I have been bringing him books, though I know he can't read them.

"What did you like about that book?" he asks with his old scorn as I retrieve *A Place of Greater Safety* from a couch littered with unopened bills and bulletins from his building announcing luncheons and bingo nights.

"This might happen to you, too," he informed me on that visit, his green eyes bright below his disheveled, still-thick gray hair. His world had by then shrunk to an upholstered chair full of burn holes and a flickering TV, often turned to a baseball game, though he loathes sports.

"No, it won't," I protest. "It's alcoholic dementia," I said. "You pickled your brain in Budweiser."

"You hope I did," he says with his old acuteness. I found a shirt in his closet and put it on him, buttoning it up. It strained over his stomach, enlarged by liver failure, but his limbs have become mere twigs. He looks like Humpty Dumpty, a wizened egg.

After the laundry room caper, he was taken to the hospital, where a sign above his bed said "Fall Precautions." A "sitter" stayed in the room, watching him lest he decide to take off. They were watching Humpty.

As he lay there, incoherent, I watched his hands twitch on the blanket and remembered that he had talked to me about the decline that comes before the end.

"I have never believed that people who have time to prepare themselves for death are fully alive when death claims them," he said. "Their lives are already shuttered down, so that the big event passes almost unnoticed."

He had rolled a cigarette and now he lit it, looking at me through the blue smoke.

"Loved ones, or those pretending to be loved ones, look down upon that ravaged face, those limp hands, thinking they are in full possession of what's happening, but of course they aren't. They don't know what is happening.

"Death began months before, to which the last lurch — up but not quite over — of the heart is anticlimax, according to the provisions laid down by the law, which ordains you can't seal them in a box until there is no possibility they can hear that first spatter of earth over them.

"I want to make a compact with you. Keep your eyes on the first joint of my little finger. If it moves at all, Dare, that will mean I was conscious of what was happening up until the time the doctor listened and shook his head."

I am looking now at the joint of his little finger as his hands twitch above the blanket, unconsciously rolling cigarette papers.

He grabs my arms and kisses my wrist. The sitter in the chair is moved by this, but I know he is licking the cigarette paper.

I sit on his bed, still watching.

What he didn't say was what to do if I saw that finger moving.

My Fodder My Father

THE BACKS of Dad's hands shine in the light from the window, the skin so loose and transparent it looks as if his hands were covered in Saran Wrap. Underneath the shine they're bloody and bruised from the IVs.

He talks to me incoherently, something about his tools, while a man screams in pain from the next bed, behind a curtain.

I murmur back to him, break off pieces of a Kit Kat bar and give it to him. At the same time I am listening to the action in the next bed, where an old woman in a wheelchair is trying to comfort the man shouting in pain. "I feel as if you are my own son," she says, "I don't want you to die."

"I don't want to die either," the man gasps. A nurse brings him a pain pill and the man gradually grows quieter. I wanted to write down what I just heard.

My friend Janis types in a pool of sunshine in her third-story office at home, writing a book about the frightening month she and her husband spent in Moscow trying to adopt a fifteen-month-old Russian boy they called Alex.

Now four-year-old Alex rushes into her office after preschool, and she says he can stay if he plays quietly on the rug and doesn't make noise.

"It's as if I say, 'Go away, Alex, so I can write about how much I love you,' " Janis says to me ruefully, knowing I will understand.

We all know about this. On the day I picked up my fifteen-year-old at a police station, I noticed how the vending machine in the lobby kept flashing "Have a Nice Day" in red digital letters while they were fetching her for me.

I was crying — she'd been riding in what turned out to be a stolen car that had lost its brakes, and she could have been killed. But I was also, at the back of my mind, taking note of that detail, the flashing vending machine.

My dad would not mind that I jot notes at his bedside.

I have brought him his yellow pad and a few of his pens in case he wants to jot something down himself, maybe continue the musings about King Lear and his treatment from his ungrateful daughters that he was writing when he lost his wits and awoke tied to a hospital bed with white fabric.

"The scribbler gathers his ammunition from the blasted scenes of battles he has lost," he wrote to me. He has lost this battle, as he lies addled from advanced liver disease.

"I am doomed," he says almost comically when I ask how he is. He is doomed, but you can tell he likes how that sounds. He reminds me of the father I read about once in the *Atlantic Monthly*, who committed suicide and left a note that said, "I have decided to quit smoking."

Lorrie Moore's baby is found to have cancer. "Take notes," says her husband as he collapses in tears on hearing the news. "We're going to need the money."

"Take notes?" she asks. "I do the careful ironies of daydream. I do the marshy ideas upon which intimate life is built. Our baby with cancer?" — but we are reading her story in the *New Yorker*.

I have student who write about making their own funeral arrangements, extracting that last triumph, squeezing meaning from life's most painful passages.

Shrinks say this is distancing. Like that's a bad thing, when your father is dying, and there isn't a damned thing you can do about it — you can't, and he can't. Except take notes.

As I am gathering up my purse to leave the nursing home, he looks at me and says in a quiet voice, "Don't leave me here by myself."

His words clutch at my throat as I leave him sprawled on his narrow bed.

But even as I walk blinking into the sunshine, I am mentally memorizing the sentence.

Dad Can't Seem To Stick Around

I AM SITTING on the bed in my dad's room at the nursing home, breaking off pieces of a Kit Kat bar and giving them to him. "People die like flies in horrible ways every day on the evening news," he said to me a few months ago, after a bout with pneumonia, "but this is me we're talking about. I'll still take all the life I can get, in whatever form it comes in."

Even now, Dad? I almost say out loud, looking around his room, three beds side by side, each guarded by metal railings. Dad cocks his head at me. His thick hair is powdery, as if it would fall into dust if you touched it. Dad doesn't say much of anything now. I talk to him, and he looks at me. He's wearing pink sweatpants that end at midcalf. I forgot to write his name in his clothes, and they all disappeared.

Bored with the one-sided conversation, I read his dietary instructions — no protein — and a sign above his neighbor's bed: "Feed slowly, in small bites." I wheel Dad out to the hall and show him a sign posted on the wall: "The Day Is Saturday. The Season is Summer. The Weather is Hot. The Next Holiday is the Fourth of July." We are both soothed by print.

He looks at it. "This job doesn't pay very much, but it's interesting," he comments cheerfully. A ring of people in wheelchairs is watching MTV (the Backstreet Boys) on a large-screen TV.

It's the weekend, so everybody's up and dressed. A man in a red shirt, with cane, shuffling around, says he's looking for his room. A woman in green in a wheelchair scolds him. "You'll fall. Please sit down! There's a chair right behind you!" The man obediently turns. No chair behind him. I slide one in, just in time.

I should be doing something, baking files into a cake or something. "What should I do, Dad?" I ask aloud. "You're the escape artist. Do your Houdini thing."

I was ten the summer he left, heading down the bright highway to Baja. One day when he'd been gone a month, my older sister

Mickey and I took the forest trail that cut across the ridge to the swimming hole at the dam. We played for a long time on the logs that floated in the pond, trying to balance on them like lumber-jacks, then lay on the rocks at the swimming hole, shivering as the breeze and the hot sun vacuumed the water droplets from our skin. We were starving, but had forgotten to bring anything for lunch. Across the way, a man and woman were cutting a huge watermelon into slices for their kids.

I shut my eyes, trying to forget my hunger. Then a shadow fell across us, and a man's gentle voice said, "You kids hungry?" It was the father from across the way, bringing us each a long, thin slice of watermelon.

I reached for it eagerly and bit into the sweet red flesh. I wondered how the man had figured out, from way across the rocks, how hungry I was, and how I had been longing for that watermelon. I suddenly missed my father, yearned to smell his familiar smell of tobacco and wood shavings, hear his light tread as he headed to the bathroom at dawn. I ate the watermelon hungrily, feeling the juice running over my jaw, but it wasn't enough. It wasn't nearly enough.

I found him again in adulthood, by accident, walking right into him at the San Francisco Public Library. Over the years, we pasted together an on-again, off-again relationship. I was often furious with him, and he with me, but Dad said once, "Make a wonderland of your own bog. It's the only way." He was my bog — the only Dad I was ever likely to have. As he got older and frailer, I'd come over, make him oatmeal, renew his prescriptions, vacuum up his tobacco. He comforted me when I had trouble with the kids.

I just about had him convinced that fatherhood was a connection that even he couldn't break when he started to leave again.

I park him in his room, hand him a paper bag into which I have broken more bars of Kit Kats. "Take it easy," he says in his old way.

Sure, Dad. You, too.

The Last Chapter

EARLY SUNDAY MORNING, the phone rang, waking us up. A voice with a Spanish accent announced, "Resident Eugene Thomas Daly passed away at 5:30 this morning."

"Who was that?" Bill asked sleepily.

"My father died," I said, and crawled into his arms.

Dad once spoke of his death as "my house showering down the abyss." I seemed to see it before me now, a house cascading over a cliff, crumpling and falling silently until it was lost from view.

Oh, Dad. I closed my eyes again.

In the years just before he died, he seemed to be my dad alone. He sent me his writing, and I found him doctors, brought him books and goldfinches and cable boxes. He and I were thrown together by biology. We struggled to make the most of that, and once in a while, for the space of a phone call on a Monday morning or a quiet drive out to the country, we pulled it off.

"Our alliance allowed me to recoup some of my agonizing losses as an arrant father," he wrote to me once, "a chance to use the oddments crammed in my head to impress and delight a daughter who had straggled back to me."

"You wanted some kind of father," he said, "and you got some kind of father."

I did, too. If we didn't get what we wanted from each other, we at least learned to settle for what we could get. It was more than either of us had hoped for—a lot more. I got the kind of dad who would buy a typewriter just so he could type up a list of his favorite words.

"He's your dad, too," I told my brothers and sisters, when he made one of his explosive appearances in Marin County, drunk, wearing bedroom slippers, his truck wheezing at the curb.

I was alone with him so long, I thought he was mine. My twin sister Adrian helped, but she lived too far away.

And now he's dead. I had thought I would be alone with this too, putting his cremation on my Visa card, maybe keeping him in a jar on my mantel. but Adrian happened to be at my house when I got the call, and together we called my mother, his other children, and Dad's sister Frances.

My oldest brother, Sean, got on a plane and came down from Washington. Shannon, my other brother, picked up Dad's ashes at the funeral home and took him for a ride up Mt. Tamalpais, with the green-wrapped box on the seat beside him. "He was always asking me to come by and take him for a ride," Shannon said. Dad enjoyed that ride. I know he did. He was the one, after all, who said, "There's always something you can do, even when the person you're trying to make up with is long gone."

We held the wake on a boat on the bay at sunset, the whole family on board—his sister, five of his kids, their kids, our mother. Sean remembered that Dad had taken him fishing. Shannon remembered playing their guitars together. I read from his journal. He wrote to me that "what you and I dignify as a writing consortium is really two half-demented spies wedging bits of coded messages in the cracks of isolated telephone poles," but it did seem to get us somewhere. After ten years of furious correspondence, I now know what he was thinking as he steamed toward Hawaii on a troopship at the age of twenty, and why he tried to burn down the house when I was nine. I know more about his spectacular departures and ignominious returns. Why he always left, and why he always came back.

Until now, at least. We celebrated him, and hugged one another—some of us, anyway; we were still Dalys. Then at sunset we poured the fine white powder that was our Dad into the water. He showered down into the brine, falling through our fingers.

We headed back in, to what would turn from quiet talking to a dance party, complete with sisters playing dice at the bar, brothers playing "House of the Rising Sun" on the piano, and grandsons dancing like go-go boys on a tabletop.

"Make a wonderland of your own bog," Dad once told me. "It's the only way."

Acknowledgements

I would like to thank:

—Matt Wilson and the *San Francisco Chronicle* for their generous permission to publish these columns.

—Andrea Behr of the *Chronicle* for brilliant copy editing and headline writing (all the good ones are hers).

—My mother, my father, my brothers and sisters —Sean, Connie, Mickey, Adrian, Shannon and Robin — my kids, Morgan and Patrick, and their father Jim for their support and for letting me write about them.

—Ginny McReynolds, Donna Levin, and Janis Newman, my talented writing partners.

—My husband, Bill LeBlond, who has been my unpaid, unsung editor, reading every scribbled effort in rough draft, often making suggestions that coax me to unfold the piece of paper I've just balled up and thrown away.

—My readers, who changed the writing of these columns from a job into a conversation.